SHAKESPEARE FOLIOS AND QUARTOS

SHAKESPEARE FOLIOS AND QUARTOS

A STUDY IN THE BIBLIOGRAPHY OF SHAKESPEARE'S PLAYS
1594-1685

BY ALFRED W. POLLARD

WITH 37 ILLUSTRATIONS

A Marandell Book

COOPER SQUARE PUBLISHERS, INC.
NEW YORK
1970

Originally Published 1909
Published by Cooper Square Publishers, Inc.
59 Fourth Avenue, New York, N. Y. 10003
Standard Book Number 8154-0322-4
Library of Congress Catalog Card No. 72-114087

Printed in the United States of America
by Noble Offset Printers, Inc.   New York, N. Y. 10003

PREFACE

THIS study in the bibliography of Shakespeare would hardly need a preface were it not for the extent of my obligations to one friend and the strenuous opposition in which I find myself to another. To ignore anything which Mr Sidney Lee has written about Shakespeare would be a greater discourtesy than anything (unless my pen has run away with me without my knowing it) which is here set down in antagonism to his views. Mr Lee is not only my immediate predecessor in this particular field, but he has also expressed with courageous frankness and his usual ability an attitude towards the earliest publishers and editors of Shakespeare which has long been very widely held, and under cover of his authority is likely to become universal if no one sallies forth to attack it. He has placed himself at the head of the bibliographical pessimists, and in the name of (I hope) a healthy and hardy optimism I find myself opposed to him at almost every point. The pessimists, of whom Mr Lee has made himself the champion, seem to me to have piracy on the brain. They depict it as the ruling element in the book-market of Shakespeare's day, Shakespeare and his fellows as submitting to it with what I should account a craven and contemptible helplessness, and the early editions of his plays as so deeply tainted with fraud and carelessness that we can never say where the mischief ends. As for the Elizabethan printers and publishers they are set down as equally stupid and dishonest, and none escape condemnation. To me the printers and publishers seem as a rule to have been honest men, though there were black sheep among them, and though a peculiar literary foppery of the day now and again enabled a decent man to quiet his conscience when a chance presented itself of turning a doubtful penny; piracy seems an exceptional incident, to which plays were indeed inconveniently exposed, but which the players, especially those of Shakespeare's company, combatted with considerable success; the pirated editions are few and clearly distinguishable from the honest ones, and they have left no trace whatever on our present texts.

When we pass to a later stage there is the same opposition. To the pessimists every stage, every incident, in the editing of the First Folio is deplorable. The materials for it, we are told, were, in the first place, the prompt copies made by the playhouse scrivener, in which the author's text might have been subjected to erasures and additions at the manager's will; secondly the even less complete and less authentic transcripts in private hands; and lastly the quartos, tainted with all the carelessness, incapacity and surreptitiousness already described. In arranging and printing this deplorably defective copy, the chief qualities displayed by the editors were clumsiness and an excessive and inexplicable haste. All editorial professions are regarded as "trade conventions," "work-a-day publishing advertisements," to which no attention need be paid. In a word the advertisers are only to be believed when they are abusing someone else.

Now, that there are possibilities of truth in all or most of these statements optimism itself cannot deny. What it may very cheerfully combat is the presentation of these possibilities as a complete and faithful picture. Optimism thinks the part assigned to the playhouse scrivener and the importance of the private transcripts dangerously exaggerated; it has heard of a prompt-copy in an author's autograph; it remembers that Shakespeare was himself an actor and manager as well as a playwright; it believes in the human dislike to throwing property away, even when it seems to have become useless. Lastly, it recognizes the editors as busy men with no love for tinkering manuscripts or for proof-reading, but it finds that they exercised care and discrimination in forming their canon, in substituting good texts for bad ones and in restoring passages which had been omitted. Doubtless everything might have been much better done, but, doubtless, everything might have been much worse, and optimism even dares to believe that there was some shred of genuine enthusiasm among the editors and publishers, and would rather take a reasonable discount off the prefatory professions than treat them as mere advertising lies.

Such is the theory which runs all through this study as compared with Mr Lee's, and the opposition necessarily results in a series of attacks, in which I hope I have succeeded in keeping the button securely on my foil. No doubt, if Mr Lee finds time to discuss my objections, I shall have to acknowledge plenty of hits, but I am quite sure that this more cheerful view of the fate of Shakespeare's text is worth setting out, and I have done my best to present it honestly.

The second object of this preface is to express my deep obligations to my friend Mr Walter Wilson Greg for constant and generous help and sympathy. In some sections of this study Mr Greg and I have been fellow-hunters, communicating our results to each other at every stage, so that our respective responsibilities for them have become hopelessly entangled. In others he has been distinctly my leader. If it had not been for his ungrudging permission to use his work as my own, I should have been hampered at every turn. For the final presentation of my case I alone am responsible, but he has spared no pains to keep me in the right path, and without his comradeship I should never have finished my task. I hope that the chapter in which our work is most intertwined, that on "The Quartos of 1619," with its story of an attempted Shakespearian collection prior to that of 1623 and of the false dates on some of the most famous Shakespeare quartos, may retain in my narrative some of the keen interest with which the new facts were unravelled.

ALFRED W. POLLARD

April 5, 1909

CONTENTS

NOTE

REACTERS of advance copies have supplied me with some corrections, two of which are of considerable importance.

(i) The date of Pavier's entry of Henry V as "formerly printed and sett over" to him, wrongly given on p. 67 as 1602, was really, as stated in the Bibliography (p. 38), 14 August, 1600. Thus it was ten days, not two years, after the staying order that Pavier, with the connivance of the Master of the Stationers' Company, from whom he was buying copyrights, slipped in a false entry of this play under the guise of a transfer, and the discreditable transaction is made a good deal worse than I thought it.

(ii) From failing to remember a *caveat* in a preface, I have omitted to search for Quartos published between 1664 and 1685. The few that were issued seem all to be connected with current theatrical revivals, and belong to another chapter in Shakespeare Bibliography, which I hope one day to write. But the facts that a *Macbeth* was printed for "P. Chetwin" in 1674 and a *Hamlet* for J. Martyn and H. Herringman in 1676 show that the publisher of the Third Folio exercised his copyright in the year of his death, and that one of the publishers of the Fourth Folio had acquired an interest two years later.

Other errata are:

p. 38, line 2. *This should precede the heading* HENRY V.

p. 57, underline. *For* SECOND EDITION *read* FIRST EDITION (SECOND ISSUE).

p. 83, line 24. *For* True Contention *read* Whole Contention.

p. 98, line 24. *For* is *read* is not.

p. 117, line 30. *For* even *read* even if.

p. 159, line 7. *For* 1753 *read* 1653.

A. W. P.

SHAKESPEARE FOLIOS AND QUARTOS

SHAKESPEARE FOLIOS AND QUARTOS

CHAPTER I. THE CONDITION OF PUBLISHING IN SHAKESPEARE'S DAY.

THE address "To the great Variety of Readers," prefixed to the First Folio edition of Shakespeare's plays over the signatures of his Friends and Fellows, John Heminge and Henry Condell, fulfils the accepted requirement of every literary composition in having a beginning, a middle and an end. The beginning is a most tradesmanlike exhortation to buy the book. The end attempts to coerce the reader's judgement by suggesting that if the plays (which on the previous leaf had been called "these trifles") were not liked, the fault lay in his lack of understanding. The middle, though it is the fashion to regard it as only an advertisement, is also the only contemporary account we possess of the editing of the First Folio, and as such deserves quotation.

It had bene a thing, we confesse, worthie to haue bene wished, that the Author himselfe had liu'd to haue set forth, and ouerseen his owne writings; But since it hath bin ordain'd otherwise, and he by death departed from that right, we pray you do not envie his Friends, the office of their care, and paine, to haue collected & publish'd them; and so to haue publish'd them, as where (before) you were abus'd with diuerse stolne, and surreptitious copies, maimed and deformed by the frauds and stealthes of iniurious impostors, that expos'd them: euen those, are now offer'd to your view cur'd, and perfect of their limbes; and all the rest, absolute in their numbers, as he conceiued them. Who, as he was a happie imitator of Nature, was a most gentle expresser of it. His mind and hand went together: And what he thought he vttered with that easinesse, that wee haue scarse receiued from him a blot in his papers.

Ben Jonson in his guilelessness deplored the absence of more blots; our own more sceptical generation doubts vehemently whether a single leaf in Shakespeare's autograph, blotted or unblotted, had been at the disposal of Messrs Heminge and Condell, or of whoever else may have acted as editor, in preparing the Folio for the press. In any case it is certain that for several of the plays use was made of the extant printed quarto editions, sometimes considerably, sometimes only slightly, emended. Undoubted errors in the quartos are repeated in the Folio in a way which defies any explanation save that a copy of the quarto (usually of the latest edition) was handed to the compositors of the Folio to work from, and thus any general condemnation of the quartos as unauthentic seriously undermines the authenticity of the Folio. Messrs Heminge and Condell breathe no word of any use having been made of the quartos. Their only concern was to suggest that the Folio edition was the book to buy, and so they launched the phrase as to the "diuerse stolne and surreptitious copies, maimed and deformed by the frauds and stealthes of iniurious impostors," which has figured so prominently in every critical edition of Shakespeare that has since been issued.

It may have been observed that Heminge and Condell merely allude to "diuerse copies." They give no indication as to which, or how many, are included in their condemnation. Modern critics and editors have imitated them in this respect, interpreting the attack (as with the sale of the First Folio in view it was doubtless intended to be interpreted) as involving all the quarto editions in a general atmosphere of fraud and surreptitiousness. Mr Sidney Lee expresses this commonly accepted view by first singling out (quite rightly) a few quartos for special condemnation as obviously pieced together from shorthand notes, and then asserting that " the greater number of the quarto editions of Shakespeare's plays which were published in his lifetime seem to have been printed from more or less imperfect and un-authorized playhouse transcripts which were obtained by publishers more or less dishonestly." After instancing six plays as notably defective, he enumerates eight others in which comparatively few faults are visible, and admits that "in these cases the authoriz'd playhouse transcript or 'prompt-copy' may have been at the publisher's disposal," * but he makes this admission apparently solely on the internal evidence of the text, without any mention of even the possibility of there being any external criterion by which this internal evidence could be supported.

As to how these "stolne and surreptitious" editions were brought out, Mr Lee is very explicit. In some cases, he tells us, plays were taken down by shorthand writers, but, "More frequently the publisher would bribe a scrivener, or perhaps an actor, into procuring for him a rough copy of the play which had been carelessly transcribed for some subordinate purpose of the playhouse." Even with the introduction of the words "or, perhaps," to suggest that Mr Lee's imagination has not been wholly idle, a statement so confident and comprehensive as this should surely have been supported by the quotation of at least one case in which a scrivener or actor is known thus to have betrayed his employers. Even an indication of what "subordinate purpose of the playhouse" a rough copy of the play, whether carelessly or carefully transcribed, would be likely to serve, would be welcome. It takes some time and trouble to copy a play, however roughly; and after one such transcript had been dishonestly used, some care would presumably have been taken to prevent any similar accident in the future. And yet Mr Lee asserts categorically that robberies of this kind occurred " more frequently " than the piracies by shorthand, which would be much more difficult to stop, and as to which we have good evidence both internal and external.†

While differing from Mr Lee as to these supposed fraudulent sales of manuscripts, or at least as to the frequency of them, we are thus in agreement with him as to plays being liable to be pirated by shorthand writers, or men with quick memories, and it is evident that in a condition of affairs in which such piracies were possible the rights of authors were very imperfectly protected. This was certainly the case throughout the whole of Shake-

---

* Mr Lee ends his sentence: " but none give absolutely convincing evidence at all points of complete authenticity." This is surely superfluous. Even a statement in Shakespeare's autograph that he had corrected the proofs would hardly justify all these adjectives without a certificate of his competence as a proof-reader.

† See the passages from Heywood quoted in Note A.

speare's career and for many years after his death, but not quite to the extent that Mr Lee describes. He tells us in one statement that "in the absence of any statutory prohibition, [publishers] freely enjoyed the right of publishing any MS., whatever might be the channel through which it reached their hands, provided that they purchased a licence for its publication of the Stationers' Company." In another sentence we have the astounding assertion, for which I doubt strongly whether a shred of evidence can be produced, that before an unauthorized text could be superseded "it was needful to conciliate and perhaps to compensate the piratical publisher, who was first in the field and had it in his power on an appeal to the Stationers' Company to prevent the substitution of a genuine version by a second publisher for his own corrupt but fully licensed property."* It is strange that while thus emphasizing, not quite accurately, the "purchase" of a licence and the "fully licensed property" thus acquired by the pirate, Mr Lee should have omitted all reference to the twin facts which, surely, rule the situation (a) that a licence could not always be obtained, whether by payment or otherwise, and (b) that the plays which he himself singles out as the worst piracies were never licensed at all.

Mr Lee is vigorous in his condemnation of the members of the Stationers' Company. "No conscientious scruple deterred [them]," he asserts, "from defying the natural sentiment which would assign to the author some exercise of control over the public fortunes of the written product of his brain." Sweeping as is this statement, it is not necessary to deny it, though it might plausibly be argued that these, like Robin Hood, were honest thieves, who seldom stole from a poor man, even (it may be) doing little more than possess themselves of what was left in their way for this very object. It will suffice for our purpose to show that, if not honest, they were at least prudent, careful tradesmen, with a wholesome fear of colliding with authority, and that this fear gave authors and theatrical companies a good deal more real protection than a strictly logical view of the situation may seem to imply. To demonstrate this it will be necessary to explain briefly the functions of the Stationers' Company and how they were carried out. At the same time some evidence will be offered to show that by the time that Shakespeare began to write authors were already being paid for literary work, and were not altogether without means of protecting it, and that players in general, more especially those of the Chamberlain's company, to which Shakespeare presumably sold his work, if on the one hand they were unusually open to attack, on the other possessed some special means of defence. When the ground has thus been cleared of some current misconceptions and exaggerations, it will be possible to consider with a better hope of success what actually happened in the case of Shakespeare's plays. The inquiry, it must be repeated, though con-

---

* At the cost of anticipating I may note at once that it would be much nearer the truth to say that the publication of a surreptitious edition left an author free to do exactly what he liked. The existence of an edition already in print absolved him from the need of a licence, and we find him simply reprinting his own text without registration or any other formality. This is what Nashe did when Richard Johnes took advantage of his absence to register and print his *Pierce Pennilesse*. Mr Lee, if he will read Nashe's letter to his authorized publisher, J[ohn] B[usby], will hardly contend that Nashe had found it "necessary to conciliate" Johnes. Of course, "to stay" or confiscate a surreptitious issue was a much more serious matter.

cerned directly only with the authenticity of the quartos is of the highest importance for any valuation of the text of the Folio, on which all modern editions are mainly based. Heminge and Condell claim that the plays previously issued in pirated editions were in the Folio presented "cured and perfect in their limbs." If plays of which the text in the quartos and Folio are in general agreement are included among the pirated quartos, then this claim was unjustified, and we have no proof of the exercise of any editorial care. The reassuring conclusion which it is hoped may be established is that the claim was strictly and accurately true. Not all, but only some of the quartos ought to be treated as "stolne and surreptitious," and no use was made of these in printing the Folio, good texts being substituted for the bad ones.

The grant of a charter to the Stationers' Company by Philip and Mary in 1557 was a clever piece of Tudor statecraft. The Company had in some form, of which very little is known, been in existence for over a century and a half. The cessation of such unscrupulous competition as that which can be traced in the publications of Pynson and Wynkyn de Worde in the early years of the sixteenth century seems to show that it had already gradually enforced some kind of harmony upon its members, and it was now to be given much greater powers of doing this. Under the new charter, save for some reservation of the rights of the two Universities, no one not a member of the Stationers' Company could lawfully possess a printing press, and the members of the Company collectively thus enjoyed a nearly absolute monopoly and also full power to manage their own affairs. The motive of the Crown in conferring these favours on the London printers was, of course, selfish. A censorship of the press had already been established, but it was entrusted to some of the busiest people in the kingdom and had apparently proved unworkable. Henceforth every printer, press and fount of type were under control, and the production of books in any way obnoxious to the Crown was rendered much more difficult. By the fifty-first Injunction of 1559 various dignitaries, including the Archbishop of Canterbury and the Bishop of London, were once more appointed to act as censors or licensers,* but

---

*It may be worth while to quote this Injunction as a capital instance of the wide difference between the regulations nominally governing the book trade and the real practice.

"51. Item because there is great abuse in the Printers of bookes, which for couetousnes cheefely regard not what they print, so they may haue gaine, whereby ariseth great disorder by publication of vnfruitefull, vaine, and infamous bookes and papers, the Queenes maiestie straitlye chargeth ánd commaundeth, that no manner of person shal print any manner of booke or paper, of what sort, nature, or in what language soeuer it be, excepte the same be firste licensed by her Maiestie, by expresse wordes in writing, or by six of her priuie counsel: or be perused and licensed by the Archbishops of Canterburie and Yorke, the Bishop of London, the Chauncelors of both Vniuersities, the Bishop being Ordinarye and the Archdeacon also of the place, where any such shal be printed, or by two of them, wherof the Ordinarie of the place to be alwayes one. And that the names of such as shall allowe the same to bee added in the end of every such worke, for a testimonie of the alowance thereof. And because many pamphlets, playes and ballads, bee oftentimes printed, wherein regarde woulde bee had, that nothing therein should be either heretical, seditious, or vnseemely for Christian eares: her Maiestie likewise commaundeth, that no manner of person shall enterprise to print any such excepte the same bee to him licensed by suche her Maiesties Commissioners, or three of them, as be appointed in the Cittie of London, to heare and determine diuers causes Ecclesiasticall, tending to the execution of certain statutes, made the last Parliament for vniformitie of order in Religion. And if any shall sell or vtter any maner of bookes

with a company of tame monopolists as intermediaries the licensing difficulty was easily surmounted. No member of the Company would be likely to print a book in any way obnoxious to the Crown, and works which from their title or subject appeared liable to any doubt would be taken to the deputies of the Archbishop or Bishop of London for an imprimatur before being brought to the Company for entry in its register. For books obviously harmless the Wardens of the Company were allowed to act as licensers. Hence the slight confusion exemplified in Mr Lee's phrase as to "purchasing a licence of the Stationers' Company." We have no record of any fee having to be paid for a licence, although the poor devil whose book was considered doubtful very probably had to spend much money on porters and ushers before he could get a licence from headquarters. The sixpence per book paid to the Stationers' Company was paid for a separate and subsequent transaction, its entry on the register "for the copy" of the printer or publisher who brought it, i.e., as his copyright, which every other member of the Company was bound to respect. This copyright could not be obtained unless the book was certified "under the hands" of the wardens or of some higher authorities as duly licensed. Once obtained it was considered, by the custom of the Company, to hold good for ever.

Although in these arrangements of the censorship and the Stationers' Company no provision was made for safeguarding the rights of authors, the commendable practice of paying authors for their work had greatly increased by the end of the sixteenth century. At the beginning of the century probably the only literary work for which payment was made was that of such men as Robert Copland, who made translations and wrote prefaces, and occasionally small books, for the printers with whom they were connected. By Shakespeare's time men like Nashe and Greene lived by their pens, and, though they endured many privations, probably suffered rather from the irregularity of their earnings than from a bad rate of pay. " Glad was that printer," wrote Nashe of Greene, " that might bee so blest to pay him deare for the very dregs of his wit," and the work of "a night and a day" sufficed to turn out a pamphlet. Nor was it by any means only the catchpenny pamphleteer who could find a market for his writings. As early as 1582 we have a very remarkable assertion of the custom of paying learned authors in a letter from Thomas Norton, the City Remembrancer, to George Goring, a patron of the malcontent printer, John Wolf, who refused to respect the privileges, granted by the Queen, giving a favoured printer or publisher the

or papers, being not licensed, as is abouesayde : that the same partie shalbe punished by order of the saide Commissioners, as to the qualitie of the fault shalbe thought meete. And touching all other bookes of matters of religion, or pollicie, or gouernaunce, that hath bene printed eyther on this side the Seas, or on the other side, because the diuersitie of them is great, and that there nedeth good consideration to be had of the particularities thereof, her Maiestie referreth the prohibition or permission thereof, to the order whiche her sayde Commissioners within the Cittie of London shall take and notifie. According to the whiche, her Maiestie straitly commaundeth all maner her subjectes, and specially the Wardens and company of Stationers to be obedient.

"Prouided that these orders doe not extende to any prophane aucthours, and works in any language that hath ben heretofore commonly receiued or allowed in any the vniuersities or schooles but the same may be printed and vsed as by good order they were accustomed."

Regulations such as these were absolutely unworkable and consequently were systematically ignored.

5

sole right of printing a particular class of book. Norton and a Dr Hammond had been appointed by the Privy Council to inquire into the matter, and on Goring, who apparently had interest with the Lord Treasurer, intervening on behalf of Wolf, Norton wrote to him an account of the extant privileges, ending:

> Otherwise we finde none to haue privilege, but generally as your man, and all other printers haue, which is to haue the sole printing of such bookes as any learned man shall make at their charge or geue vnto them. And it were greatly to the hurt of the vniuersities and learning to take from them the reward for trauailing in making or translating of bookes, which must nedes be if he that rewardeth the Learned man shold not haue the profit thereof. (Arber, ii, 776.)

Four years later (May 4, 1586) the Patentees in a petition to the Privy Council advance the same argument (Arber, ii, 805): "If privileges be revoked, no bookes should at all be prynted within short tyme, for comonlie the fyrst prynter is at charge for the Authors paynes, and somme other suche like extraordinarie cost, where an other that will print it after hym, commeth to the Copie gratis, and so maie he sell better cheaper then the first prynter, and then the first prynter shall never vtter his bookes." They go on to point out (with the same confusion between privileges and copyright) that it is always easy to improve a book in reprinting it, so that a pirate would have other advantages; but the prime reason on which they base their contention, that no one would print books if any one might reprint them, is this obligation on the first printer to pay his author and thereby add to the cost of the book.

The argument here used first by the Commissioner of the Privy Council and afterwards by the Patentees shows that the practice of paying authors was becoming common, and as a matter of fact only a year or two after this we find at least one author being paid by his publisher on quite a handsome scale. This was the Rev. William Fulke, who, finding the resources of his own library too limited to enable him to confute all the arguments, glosses and annotations in the text of the New Testament "translated by the Papists of the traiterous Seminarie at Rhemes," journeyed to London, and quartered himself with two servants and their horses, for nine months, on his publisher, George Bishop; was supplied by him with the books he wanted, and finally received in hard cash £40, while £10 more was subsequently paid to his executors for some additional notes written for a new edition. Fulke's ponderous volume remained a standard work for half a century, and we may hope that the plucky publisher was rewarded for his outlay. But when a theologian could win board and lodging for himself and his servants and the considerable sum (allowing for the altered value of money) of £40 or £50 for his pains, an author's property in his literary work had become a tangible asset, and it is difficult to believe that printers and publishers could appropriate it at pleasure by surreptitiously obtaining a copy of the manuscript.

How the theory arose that valuable copyrights might be obtained by the simple process of stealing a manuscript and "purchasing a licence" for it by the payment of vj^d at Stationers' Hall is not difficult to see. In the letter to Goring, which we have already quoted, Thomas Norton mentions as an alter-

native to a publisher paying for a book the possibility of the author giving
it to him. Then, as now, there were no doubt books which an author was
glad to get printed at his publisher's risk without being paid for them, because any probable profits would only be enough to pay for the risk. But
this giving of books to publishers was also encouraged by the feeling, which
lasted to Byron's time, that it was beneath the dignity of a man of fashion
to be paid for literary work. In Shakespeare's days this fancy sometimes took
the extremer form of objecting, or pretending to object, altogether to publication, the fashionable course to take being that of circulating a book among
the author's friends by means of manuscript copies. Sir Philip Sidney, whose
authority in such a matter would carry a weight which can hardly be exaggerated, did not allow any of his writings to be printed during his life. After
his death the transcripts of them were less carefully guarded, and, perhaps by
the connivance of friends who wished to force the hands of his family, publishers were able to lay hands on them, though not to their own profit. In
dedicating the first edition of his *Essays* to his brother Anthony, Francis
Bacon asserted that he published them himself because an unauthorized
edition was being prepared, and "to labour the staie of them had bin trouble-
some and subject to interpretation." In writing this Bacon probably meant
that to invoke the help of one of the great officers of state, or even of the
Master of the Stationers' Company, to prevent a handful of Essays appearing in print might have suggested that he attached too much importance
to them, or, on the other hand, that they contained something of which he
was ashamed. He took the sensible course, and, as the question of publication had been raised, sent them to press himself.* Minor authors, desiring
to be strictly correct in their behaviour and yet yearning to see themselves
in print, may have wondered wistfully when the piracy was going to begin,
and cursed the carefulness with which their friends guarded their manuscript copies. If a pirate did not appear of his own accord, a judicious inter-
mediary might produce one, or at least a rumour of one, which would be
sufficient to justify action similar to that of Bacon. Had the fashion lasted
long enough, "to forestall the pirates" might have become as hackneyed
an excuse for publication as "at the urgent entreaty of valued friends." While
it was in vogue, it may no doubt have had a disturbing influence on publishers' morality. *Volenti non fit injuria:* to help an author to immortality must
surely be a kindness in which he would acquiesce, did his dignity allow!
Perhaps some Elizabethan publishers may have made such excuses to themselves for printing books which the writers really desired to suppress, or to
publish in their own way, and yet I cannot help believing that surreptitious
printing was something of a bogey, far more talked about than practised,
and that (outside the disputed category of plays) to find half a dozen instances
where it was practised to the detriment of a professional author, i.e. one
known to take money for his writings, would be very far from easy.

As we have seen, in the dedication of his *Essays*, Bacon tells his brother
that "to labour the staie of them had bin troublesome," and the three cases
in which the higher powers were invoked to prevent the illegitimate printing
of the works of Sir Philip Sidney show that this was no idle excuse. It was by

*See Note B at end of chapter.

complaint to the Archbishop of Canterbury, or his deputy in licensing matters, Dr Cosin, that the Sidney family, by the help of Fulke Greville, frustrated an intended edition of the *Arcadia* and were able to entrust it to a publisher of their own choice, William Ponsonby. It was by complaint to the Lord Treasurer that they brought Thomas Newman to book for printing *Astrophel and Stella* with an objectionable appendix of other men's work. Finally, when Ponsonby found that his nine-shilling edition of Sidney's *Arcadia* and miscellaneous writings was being supplanted by the sale in England of copies of the Edinburgh edition of 1599 at six shillings, it was from no less a tribunal than the Court of Star Chamber that he had to seek redress for his grievance. The Stationers' Company was allowed to act, on sufferance, as a licensing authority, but essentially it was only a trade society with no power save over its own members. The determination of the Crown to keep the control of the press entirely in its own hands removed all questions connected with printing from the jurisdiction of the ordinary law. It was thus to the Privy Council itself, or to some one of its most distinguished individual members, that all complaints had to be taken. No doubt, to obtain a hearing might be difficult, but the hearing once gained there would be no appeal from the decision. If an honest man might pocket a wrong rather than appear as a suitor before so august a body, this was certainly also not a court before which a thief would care to be cited. Moreover, it was essentially a court, not of law, but of common sense, where proof of a substantial wrong done could not be met by quibbles on an indictment or other subterfuges. If, as has been suggested, the amount of wrong done to professional authors was really much less than might have been expected from the absence of any legal protection for their rights, may we not conjecture that fear of the powers of the Privy Council acted as a real deterrent to theft? If so, it is well to note that for obtaining the help of the Privy Council the players had one great advantage over ordinary authors.

To escape from the statute which otherwise condemned them as rogues and vagabonds, the Elizabethan actors were compelled to put themselves under the protection of some nobleman. In an ordinary action at law the patron could not have helped them much; in an appeal to the Privy Council the request of the Lord Chamberlain or the Lord Admiral could hardly have failed to obtain a hearing for any genuine grievance. No doubt, the players would have been reluctant to trouble their patron for any trifling cause, and might have submitted to the piracy of a play now and again rather than invoke his aid. But on the generally accepted hypothesis the wrong done to them was recurrent, and the lost value of the copyrights of a succession of popular plays must have amounted to some hundreds of pounds, the equivalent of some thousands as money now passes. This loss, we are asked to believe, was endured with absolute patience, varied only by an occasional grumble at the thieves. Yet Elizabethan Englishmen were not so different from the Englishmen of to-day as to make it likely that they would thus tamely endure a pecuniary wrong.

As against our suggestion of the inherent improbability of the players having acquiesced in any wholesale attack on their property we find set up the counter-suggestion that it is inherently improbable that they would ever willingly have allowed an actable play to be printed. Thus Mr Sidney Lee remarks: "The theatrical manager viewed the publication of plays as injurious to his interests, and until a play had wholly exhausted its popularity on the stage he deprecated its appearance in print." Mr Lee is, of course, translating various bits of evidence into his usual positive and rounded statement, and, while broadly taken the statement is undeniably true, the process does not make for precision. Presumably, when a play had "wholly exhausted its popularity on the stage," the assertion that "the theatrical manager viewed the publication of plays as injurious to his interests" would cease, in this case, to be true, and it seems à *priori* probable that even before a play had become quite unactable there may often have been a moment when the possible harm done by publication was outbalanced by the possible profit from its sale to a publisher. It seems not unlikely, indeed, that in some cases the publication of the text of a play might revive interest in its performance. Certainly from the Restoration to the end of the eighteenth century successful plays were usually printed. It must be remembered also that the sooner a a play was sold the higher would be the price paid for it. We know from the preface to Middleton's *Family of Love* (1608) that old plays did not sell well: "when they grow stale they must be vented by Termers and Cuntrie chapmen." As to what the copyright of a play would be worth we have no other guide than the fact that a popular play often went through several editions, and that even at the price of 6d. a copy this must have meant a profit which might well seem considerable at a time when the highest price which we know to have been paid to a dramatist for any one play is £20, while from £6 to £10 seems to have been a common payment.*

If we look at this question of the sale of plays from another side, we may get more light on it than these probabilities afford. It may surely be taken for granted that no one save the players themselves could sell plays in batches, and if we find plays appearing in print in such batches, and at the very times when it would obviously be to the convenience of the players to sell them, then we have a very strong argument that it was from the players that they were obtained. Now, in the eight years 1585–1592 only nine plays were entered for publication on the Stationers' Register. In the last of these years, 1592, the theatres were closed, owing first to riots and subsequently to the plague, from the end of June to December; but the players doubtless hoped for better times, and only three plays were entered. In 1593, however, plague again broke out, and the theatres were closed for an even longer time, viz., from April to December 22, a period of nearly eight months. It is, therefore, very significant that a few months later we find a nearly similar period beginning (October 8, 1593–July 20, 1594), during which no fewer than twenty-eight plays were entered on the Register, suggesting the inference that they had been sold by the players during the time that the theatres were closed and were now being registered as they were got ready for publication. After July, 1594, there is a pause of some months, and then between April, 1595, and January, 1596, nine plays are entered. In the rest of 1596 and in the three years 1597–1599 we have only nine more entries, but in 1600 the number again rises suddenly to twenty-eight. The theatres

*See Note C.

9

were not closed that year because of the plague, but, apparently, there was trouble of another kind, since in response to complaints from the Puritan party, the Lords of the Privy Council on June 22 issued an order directing that only two theatres should be allowed for the future, and that these should be closed during Lent and at other times only give two performances in each week. The players must have been pretty well used to being threatened in this way, and the coincidence here is not as strong as in 1593; but, putting coincidences altogether out of the question, such an outpouring of plays as we find between October, 1593, and July, 1594, and again in 1600, points strongly to the publishers having obtained them in those years from the only source where they could exist in quantities, that is from the companies of players. These, who bought plays outright from their authors, had every reason to keep them to themselves as long as the exclusive acting rights in them were more valuable than the copyright, but had no reason to refuse money for them when this had ceased to be the case, or when there was, or was likely to be, no opportunity of acting them. We cannot suppose that an army of shorthand writers invaded the theatres at these two periods. If there had been a great burglary at the theatres, the whole affair would have been too notorious. When we find twenty-eight plays apiece entered in each of these two periods, and only twenty-six altogether in the fourteen other years at the close of the century, surely we have strong *prima facie* evidence that the sale to publishers of plays afterwards duly entered on the Stationers' Registers was regulated by their lawful owners.

It may be most freely and willingly admitted that the theory that any-one could steal and print an Elizabethan play and obtain copyright in it by paying sixpence to the Stationers' Company, to the exclusion of the author and his assigns, does not conflict with the official functions either of the Censors of the Press or of the Stationers' Company. Neither the one nor the other were legally bound to show any consideration to authors. What the theory, when extended to cover not an isolated instance but a whole series of depredations, conflicts with is common sense and the English character. It is understood that in this happy land if various people in authority, from His Majesty the King downwards, did all the things they are legally entitled to do, the Constitution would be in a sad plight. But these mysterious possibilities remain unfulfilled, and while they are unfulfilled no one troubles to obtain paper guarantees against them, with the result that future historians will perhaps gravely argue that of course they happened. No doubt there were similar possibilities within the reach of the worthy Stationers of London, but, perhaps, after what has been said, it will be allowable to approach the consideration of the quarto plays and the entries of them in the Stationers' Registers without taking it for granted that their publication was attended by systematic fraud, in which various respectable people, who had nothing to gain from it, are supposed to have cheerfully acquiesced.

NOTE A.

The two passages from Heywood as to plays being pirated are so often referred to that, as they are both rather inaccessible, it may be well to quote them here in full. The first is the preface to *The Rape of Lucrece* (London: N. Butter, 1630): "To the Reader.—IT hath beene no custome in mee of all other men (courteous Reader) to commit my plaies to the presse: the

reason though some may attribute to my owne insufficiencie, I had rather subscribe in that to
their seueare censure then by seeking to auoide the imputation of weaknes to incurre greater
suspition of honestie: for though some haue vsed a double sale of their labours, first to the Stage,
and after to the presse, For my owne part I heere proclaime my selfe euer faithfull in the first,
and neuer guiltie of the last: yet since some of my plaies haue (vnknowne to me, and without
any of my direction) accidentally come into the Printers hands, and therefore so corrupt and
mangled, (coppied only by the eare) that I haue bin as vnable to know them, as ashamed to
chalenge them, This therefore, I was the willinger to furnish out in his natiue habit: first being
by consent, next because the rest haue beene so wronged in being publisht in such sauadge and
ragged ornaments: accept it courteous Gentlemen, and prooue as fauorable Readers as we haue
found you gratious Auditors.   Yours T. H."

The second passage occurs in Heywood's *Pleasant Dialogues and Drammas* (London, R. O. for
R. H. and solde by T. Slater, 1637). This is headed:

"A Prologue to the Play of Queene Elizabeth as it was last revived at the Cock-pit, in which
the Author taxeth the most corrupted copy now imprinted, which was published without his
consent."

Prologue.

Playes have a fate in their conception lent,
Some so short liv'd, no sooner shew'd than spent;
But borne to-day, to morrow buried, and
Though taught to speake, neither to goe nor stand.
This: (by what fate I know not) sure no merit,
That it disclaimes, may for the age inherit.
Writing 'bove one and twenty; but ill nurst,
And yet receiv'd as well perform'd at first,
Grac't and frequented, for the cradle age,
Did throng the Seates, the Boxes, and the Stage
So much; that some by Stenography drew
The plot: put it in print: (scarce one word trew:)
And in that lamenesse it hath limp't so long,
The Author now to vindicate that wrong
Hath tooke the paines, upright upon its feete
To teache it walke, so please you sit, and see't.

In the first of these passages Heywood alludes, first to the dishonesty of some playwrights who,
after selling their plays to the actors, make a further profit by secretly supplying copies to printers
desirous of publishing (piratical) editions. As some of his own plays have been printed in a mangled form, "coppied only by the eare," he has obtained the consent of the actors to issue an
authorized edition of his *Lucrece*. In the prologue to the play of *Queene Elizabeth* (i.e., *If you
know not me, you know no bodie; Or, The troubles of Queene Elizabeth*), of which seven
editions of Part 1, and four of Part 2 were published before 1637, Heywood repeats his complaint, and says that this play has been so deformed by the stenographers, that he has taken
pains to amend it for a revival. As *If you know not me*, etc., was first published as early as 1605,
the statement of its having been printed by means of stenography is good evidence as to what
went on in the early years of James I. During these years the players published very few plays
of their own accord, and the temptations to piracy must therefore have been all the greater.

NOTE B.

After writing this preface, which he dates "from my Chamber at Graie's Inne this 30 of
Januarie, 1597," Bacon helped his publisher to secure the copyright. The intending pirate was
Richard Serger, to whom on January 24, 1596/97 was "Entred for his copie vnder thande of
Master Warden Dawson a booke entituled Essayes of M. F. B. with the prayers of his Sove-
reigne." Against this entry (in which the designation of the author by initials probably betrays
the pirate's tremors) is written in the margin of the Register, "cancellatur ista intratio per curiam
tentam 7 februarij." Meanwhile, on February 5, Humfrey Hooper, Bacon's authorized publisher,
"Entred for his copie vnder thandes of Master Frauncis Bacon, master Doctor Stanhope, master
Barlowe, and master Warden Lawson, A booke intituled Essaies, Religious meditations, Places of
Perswasion and Disswasion by master Frauncis Bacon." Two days after this the book was already
on the market, since the copy in the British Museum bears the inscription: "Septimo die Febru-
arii, 39 E.R. pretium xx^d," where "39 E.R." of course stands for the thirty-ninth year of
Queen Elizabeth, which ran from November 17, 1596, to November 16, 1597. Moreover the

price paid for the tiny book suggests that the pretty vellum binding with a gold fillet and a flower in the centre was already covering it.

NOTE C.

As a proof of the objection of the players to their plays being printed, it is usual to quote an entry in Henslowe's Diary : " Lent vnto Robarte Shawe the 18 of March, 1599, to geue vnto the printer, to staye the printing of patient gresell, the some of xxxxˢ." *Patient Grissill* (for which the joint authors, Dekker, Chettle and Haughton, received £10 10s.) was eventually published in 1603, but according to the usual interpretation of the entry the players thought it better in 1599 to buy off a piratical printer at the earlier date with a couple of pounds, than to allow it to be printed or to be at the trouble of getting the play stayed by authority. As it is certain that some plays were pirated, there is no impossibility in this, but the entry may equally well be explained as caused by the revocation of a permission to print previously given, the forty shillings being the compensation offered to the printer, either for pages he had set up, or for surrendering his bargain.

CHAPTER II. A BIBLIOGRAPHY OF THE QUARTO EDITIONS OF SHAKESPEARE'S PLAYS PUBLISHED PREVIOUSLY TO 1623 WITH THE ENTRIES RELATING TO THEM IN THE REGISTERS OF THE STATIONERS' COMPANY, AND NOTES.

AS this bibliography contains some unusual particulars, a few words of explanation as to each of its features may be prefixed. In every case where a play was entered in the Register of the Stationers' Company the entry has been quoted (in italics) before the edition which it covers. In the same way all transfers are entered in their chronological order, so that a complete history is given of each of the plays printed in quarto down to the date of the publication of the First Folio.

When a facsimile is not given, the transcript of the title is printed in such a way as to show roughly the types used. The "collation," e.g., A-K⁴, indicates that the book is made up of the number of sheets denoted by the letters and that each sheet has the number of leaves denoted by the index figure, A-K⁴ being equivalent to ten sheets of four leaves each, i.e., forty leaves or eighty pages. Head-titles, that is the name of the play as set forth at the beginning of the text, and Running-titles, the form used at the top of each page or pair of pages, are added partly for any additions, or differences, which they may offer as compared with the information given on the titlepage, partly because they may possibly contain some evidence as to the typographical habits of the printer. The presence or absence of Division into Acts and Scenes is noted because it has been claimed that this offers important evidence as to the source of the copy which the printer used; Stage directions, other than simple exits and entrances, for the same reason, directions of a kind already represented being sometimes omitted. The next two notes, which treat directly of the source of the quarto text and its relations to subsequent editions including the First Folio, are so intimately connected with the conclusions which it is desired to elicit from our whole investigation, that to give my own views might easily involve a *petitio principii*. Except therefore when otherwise stated, they represent the conclusions of the editors of the Facsimile Quartos, a distinguished body of students, whom I have the more confidence in citing because they express with various degrees of strength that belief in the unauthorized and surreptitious nature of the quarto editions taken indiscriminately to which I am strongly opposed. Finally, in the case of the quartos which are typographically anonymous, the name of the printer, where this has been ascertained, is supplied in the last note, with a brief indication of the evidence on which the ascription is based. This evidence I have everywhere examined and tested for myself, but some of it was first brought to light by Mr H. R. Plomer in the article on "The Printers of Shakespeare's Plays and Poems," which he wrote at my request for *The Library* of April, 1906 (New Series, vol. VII, pp. 149–166).

TITUS ANDRONICUS

Entry in Stationers' Register:

1593/94] *vj⁰ die ffebruarii. John Danter. Entred for his copye vnder thandes of bothe the wardens a booke intituled a Noble Roman Historye of Tytus Andronicus. vjᵈ.*

The next entry to this, under the same date, is "John Danter. Entred alsoe vnto him by warraunt from Master Woodcock the ballad thereof, vjᵈ." Until the beginning of 1905 it was generally supposed that the entry of the play referred to an early version of it, and that the edition of 1600, which was believed to be the first with the received text, was a recast of this. The discovery, in Sweden, of a copy of a 1594 edition, printed by Danter, with substantially the same text as that of 1600, proved this theory to be erroneous.

THE | MOST LA- | mentable Romaine | Tragedie of Titus Andronicus: | As it was Plaide by the Right Ho- | nourable the Earle of *Darbie*, Earle of *Pembrooke* | and Earle of *Suffex* their Seruants. [Danter's device and motto: Aut nunc aut numquam.] LONDON, | Printed by Iohn Danter, and are | to be fold by *Edward White & Thomas Millington*, | at the little North doore of Paules at the | figne of the Gunne. | 1594.

Collation: A-K⁴, unpaged.

Head-title: [Head-piece, with I.D in centre] The most Lamen- | table Roman Tragedie of | *Titus Andronicus:* As it was Plaide by | the Right Honourable the Earle | of *Darbie*, Earle of *Pembrooke*, | and Earle of *Suffex* their Seruants.

Running-title: The most Lamentable Tragedie | of Titus Andronicus.

Division into Acts and Scenes: none.

Stage directions: believed to be same as in the second edition, q.v.

Relation to subsequent editions: copied by the quartos of 1600 and 1611 and through them by the First Folio, which has, however, additional stage directions, corrections balanced by new misprints and the addition of Act IV., Scene 2, omitted, no doubt accidentally, from this and the subsequent quartos.

SECOND EDITION

The moft lamenta- | ble Romaine Tragedie of *Titus* | *Andronicus*. | As it hath fundry times beene playde by the | Right Honourable the Earle of Pembrooke, the | Earle of Darbie, the Earle of Suffex, and the | Lorde Chamberlaine theyr | Seruants. [Ornament] AT LONDON, | Printed by I.R. for Edward White | and are to bee folde at his fhoppe, at the little | North doore of Paules, at the figne of | the Gun. 1600.

Collation: A-K⁴, unpaged.

Head-title: The moft lamentable Romaine | Tragedie of *Titus Andronicus*: As it was plaid | by the Right Honorable the Earle of Darbie, Earle | of Pembrooke, and Earle of Suffex | theyr Seruants.

Running-title: The moft lamentable Tragedie | of Titus Andronicus.

Division into Acts and Scenes: None.

Stage Directions*: I, i. They goe vp into the Senate houfe.—Sound Drummes and Trumpets, and then enter two of Titus fonnes, and then two men bearing a Coffin

* Unlefs where otherwife indicated all stage directions are printed in italics, with proper names sometimes in roman.

couered with blacke, then two other ſonnes, then Titus Andronicus, and then
Tamora the Queene of Gothes and her two ſonnes, Chiron and Demetrius, with Aron
the More, and others, as many as can be [:] then ſet downe the Coffin, and Titus
ſpeakes.—They open the Tombe.—Sound Trumpets and lay the coffin in the
Tombe.—Enter aloft the Emperour with Tamora and her two ſonnes, and Aron the
Moore.—The brother and the ſonnes kneele.—They put him in the tombe.—They
all kneele and ſay.—Enter the Emperour, Tamora and her two ſonnes, with the
Moore at one doore. Enter at the other doore Baſcianus and Lauinia, with others.
II, i. Enter Chiron and Demetrius brau[l]ing.—they draw.—Enter Titus Andro-
nicus and his three ſonnes, making a noyſe with hounds & hornes.—Heere a cry of
Houndes, and winde hornes in a peale, then enter Saturninus, Tamora [&c.] II, iii.
She giueth Saturnine a Letter.—Enter the Empreſſe ſonnes, with Lauinia, her
handes cut off, & her tongue cut out and rauiſht. III, i. Enter the Iudges and
Senatours with Titus two ſonnes bound paſſing on the Stage to the place of execu-
tion, and Titus going before pleading.—Andronicus lieth downe, and the Iudges
paſſe by him.—Enter Lucius, with his weapon drawne.—Hee cuts off Titus hand.—
Enter a meſſenger with two heads and a hand.—IV, i. Enter Lucius ſonne and
Lauinia running after him, and the boy flies from her with his bookes vnder his
arme.—He writes his Name with his ſtaffe, and guides it with feete and mouth.—
Shee takes the ſtaffe in her mouth, and guides it with her ſtumps and writes. IV, ii.
Enter Aron, Chiron, and Demetrius at one doore, and at another doore young
Lucius and another, with a bundle of weapons and verſes writ vpon them.—
He kils her.—IV, iii. Enter Titus, old Marcus, young Lucius, and other gentlemen
with bowes, and Titus beares the arrowes with Letters on the endes of them.—He
giues them the arrowes.—Enter the Clowne with a baſket and two pidgions in it.
IV, iv. Enter Emperour and Empreſſe, and her two ſonnes, the Emperour brings
the Arrowes in his hand that Titus ſhot at him.—Hee reades the Letter.—V, ii.
They knocke and Titus opens his ſtudie doore.—Enter Titus Andronicus with a
knife, and Lauinia with a Baſon. V, iii. Sound Trumpets, enter Titus like a Cooke,
placing the meate on the table, and Lauinia with a vaile ouer her face.—He ſtabs
the Empreſſe.

Relation to other editions: Reprinted from the first edition. Danter, the printer of the
first edition, who had entered the play "for his copie," had died in 1597, and
Edward White, one of the publishers of the first edition, does not appear to have
troubled to register a formal transfer. In 1594 and 1596 Danter had sold two copyrights to Cuthbert Burby on condition of being employed to print the books, and to
obtain something to print may have been his only reason for entering *Titus Andronicus.* If so, White may have bought the copyright without registering it.

Printer: I. R. are the initials of Iames Roberts.

Attempted Assignment:

1602] 19 *Aprilis . . . Thomas pavier. Entred for his copies by aſſignement from
Thomas Millington theſe bookes folowinge, Saluo Jure cuiuscunque,*

viz.

A booke called Thomas of Reading	*vj*[d]
The first and second parte of Henry the vj[t] ij bookes	*xij*[d]
A booke called Titus and Andronicus	*vj*[d]

Entred by warrant vnder master Setons hand

Pavier seems to have been anxious about this time to pick up Shakespeare copyrights, and Edward White's failure to register a formal transfer from Danter's widow
no doubt encouraged him to bargain for the rights, if any, of the other seller of the
1594 edition, Thomas Millington. Until the rediscovery of that edition there was no
clue to Millington's connexion with the book. Pavier's attempt was unsuccessful, as
the copy remained with Edward White, as shown by the next entry. Nevertheless we
find his claim to the play reiterated at a later date.

THE
Tragedie of King Richard the second.

As it hath beene publikely acted by the right Honourable the Lorde Chamberlaine his Seruants.

LONDON

Printed by Valentine Simmes for Androw Wife, and
are to be fold at his fhop in Paules church yard at
the figne of the Angel.

1 5 9 7.

TITLEPAGE OF THE FIRST EDITION OF "KING RICHARD II"
16

THE
Tragedie of King Richard the second.

As it hath beene publikely acted by the Right Honourable the Lord Chamberlaine his seruants.

By William Shake-speare.

LONDON
Printed by Valentine Simmes for Andrew Wise, and are to be sold at his shop in Paules churchyard at the signe of the Angel.
1 5 9 8.

TITLEPAGE OF THE SECOND EDITION OF "KING RICHARD II"

[Headpiece] THE | MOST LAMEN- | TABLE TRAGEDIE | *of Titus Andronicus.* | As it hath sundry | *times beene plaide by the Kings* | Maiefties Seruants. | [Device] London, | Printed for Eedward [sic] White, and are to be folde | at his fhoppe, nere the little North dore of | Pauls, at the figne of the | Gun. 1611.

Collation: A-K⁴, unpaged.
Head-title: The most lamentable Romaine | Tragedie of Titus Andronicus: As it was plaid | by the right honorable the Earle of Darbie, Earle | of Pembrooke and Earle of Suffex | their Servants.
Running-title: The most lamentable *Tragedie* | *of Titus Andronicus.*
Divifon into Aɛts and Scenes: None.
Source of Text: Reprinted from the second edition.
Relation to First Folio: The text follows this edition, with some additions to the stage directions, corrections balanced by new misprints, and the important addition of Aɛt III, Sc. 2.
Printer: Not identified.

RICHARD II

Entry in Stationers' Register:

1597.] 29° *Augusti. Andrew Wise. Entred for his Copie by appoyntment from master Warden man, The Tragedye of Richard the Second.* vjᵈ.

On August 15 and September 26 and 30 of this year books were entered "by warrant from master Warden man"; on August 22 it was noted that a book "entred under the hand of Master Peter Lyllie" was "entred also by appointment of master man warden"; on August 26 a book was "entred by master warden mans appointment"; on October 14 a book was "entred by direction from master Warden man." It is clear that all these phrases are synonymous, and that this is an original entry, and not, as has been suggested, a transfer.

FIRST EDITION (See Facsimile)

Collation: A-I⁴K², unpaged. A, B, C, D and I are found in two different states, corrected and uncorrected.
Head-title: None.
Running-title: The Tragedie of | King Richard the fecond.
Division into Acts and Scenes: None.
Stage Direɛtions: I, iii. The trumpets found and the King enters with his nobles, when they are fet, enter the Duke of Norfolke in armes defendent.—The trumpets found. Enter Duke of Hereford appellant in armour. I, iv. Enter the King with Bushie &c. at one dore, and the Lord Aumarle at another. III, iii. The trumpets found, Richard appeareth on the walls. v, ii. He pluckes it out of his bofome and reades it.—His man enters with his bootes. v, iii. The Duke of Yorke knokes at the doore and crieth. v, v. The mufike plaies. v, v. The murderers rufh in.—Here Exon ftrikes him downe.

SECOND EDITION (See Facsimile)

The first edition with Shakespeare's name.
Collation: A-I⁴, unpaged.
Head-title: None.
Running-title: The Tragedie of | King Richard the fecond.
Division into Aɛts and Scenes: None.
Stage Direɛtion: In this edition the Parliament scene contains the following direɛtions: Enter Bullingbrooke, Aumerle, and others.—Enter King Richard.
Source of Text: Reprinted from First Quarto with trifling correɛtions and many new misprints.

Assignment from Wise to Law:
1603.] 23 *Junij. Mathew Lawe. Entred for his copies in full courte Holden this Day. These ffyve copies folowinge* ij^s vj^d.

viz.

iij enterludes or playes.
The ffirst is of Richard the .3.
The second of Richard the .2.
The Third of Henry the .4 the firste part. all kinges.
Item master Doctor Plafordes sermons.
Item a thyng .of. no man can be hurt but by hymself.
    All whiche by consent of the Company are sett over to him from Andrew Wise.

THIRD EDITION

(A) THE | Tragedie of King | Richard the fecond. | As it hath been publikely acted by the Right | Honourable the Lord Chamberlaine | his feruantes. | By *William Shake-fpeare.* | [Device.] LONDON, | Printed by W.W. for *Matthew Law*, and are to be | fold at his fhop in Paules Church-yard, at | the figne of the Foxe. | 1608.
(B) (See Facsimile.)

These are two issues of the same edition, the latter with a new titlepage calling attention to the inclusion of the Parliament Scene (Act IV, sc. i, ll. 154–318) now first printed.
Collation: A–K⁴, unpaged. K₄ blank [?].
Head-title: None.
Running-title: The Tragedie of | Richard the Second [or *King Richard the Second*].

FOURTH EDITION

THE | Tragedie of King | Richard the Se- | cond: | *With new additions of the Parliament Sceane, | and the depofing of King | Richard.* | As it hath been lately acted by the Kinges | Maiesties feruants, at the Globe. | *By* WILLIAM SHAKE-SPEARE | [Ornament] *At LONDON,* | Printed for *Mathew Law*, and are to be fold | at his fhop in Paules Church-yard, at the | figne of the Foxe. | 1615.

Collation: A–K⁴, unpaged. K₄ blank.
Head-title: None.
Running-title: The Tragedie of | Richard the Second.
Division into Acts and Scenes: None.
Relation to First Folio: the Folio text was set up from a copy of this edition, corrected by a better text, and divided into Acts and Scenes.

RICHARD III

Entry in Stationers' Register:
1597.] 19° *Octobris. Andrewe wise. Entred for his copie vnder thandes of master Barlowe, and master warden man. The tragedie of Kinge Richard the Third with the death of the Duke of Clarence.*

FIRST EDITION (See Facsimile)

Collation: A–M⁴, unpaged. M₄ blank [?].
Head-title: None.
Running-title: **The Tragedy | of Richard the third.**

19

THE
Tragedie of King
Richard the Second:

With new additions of the Parliament Sceane, and the depofing
of King Richard.

As it hath been lately acted by the Kinges
Majefties feruantes, at the Globe.

By William Shake-fpeare.

AT LONDON,
Printed by W. W. for *Mathew Law*, and are to
be fold at his fhop in Paules Church-yard,
at the figne of the Foxe.
1 6 0 8.

TITLEPAGE OF THE SECOND ISSUE OF THE THIRD
EDITION OF "KING RICHARD II"

THE TRAGEDY OF
King Richard the third.

Containing,
His treacherous Plots againſt his brother Clarence:
the pittiefull murther of his iunocent nephewes:
his tyrannicall vſurpation : with the whole courſe
of his deteſted life, and moſt deſerued death.

As it hath beene lately Acted by the
Right honourable the Lord Chamberlaine his ſeruants.

AT LONDON
ꟼ Printed by Valentine Sims , for Andrew Wiſe,
dwelling in Paules Chuch-yard , at the
Signe of the Angell.
1597.

TITLEPAGE OF THE FIRST EDITION OF
"KING RICHARD III"

Division into Acts and Scenes: None.

Stage Directions. i, ii, Shee fpitteth at him.—Here fhe lets fall the fword. i, iv, He
readeth it. iii, ii, He gives him his purfe.—He whifpers in his eare. iii, vi, Enter a
Scrivener with a paper in his hand.—Enter Glocefter at one dore, Buckingham at
another. iii, vii, Enter Rich. with two bishops aloste [*sic*]. iv, ii, Here he afcendeth
the throne.—He wifpers in his eare. iv, iv, The trumpets.—He ftriketh him.
v, iii, Richard ftarteth vp out of a dreame.—The clocke ftriketh.—he fheweth him
a paper.

Source of Text: A copy of the play slightly cut down and altered for stage representation.

Relation to subsequent editions: Each subsequent quarto reprints its predecessor, except
Q5, which was set up from a made-up copy of Quartos 3 and 4: the Folio reprints
Q6, corrected by a transcript of the original text of the play, and with division into
Acts and Scenes.

SECOND EDITION (see Facsimile)

Collation: A-M⁴, unpaged. M₄ blank [?].
Head-title: None.
Running-title: The Tragedie | of Richard the third.
Division into Acts and Scenes: None.
    The first edition with Shakespeare's name.

THIRD EDITION

THE | TRAGEDIE | of King Richard | the third. | *Conteining his treache-*
rous Plots againft his brother | *Clarence:* the pittifull murther of his innocent
Ne- | phewes: his tyrannicall vfurpation: with the | whole courfe of his
detefted life, and | most deferued death. | *As it hath bene lately Acted by the*
Right Honourable | *the Lord Chamberlaine his feruants.* | Newly augmented, |
By *William Shakefpeare.* | [Creed's Device] | LONDON. | Printed by
Thomas Creede, for Andrew Wife, dwelling | in Paules Church-yard, at the
figne of the | Angell. 1602.

Collation: A-L⁴M², unpaged.
Head-title: None.
Running-title: The Tragedie | of Richard the Third.
Division into Acts and Scenes: None.
Source of Text: Notwithstanding the words "Newly augmented," this edition contains
no new matter.

Assignment from Wise to Law:

1603.] 23. *Junii Mathew Lawe. Entred for his copies in full courte Holden this*
Day. These ffyve copies followinge   *ijˢ vjᵈ.*

                             viz.

> *iij enterludes or playes.*
> *The ffirst is of Richard the .3.*
> *The second of Richard the . 2.*
> *The third of Henry the .4. the firste part. All kinges.*
> *Item Master Doctor Plafordes sermons.*
> *Item a thyng . of . no man can be hurt but by hymself.*
>   *All whiche by consent of the Company are sett ouer to him from*
> *Andrew Wise.*

THE TRAGEDIE

of King Richard
the third.

Conteining his treacherous Plots againſt his
brother *Clarence*: the pitiful murther of his innocent
Nephewes: his tyrannicall vſurpation: with
the whole courſe of his deteſted life, and moſt
deſerued death.

As it hath beene lately Acted by the Right honourable
the Lord Chamberlaine his ſeruants.

By William Shake-ſpeare.

LONDON

Printed by Thomas Creede, for Andrew Wiſe,
dwelling in Paules Church-yard, at the ſigne
of the Angell. 1 5 9 8.

TITLEPAGE OF THE SECOND EDITION OF
"KING RICHARD III"

FOURTH EDITION

THE | TRAGEDIE | of King Richard | the third. | *Conteining his treacherous Plots againft his brother* | *Clarence:* the pittifull murther of his innocent Ne- | phewes: his tyrannicall vfurpation: with the | whole courfe of his detefted life, and | moft deferued death. | *As it hath bin lately Acted by the* | *Right Honourable* | *the Lord Chamberlaine his feruants.* | Newly augmented, | By *William Shake-speare.* | [Creed's device] LONDON, | Printed by Thomas Creede, and are to be fold by *Mathew* | *Lawe,* dwelling in Paules Church-yard, at the Signe | of the Foxe, neare S. Auftins gate, 1605.

Collation: A-L⁴ M².
Head-title: None.
Running-title: The Tragedie | of Richard the third.
Division into Acts and Scenes: None.

FIFTH EDITION

THE | TRAGEDIE | of King Richard | the third. | ... *As it hath beene lately Acted by the Kings Maiefties* | *feruants.* | Newly augmented, | By *William Shake-fpeare.* [Creed's device]. [Same imprint.] 1612.

Collation: A-L⁴M².
Head-title: None.
Running-title: The Tragedie | of Richard the third.
Division into Acts and Scenes: None.

SIXTH EDITION

THE | TRAGEDIE | *OF* | KING RICHARD | *THE THIRD.* | Contayning, *etc.* [Ornament] LONDON, | Printed by *Thomas Purfoot,* and are to be fold by *Mathew Law,* dwelling | in *Pauls* Churchyard at the Signe of the *Foxe,* | neere | *S. Austines* gate, 1622.

Collation: A-L⁴M², unpaged.
Head-title: None.
Running-title: The Tragedie | of Richard the Third.
Division into Acts and Scenes: None.
Relation to First Folio: A copy of this edition, with additions and corrections, made from a transcript of the original, formed the basis of the Folio text.

ROMEO AND JULIET

Entry in Stationers' Register: *None.*

FIRST EDITION (see Facsimile)

Collation: A-K⁴, unpaged, A-D in a large type, 32 lines to a page ; E-K, in smaller type, 36 lines to a page.
Head-title: The moft excellent Tragedie of | *Romeo and Iuliet.*
Running-title: (sigs A-D) *The moft excellent Tragedie,* | *of Romeo and Iuliet.* (Sigs E-K) *The excellent Tragedie of* | *Romeo and Iuliet.*
Division into Acts and Scenes: None until the end of Act III, Sc. 4. After this each new scene is marked off from its predecessor by a printer's ornament.
Stage Directions: I, i, They draw, to them enters Tybalt, they fight, to them the Prince, old Mountague, and his wife, old Capulet and his wife, and other Citizens, and part them. I, ii, He reads the Letter. I, v, They whifper in his eare. II, iv, He walkes by them, and fings.—She turnes to Peter her man. II, vi, Enter Iuliet fomewhat faft, and embraceth Romeo. III, i, Tibalt vnder Romeo's arme thrufts Mercutio, in and flyes.—

Fight, Tibalt falles. iii, ii, Enter Nurfe wringing her handes, with the ladder of cordes in her lap. iii, iii, Nurfe knockes.—Shee knockes againe.—He rifes.—He offers to stab himfelfe and Nurfe fnatches the dagger away.—Nurfe offers to goe in and turnes againe. iii, iv, Paris offers to goe in and Capolet calles him againe. iii, v, Enter Romeo and Iuliet at the window. | He goeth downe.—She goeth downe from the window.—She kneeles downe.—She lookes after Nurfe. iv, iii, She fals vpon her bed within the Curtaines. iv, v, All at once cry out and wring their hands.—They all but the Nurfe goe forth, casting Rofemary on her and fhutting the Curtens. v, iii, Enter Countie Paris and his Page with flowers and fweete water.—Paris ftrewes the Tomb with flowers.—Enter Romeo and Balthazar, with a torch, a a (sic) mattocke, and a crow of yron.—Romeo opens the tombe.—They fight.—Enter Fryer with a lanthorne.—Fryer ftoops and lookes on the blood and weapons.—Iuliet rifes.—She ftabs herfelfe and falles.

Relation to later editions: An imperfect report of a version of substantially the same text, but abridged (2,232 lines instead of 3,007) for a performance of little more than two hours. The faults become more prominent towards the end.

Assignment in Stationers' Register: *None.*

SECOND EDITION (see Facsimile)

Collation: A-L⁴M².

Head-title: THE MOST EX- | cellent and lamentable | Tragedie, of *Romeo* and *Iuliet.*

Running-title: The moft lamentable Tragedie | of *Romeo* and *Iuliet.*

Division into Acts and Scenes: None.

Stage Directions: i, iv, They march about the Stage, and Seruingmen come forth with Napkins.—Enter all the guefts and gentlewomen to the Maskers.—Mufick playes and they dance. i, v, One cals within Iuliet. iii, ii, Enter Nurfe with cords. iii, iii, Enter Nurfe and knocke—They knocke—Slud knock—Knocke. iii, v. Enter Romeo and Juliet aloft. Play Musicke. iv, v. Enter Will Kemp. v, 3. Whiftle Boy.—Entrer (sic) Frier with Lanthorne, Crowe and Spade.

Evidence as to source of Text: Mr Daniel has shown that lines 1-4 of Act ii, Scene iii and ll. 37-43 of Act iii, Sc. iii, could only have taken their present form from misunderstanding a carelessly corrected manuscript copy. The later stage directions show that this was, or was copied from a prompt copy.

Relations to subsequent editions: Copied by quartos of 1609 and through that by the First Folio.

Assignment from Burby to Ling:

1606/7.] 22 *Januarij. Master Linge. Entred for his copies by direccon of a Court and with consent of Master Burby vnder his hand wrytinge These . iij copies.*

viz.

> *Romeo and Juliett.*
> *Loues Labour Loste.*
> *The taminge of A Shrewe . . . .*   *xviij.ᵈ·R.*

Assignment from Ling to Smethwick:

1607.] 19. *Novembris. John Smythick. Entred for his copies vnder thandes of the wardens. these bookes followinge whiche dyd belonge to Nicholas Lynge.*

viz.

1 *Master Draytons Poemes*	*vjᵈ*
2 *Euphues golden legacie*	*vjᵈ*
3 *Master Greenes Arcadia*	*vjᵈ*
4 *Greenes neuer to late*	*vjᵈ*
5 *His Tullies loue*	*vjᵈ*
6 *A booke called Hamlett*	*vjᵈ*

A N EXCELLENT
conceited Tragedie
O F
Romeo and Iuliet.

As it hath been often (with great applause)
plaid publiquely, by the right Honourable the L. of *Hunsdon*
his Seruants.

LONDON,
Printed by Iohn Danter.
1 5 9 7

TITLEPAGE OF THE FIRST EDITION OF
"ROMEO & JULIET"

THE
MOST EX=
cellent and lamentable
Tragedie, of Romeo
and *Iuliet*.

Newly corrected, augmented, and
amended:

As it hath bene sundry times publiquely acted, by the
right Honourable the Lord Chamberlaine
his Seruants.

LONDON
Printed by Thomas Creede, for Cuthbert Burby, and are to
be sold at his shop neare the Exchange.
1 5 9 9.

TITLEPAGE OF THE SECOND EDITION OF
"ROMEO & JULIET"

7 *Three Sermons of Master Smythes* . . . . *vj^d*
8 *Wytte's common wealth* . . . . *vj^d*
9 *The taminge of A Shrewe* . . . . *vj^d*
10 *Romeo and Julett* . . . . *vj^d*
11 *Loues Labour Lost* . . . . *vj^d*
12 *Smythes common Wealth of England* . . . . *vj^d*
13 *Piers Pennyles* . . . . *vj^d*
14 *Reformation of Couetousnes* . . . . *vj^d*
15 *Figure of Fowre* . . . . *vj^d*
16 *Englishe Romane Lyfe* . . . . *vj^d*

THIRD EDITION

THE | MOST EX | CELLENT AND | Lamentable Tragedie, of | *Romeo and Juliet*. | As it hath beene fundrie times publiquely Acted, | by the KINGS Maiefties Seruants | at the Globe. | Newly corrected, augmented and | amended: | [Ornament.] LONDON | Printed for IOHN SMETHWICK, and are to be fold | at his Shop in Saint Dunftanes Church-yard, | in Fleete ftreete vnder the Dyall. | 1609.

Collation: A-L⁴ M², unpaged.
Relation to First Folio: the text follows this edition, with the usual small differences.
Printers:
Head-title: THE MOST EX | CELLENT AND | Lamentable Tragedie of | ROMEO and IVLIET.
Running-title: The moft lamentable Tragedie | of Romeo and Iuliet.
Division into Acts and Scenes: None.

HENRY IV

Entry in Stationers' Register:
1597/98.] *25° die ffebruarij. Andrew Wyse. Entred for his Copie vnder thandes of Master Dix: and master Warden man a booke intituled The historye of Henry the IIIj^th with his battaile of Shrewsburye against Henry Hottspurre of the Northe with the conceipted mirthe of Sir John Ffalstoff.* *vj^d.*

FIRST EDITION (see Facsimile)

Collation: A-K⁴, unpaged.
Head-title: THE HISTORIE OF | Henry the fourth.
Running-title: The Hiftorie | of Henrie the fourth.
Stage Directions: II, ii, They whiftle.—Here they rob them and bind them.—As they are fharing the Prince & Poins fet upon them, they all runne away, and Falftalffe after a blow or two runs away too, leauing the bootie behind them. II, iv. He drinketh.— He fearcheth his pocket, and findeth certaine papers. III, i. Glondower fpeakes to her in Welfh, and fhe anfweres him in the fame [&c.].— The muficke playes.—Here the ladie fings a welfh fong. III, iii, Enter the prince marching, and Falftalffe meetes him playing upon his trunchion like a fife. v, iii. Here they embrace, the trumpets sound, the king enters with his power, alarme to the battel, then enters Douglas, and Sir Walter Blunt. v, iii. The Prince drawes it out, and finds it to be a bottle of Sacke.—He throwes the bottle at him. v, iv. They fight, the king being in danger, Enter Prince of Wales.—Enter Douglas, he fighteth with Falftalffe, he fals down as if he were dead, the Prince killeth Percy.—He fpieth Falftalffe on the ground.—Falftalffe rifeth up.—He takes up Hotspur on his backe.—A retraite is founded.

Relation to subsequent editions: Each quarto copies its predecessor, and the First Folio the quarto of 1613.

SECOND EDITION

THE | HISTORY OF | HENRIE THE | FOVRTH | . . . Newly cor-rected by *W. Shake-ſpeare.* | [Device] AT LONDON, | Printed by *S. S.* for *Andrew Wiſe* dwelling | in Paules Churchyard, at the ſigne of | the Angell. 1599.

Collation: A-K⁴, unpaged.
Head-title: THE HISTORIE OF | Henry the fourth.
Running-title: The Hiſtorie | of Henry the fourth
Division into Acts and Scenes: None.
Printer: S.S. are the initials of Simon Stafford.

Assignment from Wise to Law:
1603.] 23 *Junij. Mathew Lawe. Entred for his copie in full courte Holden this Day. These ffyve copies followinge*   *ij, vjᵈ*

viz.

iij enterludes or playes.
The ffirst is of Richard the . 3.
The second of Richard the . 2.
The third of Henry the . 4 . the first parte.
all kinges
. . . *all whiche by consent of the Company are sett over to him from Andrew Wise.*

THIRD EDITION (see Facsimile)

Collation: A-K⁴, unpaged.
Head-title: THE HISTORIE OF | Henry the fourth.
Running-title: The Hiſtorie of | Henry the fourth.
Division into Acts and Scenes: None.

FOURTH EDITION

THE | HISTORY OF | Henry the Fourth, | . . . [Ornament] LON-DON, | Printed for *Mathew Law,* and are to be ſold at | his ſhop in Paul's Churchyard, neere vnto S. | *Auguſtines* gate, at the ſigne of | the Foxe. 1608.

Collation: A-K⁴, unpaged.
Head-title: THE HISTORIE OF | Henry the fourth.
Running-title: The Hiſtory of | Henrie the fourth.
Division into Acts and Scenes: None.

FIFTH EDITION

THE | HISTORY OF | Henrie the fourth | . . . [White's device] LON-DON, | Printed by *W. W.* for *Mathew Law,* and are to be ſold | at his ſhop in Paules Church-yard, neere vnto S. | Auguſtines Gate, at the ſigne of the Foxe. | 1613.

Collation: A-K⁴, unpaged.
Head-title: The Hiſtorie of | Henrie the fourth.
Running-title: The Hiſtorie of | Henry the fourth.
Division into Acts and Scenes: None.
Relation to First Folio: The text of the play in the First Folio was set up from a copy of this edition.

THE
HISTORY OF
HENRIE THE
FOVRTH;

With the battell at Shrewsburie,
betweene the King and Lord
Henry Percy, furnamed
Henrie Hotſpur of
the North.

With the humorous conceits of Sir
Iohn Falſtalffe.

AT LONDON,
Printed by *P. S.* for *Andrew Wiſe,* dwelling
in Paules Churchyard, at the ſigne of
the Angell 1598.

TITLEPAGE OF THE FIRST EDITION OF "THE HISTORY OF
HENRY IV"

THE
HISTORY OF
Henrie the fourth,

VVith the battell at Shrewsburie,
betweene the King, and Lord
Henry Percy, surnamed Henry Hot-
spur of the North.

With the humorous conceits of Sir
Iohn Falstalffe.

Newly corrected by *W. Shake-speare.*

LONDON
Printed by Valentine Simmes, for *Mathew Law* , and
are to be solde at his shop in Paules Churchyard,
at the signe of the Fox.
1 6 0 4.

TITLEPAGE OF THE THIRD EDITION OF "THE HISTORY OF
HENRY IV"

Sɪxᴛʜ Eᴅɪᴛɪᴏɴ

THE | HISTORIE | *OF* | Henry the Fourth | ... Newly correct̗ed. | By *William Shake-ſpeare.* | [Ornament] Lᴏɴᴅᴏɴ, | Printed by *T. P.* and are to be ſold by *Mathew Law,* dwelling | in *Pauls* Church-yard, at the Signe of the *Foxe,* neere | S. *Auſtines* gate, 1622.

Collation: A-K⁴, unpaged.
Head-title: The Hiſtorie of | *Henry the Fourth.*
Running-title: The Hiſtorie of | Henry the Fourth.
Division into Act̗s and Scenes: None.

   Although this 1622 edition probably appeared before the Folio was printed the quarto was not used for the text. In this edition a stop was for the first time placed after the words "newly correct̗ed" in the titlepage.
Printer: T. P. are the initials of Thomas Purfoot, who printed an edition of *Richard III* for Matthew Law in this same year.

LOVE'S LABOUR'S LOST
Entry in Stationers' Register: None.

Fɪʀsᴛ [?] Eᴅɪᴛɪᴏɴ (see Facsimile)
Collation: A-I⁴ K², unpaged.
Head-title: None.
Running-title: A pleaſant conceited Comedie | called Loues Labor's loſt.
Division into Act̗s and Scenes: None.
Stage Direct̗ions: ɪv, iii. Enter Berowne with a paper in his hand, alone.—He ſtandes a ſide. The King entreth.—Enter Longavill. The King ſteps a ſide.—He reads the Sonnet.—Dumaine reads his Sonnet.—He reads the letter.—v, i. Draw-out his Table-booke. v, ii, Sound Trom.—Enter Black-moores with muſicke, the Boy with a ſpeach, and the reſt of the Lordes diſguyſed.
Printer: W. W. are the initials of William White.
Relation to First Folio: Reprinted in the Folio, with division into Act̗s and Scenes.

Assignment from Burby to Ling:
1606/7.] 22 *Januarij. Master Linge. Entred for his copies by direccon of A Court and with consent of Master Burby vnder his handwrytynge   These iij copies.*
                                 viz.

   Romeo and Juliett.
   Loves Labour Loste.
   The taminge of A Shrewe. . . . . *xviijᵈ* R.

Assignment from Ling to Smethwick.
1607.] 19 *Novembris. John Smythick. Entred for his copies vnder thandes of the wardens, these bookes followinge whiche dyd belong to Nicolas Lynge.*
                                 viz. . . . .

   6 *A booke called Hamlett . . .*
   9 *The taminge of A Shrewe*
   10 *Romeo and Julett.*
   11 *Loves Labour Lost.*

   The full entry is given under *Romeo and Juliet.* As regards *Loves Labors Lost,* Smethwick is not known to have made any use of his rights until 1631, when he published a quarto edition.

A
PLEASANT
Conceited Comedie
CALLED,
Loues labors loſt.

As it vvas preſented before her Highnes
this laſt Chriſtmas.

Newly correĉted and augmented
By *W. Shakeſpere.*

Imprinted at London by *W.W.*
for *Cutbert Burby.*
1598.

TITLEPAGE OF THE FIRST (?) EDITION OF
"LOVE'S LABOUR'S LOST"

(A)

1598.] xxij, Julij. James Robertes. Entred for his copie vnder the handes of bothe the wardens, a booke of the Marchaunt of Venyce or otherwise called the Jewe of Venyce, Prouided that yt bee not prynted by the said James Robertes or anye other whatsoeuer without lycence first had from the Right honorable the lord Chamberlen. vj^d

This entry will be repeated in its connexion with *The Merchant of Venice*, but it is inserted here because, according to a possible interpretation, it was made not in view of, but to prevent, publication.

(B)

1599. June 1.] . . . That noe Satyres or Epigrams be printed hereafter. That noe Englishe historyes be printed excepte they bee allowed by some of her Maiesties priuie Counsell.
That noe playes be printed excepte they bee allowed by suche as haue aucthorytie.
That all Nasshes bookes and Doctor Harvyes bookes be taken wheresoeuer they maye be found and that none of theire bookes bee euer printed hereafter. . . .

     Jo. Cantuar.
     Ric. London.

.... Die veneris Primo Junij, xlj° Regin. The Commaundementes aforesaid were Delyuered att Croyden by my Lordes grace of Canterbury and the Bishop of London vnder theire handes to master Newbery master Binge and master Ponsonby wardens. And the said master and wardens Did there subscribe two Coppies thereof, one remaynynge with my Lords grace of Canterbury and the other with the Bishop of London.

The inclusion of plays in this drastic order is of some little importance, as until the storms which had evoked it were blown over the Wardens of the Stationers' Company would be bound to use more than ordinary care before entering the plays brought to them.

(C)

My lord chamberlens mens plaies Entred
viz.

27 May 1600   *A moral of clothe breches and veluet hose*
To master
Robertes

27 May   *Allarum to London*
To hym.

4 *Augusti*

As you like yt, a booke
Henry the ffift, a booke   *to be staied*
Euery man in his humour, a booke
The Commedie of muche A doo about nothing a booke

These entries (which are in different hands) occur on a fly-leaf of Register C. (Arber iii, 37), and in 1603 other provisional entries of books for which further authority was needed were written before and after them. The marginal references are explained by two entries on fol. 59 of the Register (Arber iii, 161): (i) "27. maij. Master Robertes. Entred for his copye vnder the handes of the wardens, A morall of Clothe breches and veluet hose, As yt is Acted by my lord Chamberlens seruantes. Provided that he is not to putt it in prynte Without further and better Aucthority... vj^d." (ii) "29 Maij ... Master Robertes. Entred for his copie vnder the hands of the Wardens, the Allarum to London, prouided that yt be not printed without further Aucthoritie ... vj^d." As there is no bookseller's name to the staying entries, it is clear that they were made directly at the instance of "my lord chamberlens men."

THE MERCHANT OF VENICE

Entries in Stationers' Register:

1598.]*xxij° Julij. James Robertes. Entred for his copie vnder the handes of bothe the wardens, a booke of the Marchant of Venyce, or otherwise called the Jewe of Venyce, Prouided, that yt bee not prynted by the said James Robertes or anye other whatsoeuer without lycence first had from the Right honorable the lord chamberlen.* vj^d.

1600.] *28 octobris. Thomas haies. Entred for his copie under the handes of the Wardens and by Consent of master Robertes. A booke called the booke of the merchant of Venyce ..* vj^a.

FIRST EDITION (see Facsimile)

*** Until 1908 this was usually considered the second. See the note to the next entry, and Chapter IV (The Quartos of 1619).

Collation: A-I¹ K², unpaged.
Head-title: The comicall Hiftory of the Mer- | chant o^f Venice.
Running-title: The comicall Historie of | the Merchant of Venice.
Divisions into Acts and Scenes: None.
Stage Directions*: II, i. Enter Morochus a tawnie Moore all in white, and three or foure followers accordingly, with Portia, Nerriffa, and their traine. II, ii. Enter old Gobbo with a basket. III, ii. A Song, the whilst Baffanio comments on the caskets to himfelfe. III, ii. l. 239. He opens the letter. v, i. Muficke playes.
Printer: I. R. are the initials of Iames Roberts, who would naturally have bargained with Heyes that in consideration of his surrender of his rights under the entry of 1598 he should have the book to print.

SECOND EDITION (see Facsimile).

Collation: A-K⁴, unpaged.
Head-title: The Comicall Hiftory of the | Merchant of Venice. [Under headpiece of Royal Arms.]
Running-title: The Comicall Hiftory of | the Merchant of Venice.
Source: Reprinted from the Heyes Quarto of 1600.
Printer: William Jaggard in 1619.

*** See Chapter IV, "The Quartos of 1619."

Assignment from Estate of Thomas Heyes to Lawrence Heyes:
8° *Julij* 1619. *Laurence Hayes. Entred for his Copies by Consent of a full Court their two copies following which were the Copies of Thomas Haies his fathers*
vizt
A play called *The Merchant of Venice*,
And the Ethiopian History . . . . xij^d

* Many of the Directions in this edition are in roman with names in italics.

The moſt excellent

Hiſtorie of the *Merchant of Venice*.

VVith the extreame crueltie of *Shylocke* the Iewe
towards the ſayd Merchant, in cutting a iuſt pound
of his fleſh : and the obtayning of *Portia*
by the choyſe of three
cheſts.

*As it hath beene diuers times aſted by the Lord
Chamberlaine his Seruants.*

Written by William Shakeſpeare.

AT LONDON,
Printed by *I. R.* for Thomas Heyes,
and are to be ſold in Paules Church-yard, at the
ſigne of the Greene Dragon.
1 6 o o.

TITLEPAGE OF THE FIRST EDITION OF "THE
MERCHANT OF VENICE"

THE
EXCELLENT
Hiſtory of the Mer-
chant of Venice.

With the extreme cruelty of *Shylocke*
the Iew towards the ſaide Merchant, in cut-
ting a iuſt pound of his fleſh. And the obtaining
of *Portia*, by the choyſe of
three Caskets.

Written by W. SHAKESPEARE.

Printed by *J. Roberts*, 1600.

HENRY V

Laurence Hayes printed an edition in 1637.

Note in Stationers' Register:

[1600] 4 *Augusti. Henry the ffift, a booke, to be staied.*

Entry in Stationers' Register: *None.*

FIRST EDITION (see Facsimile)

Collation: A-G⁴, unpaged. Last blank.

Head-title: The Chronicle Historie | of *Henry* the fift: with his battel fought | at *Agin* Court in *France.* Togither with | Auncient *Pistoll.*

Running-title: The *Chronicle Hiftorie of* | *Henry the fift.*

Division into Acts and Scenes—None.

Stage Directions: II, i, They drawe. III, ii, Enter Flewellen and beates them in. III, iii, Enter the King and his Lords. alarum. IV, vi, l. 32, Alarum soundes. IV, viii, He strikes him. V, ii. Enter at one doore, the King of England and his Lords. And at the other doore, the King of France [etc.].

Source of Text: a grossly imperfect version of the play as abridged for the stage.

Relations to subsequent editions: Reprinted twice in quarto, but ignored by the editors of the Folio.

Assignment to Pavier:

1600.] 14 *Augusti. Thomas Pavyer. Entred for his Copyes by Direction of master white warden vnder his hand wrytinge. These Copyes followinge beinge thinges formerlye printed and sett over to the sayd Thomas Pavyer.*

viz.

The Pathway to Knowledge	*vjᵈ*
The historye of Henry the Vᵗʰ with the battell of Agencourt . .	*vjᵈ*
The Spanish Tragedie.	*vjᵈ*
An Interlude Called Edward Longe Shankes	*vjᵈ*

[With eight others.]

SECOND EDITION (see Facsimile)

Collation: A-F⁴ G², unpaged.

Head-title: The Chronicle Hiftorie | of Henry the fift: with his battel fought | at *Agin* Court in *France.* Togither with | Ancient *Pistoll.*

Running-title: The *Chronicle Hiftorie* | *of Henry the fift.*

Source of Text: Reprinted from quarto of 1600 with trifling corrections.

THIRD EDITION (See Facsimile)

Collation: A-G⁴, unpaged, last blank.

Head-title: The Chronicle Hiftorie | of Henry the fift: with his battell fought | at *Agin* Court in France. Togither with | Ancient *Pistoll.*

Running-title: The *Chronicle History* | *of Henry the fift.*

Source of Text: Reprinted from the quarto of 1600.

Printer: William Jaggard in 1619. See Chapter IV, "The Quartos of 1619."

MUCH ADO ABOUT NOTHING

Note in Stationers' Register:

[1600] 4 *Augusti, The Comedie of muche A doo about nothing, a booke To be staied.*

Entry in Stationers' Register:

[1600] 23 *Augusti. Andrew Wyse, William Aspley. Entered for their copies vnder the handes of the wardens Two bookes. the one called Muche a Doo about Nothinge. Thother the second parte of the history of Kinge Henry the iiijᵗʰ with the humours of Sir John ffalstaff: wrytten by master Shakespere.* xijᵈ.

38

THE
CRONICLE

Hiſtory of Henry the fift,

With his battell fought at *Agin Court* in
France. Togither with *Auntient*
Piſtoll.

As it hath bene ſundry times playd by the Right honorable
the Lord Chamberlaine his ſeruants.

LONDON

Printed by *Thomas Creede*, for Tho. Millington, and Iohn Busby. And are to be
ſold at his houſe in Carter Lane, next
the Powle head   1600.

THE
CHRONICLE
Hiſtory of Henry the fift,
VVith his battell fought at *Agin Court*
in *France*. Togetherwith *Auntient*
Piſtoll.

As it hath bene ſundry times playd by the Right honorable
the Lord Chamberlaıne hiſſeruants.

LONDON
Printed by Thomas Creede, for Thomas
Pauier,and are to be ſold at his ſhop in Cornhill,
at theſigne ofthe Cat and Parrets neare
the Exchange. 1602.

TITLEPAGE OF THE SECOND EDITION OF "THE
CHRONICLE HISTORY OF HENRY V"

THE
Chronicle History

of Henry the fift, with his
battell fought at *Agin Court* in
France. Together with an-
cient *Piſtoll*.

*As it hath bene ſundry times playd by the Right Honou-
rable the Lord Chamberlaine his
Seruants.*

Printed for *T. P.* 1608.

Much adoe about Nothing.

As it hath been sundrie times publikely
acted by the right honourable, the Lord
Chamberlaine his seruants.

Written by William Shakespeare.

LONDON
Printed by V. S. for Andrew Wise, and
William Aspley.
1600.

TITLEPAGE OF THE FIRST EDITION OF
"MUCH ADOE ABOUT NOTHING"

THE
Second part of Henrie

the fourth, continuing to his death,
and coronation of Henrie
the fift.

With the humours of sir Iohn Fal-
staffe, and swaggering
Pistoll.

As it hath been sundrie times publikely
acted by the right honourable, the Lord
Chamberlaine his seruants.

Written by William Shakespeare.

LONDON
Printed by V.S. for Andrew Wise, and
William Aspley.
1600.

TITLEPAGE OF THE FIRST EDITION OF "THE SECOND
PART OF HENRY IV"

FIRST EDITION (see Facsimile)

Collation: A-I⁴, unpaged.

Head-title: Much adoe about | *Nothing.*

Running-title: Much adoe | about Nothing.

Division into Acts and Scenes: None.

Stage Directions: II, iii, 38. Enter grinder, Leonato, Claudio, Muficke; II, iii, 44, Enter Balthafer with muficke; IV, ii, Enter the Conftables, Borachio and the Towne clearke in gownes; V, iii, Enter Claudio, Prince, and three or foure with tapers.

Source of Text: In Act IV, Sc. ii, the names of the actors, Kemp and Cowley, are substituted for Dogberry and Verges, proving that the text was set up from a prompt copy or a transcript of one.

Relation to First Folio: The "Folio edition a copy of the quarto containing a few MS. alterations and corrections made probably years before and not specially for this purpose." In the stage directions to II, iii, 38, the name of the performer, " Jack Wilson," is substituted for " Musicke."

Printer: V. S. are the initials of Valentine Sims.

HENRY IV, PART 2.

Entry in Stationers' Register:

1600] 2 3 *Augusti. Andrewe Wyse William Aspley. Entred for their copies vnder the handes of the wardens Two bookes, the one called Muche a Doo about nothinge. Thother the second parte of the history of Kinge Henry the iiij^th with the humours of Sir John ffalstaff: wrytten by Master Shakespere.* xij^d

FIRST EDITION (see Facsimile)

(A.) *First issue. Collation:* A-K⁴ L², unpaged.

(B.) *Second issue. Collation:* A-D⁴ E⁶ F-R⁴ L², unpaged.

In this issue Sheet E was reprinted with two additional leaves to make good the omission of Act III, Scene i.

Head-title: The fecond part of Henry the fourth, | *continuing to his death, and coro-* | nation of Henry the | fift.

Running-title: The fecond part of | Henry the fourth.

Division into Acts and Scenes: None.

Stage Directions: I, i. Enter the Lord Bardolf at one doore [&c.]; I, ii. Enter Sir Iohn alone, with his page bearing his sword and buckler; II, iv. Peyto knockes at doore; III, ii. Enter the King in his nightgown alone; IV, i. Enter the Archbishop, Mowbray, Bardolfe, Hastings, within the forreft of Gaultree; IV, ii. Shout; IV, iii. Alarum. Enter Falftaffe. Excurfions; V, iii. One knockes at doore; V, v. Trumpets found and the King and his traine paffe over the ftage, after them enter Falftaffe [etc.].

Source of Text: That the text is taken from an acting version, made for use in the playhouse, is proved (a) by its omission of 171 lines found in the Folio; (b) by the use of the name of the actor " Sincklo " for the part assigned to the " Officer " in the Folio in Act v, sc. iv; (c) by signs of the text being in an unedited state as compared with that of the Folio, e.g., in its retention in I, i, 161, of the part of Sir John Umfreville merged in the Folio in that of Bardolph.

Relation to the First Folio: The Folio text was taken from an independent source. While adding 171 lines, it omits 39. The faults in the two texts seem about on a level. Mr Evans speaks of the quarto "as representing, in all probability, the earlier, purer and less sophisticated text." He nevertheless speaks of Matthew Law succeeding " to the piratical business of Andrew Wise."

A MIDSUMMER NIGHT'S DREAM

Entry in Stationers' Register:

1600] *8 octobris. Thomas ffyssher. Entred for his copie vnder the handes of master Rodes and the Wardens A booke called A mydsommer nightes Dreame. vj^d.*

FIRST EDITION (see Facsimile)

Collation: A-H⁴, unpaged.
Head-title: A | MIDSOMMER NIGHTS | DREAME.
Running-title: A Midſommer nightes dreame.
Stage Directions: I, i. Stand forth Demetrius. Stand forth Lisander. (Both these really belong to the text.) II, i. Enter a Fairie at one doore, and Robin goodfellow at another.—Enter the King of Fairies, at one doore, with his traine; and the Queen at another, with hers. III, ii, 85, Ly doun; IV, i, 138, Shoute within: they all ſtart up. Winde hornes.
Divisions into Acts and Scenes: None.
Relation to other editions: Reprinted by "Roberts."
Printer: Not identified.

SECOND EDITION (see Facsimile)

Collation: A-H⁴, unpaged.
Head-title: A | MIDSOMMER NIGHTS | DREAME.
Running-title: A Midſommer nights Dreame.
Relation to other editions: Reprinted from the edition with Fisher's name. The text used in the First Folio.
Printer: William Jaggard in 1619. See Chapter, "The volume of 1619."

THE MERRY WIVES OF WINDSOR

Entry in Stationers' Register:

1601/2] *18 Januarij. John Busby. Entred for his copie vnder the hand of master Seton, A booke called An excellent and pleasant conceited commedie of Sir John ffaulstof and the merry wyves of Windesor.* *vj^d.*
Arthur Johnson. Entred for his Copye by assignement from John Busbye, A booke Called an excellent and pleasant conceyted Comedie of Sir John ffaulstafe and the merye wyves of Windsor. *vj^d.*

Dr Arber comments on these two entries: "It is quite clear that *The Merry Wives of Windsor* was printed by J. Busby before this date, but not entered in the Registers until he came to assign it to A. Johnson." No edition, however, bearing Busby's name has ever been heard of. It seems probable that Johnson preferred that Busby should take the responsibility of entering the book.

FIRST EDITION (see Facsimile)

Collation: A-G⁴, unpaged. A1 blank save for signature.
Head-title: A pleasant conceited Co- | medie of Syr *Iohn Falſtaffe* and the | merry Wiues of *Windſor.*
Running-title: A pleaſant Comedie, of | the merry wiues of Windſor.
Division into Acts and Scenes: None.
Stage Directions: II, ii. He ſteps into the Counting-houſe . . . And ſhe opens the doore.—The Doctor writes. II, v. Ford and the Hoſt talkes. III, viii. Enter Doctor and the Host, they offer to fight.—III, x. Enter Miſtreſſe Ford, with two of her men, and a great buckbusket.—Falſtaffe stands behind the aras.—Sir Iohn goes into the basket, they put cloathes ouer him, the two men carries it away: Foord meetes it, and all the rest, Page, Doctor, Priest, Slender, Shallow.—IV, xiii. Enter M. Ford, Page, Priest, Shallow, the two men carries the basket, and Ford meets it.—IV, ii. Enter

A
Midſommer nights
dreame.

As it hath beene ſundry times pub-
lickely acted, by the Right honoura-
ble, the Lord Chamberlaine his
ſeruants.

Written by William Shakeſpeare.

¶ Imprinted at London, for *Thomas Fiſher,* and are to
be ſoulde at his ſhoppe, at the Signe of the White Hart,
in *Fleeteſtreete.* 1600.

**TITLEPAGE OF THE FIRST EDITION OF "A MIDSUMMER
NIGHT'S DREAM"**

A
Midſommer nights
dreame.

As it hath beene ſundry times publikely acted, *by the Right Honoura-*
ble, the Lord Chamberlaine his
ſeruants.

VVritten by VVilliam Shakeſpeare.

Printed by Iames Roberts, 1600.

TITLEPAGE OF THE SECOND EDITION OF "A MIDSUMMER
NIGHT'S DREAM"

A
Moſt pleaſaunt and
excellent conceited Co-
medie, of Syr *Iohn Falſtaffe*, and the
merrie Wiues of *Windſor*

Entermixed with ſundrie
variable and pleaſing humors, of Syr *Hugh*
the Welch Knight, Iuſtice *Shallow* , and his
wife Couſin M. *Slender*.

With the ſwaggering vaine of Auncient
Piſtoll, and Corporall *Nym*.

By *William Shakeſpeare*.

As it hath bene diuers times Acted by the right Honorable
my Lord Chamberlaines ſeruants. Both before her
Maieſtie, and elſe-where.

LONDON
Printed by T. C. for Arthur Iohnſon, and are to be ſold at
his ſhop in Powles Church-yard, at the ſigne of the
Flower de Leuſe and the Crowne.
1602.

TITLEPAGE OF THE FIRST EDITION OF "THE MERRY
WIVES OF WINDSOR"

A
Most pleasant and ex-
cellent conceited Comedy,

of Sir Iohn Falstaffe, and the
merry VViues of VVindsor.

VVith the swaggering vaine of Ancient *Pistoll*, and Corporall *Nym*.

Written by W. SHAKESPEARE.

Printed for *Arthur Johnson,* 1619.

TITLEPAGE OF THE SECOND EDITION OF
"THE MERRY WIVES OF WINDSOR"

Falſtaffe diſguiſed like an old woman, and miſteris Page with him, Ford beates him, and hee runnes away.—v, v. Enter Sir Iohn with a Bucks head vpon him.—There is a noiſe of hornes, the two women run away.—Enter Sir Hugh like a Satyre, and boyes dreſt like Fayries, miſtreſſe Quickly, like the Queene of Fayries: they ſing a ſong about him, and afterwardſ ſpeake. v, v. They put the Tapers to his fingers, and he ſtarts.—Here they pinch him, and ſing about him, & the Doctor comes one way & ſteales away a boy in red. And Slender another way he takes a boy in greene: And Fenton ſteales miſteris Anne, being in white. And a noyſe of hunting is made within: and all the Fairies runne away. Falſtaffe pulles of his bucks head and riſes up. And enters M. Page, M. Ford, and their wiues, M. Shallow, Sir Hugh.

Printer: T. C. are the initials of Thomas Creed.

Probable source of the Text: "The true origin of the quarto I believe to be as follows:—The play was first shortened for stage representation: to the performance the literary hack, employed by the stationer to obtain a copy, resorted with his note-book. Perhaps he managed to take down some portions of the dialogue pretty accurately in short-hand, or obtained them by the assistance of some of the people connected with the theatre; but for the larger portion of the play it seems evident that he must have relied on his notes and memory only, and have clothed with his own words the bare ideas which he had stolen."—P. A. Daniel.

SECOND EDITION (see Facsimile)

Collation: A-G⁴, unpaged.

Head-title: A | Pleasant conceited Come- | die of Sir John Falstaffe, | and the merry Wives of Windſor.

Running-title: A pleaſant Comedy, of | the merry Wives of Windſor.

Division into Acts and Scenes: None.

Printer: The device about 1608 passed from Roberts into the hands of William Jaggard.

HAMLET

Entry in Stationers' Register:

1602.]xxvjᵗᵒ Julij. *James Robertes. Entred for his copie vnder the handes of master Pasfield and master Waterson warden A booke called the Revenge of Hamlett Prince [of] Denmarke as yt was latelie Acted by the Lord Chamberleyne his servantes.* vjᵈ.

FIRST EDITION

THE | Tragicall Hiſtorie of | HAMLET | *Prince of Denmarke* | By William Shake-ſpeare. | As it hath beene diuerse times acted by his Highneſſe ſer- | uants in the Cittie of London: as also in the two V- | niuerſities of Cambridge and Oxford, and elſewhere. | [Ling's device.] At London printed for N. L. and Iohn Trundell. | 1603.

Collation: Titlepage; B-I⁴.

Head-title: The Tragicall Hiſtorie of | HAMLET | Prince of Denmarke.

Running-title: The Tragedie of Hamlet | Prince of Denmarke.

Division into Acts and Scenes: None.

Stage Directions: I, iv, Sound Trumpets. I, v, 195, The Gost vnder the stage. II, ii, The Trumpets ſound. Enter Corambis. iii, hee kneeles. enters Hamlet. III, iv, Enter the ghost in his night gowne. IV, v, Enter Ofelia playing on a Lute, and her haire downe ſinging. IV, v. A noyſe within. enter Leartes. v, i, 35, he throwes vp a ſhouel. v, i, l. 124. Enter King and Queene, Leartes, and other lordes, with a Priest after the coffin. v, i, l.141, Leartes leapes into the grave. v, i, l.143, Hamlet leapes in after Leartes. v, ii, Enter a Bragart Gentleman. v, ii, l.63, a hit. v, ii, l.64, Heere they play. v, ii, l. 67, They play againe. v, ii, l. 75, Shee drinkes. v, ii, l. 82. They catch

T H E

Tragicall Hiſtorie of
H A M L E T,

Prince of Denmarke.

By William Shakeſpeare.

Newly imprinted and enlarged to almoſt as much
againe as it was, according to the true and perfect
Coppie.

AT LONDON,
Printed by I. R. for N. L. and are to be ſold at his
ſhoppe vnder Saint Dunſtons Church in
Fleetſtreet. 1 6 0 5.

TITLEPAGE OF THE SECOND EDITION (SECOND ISSUE) OF
"THE TRAGICAL HISTORY OF HAMLET"

one anothers Rapiers and both are wounded. Leartes falles downe, the Queene falles downe and dies. v, ii, l. 95, The king dies. v, ii, l. 98, Leartes dies. v, ii, l. 108, Ham. dies.

Printer identifiable by ornament and type as Valentine Sims.

Second Edition.—First Issue.

The | Tragicall Hiftorie of | HAMLET, | *Prince of Denmarke.* | By William Shakefpeare. | Newly imprinted and enlarged to almost as much | againe as it was, according to the true and perfeƈt | Coppie. | [Ling's device] AT LONDON, | Printed by I. R. for N. L. and are to be fold at his | fhoppe vnder Saint Dunstons Church in | Fleetftreet. 1604.

Collation: Title-page; B-N⁴, O².
Head-title: The Tragedie of | HAMLET | *Prince of Denmarke* [Below the block with Royal Arms in the centre.]
Running-title: The Tragedie of Hamlet | Prince of Denmarke.
Division into Aƈts and Scenes: None.
Stage Direƈtions: I. i. Enter Barnardo, and Francesco, two centinels. I. i. 126. It fpreads his armes. I, i. l. 138. The cocke crowes. I. iv. l. 7. A florish of trumpet and 2 peeces goes of. I, iv, l. 57, Beckins. I, v, l. 148, Ghost cries vnder the Stage. II, i, Enter old Polonius, with his man or two. III, ii, l. 356. Enter the Players with Recorders. IV, iv, Enter Fortinbraffe with his Army ouer the stage. IV, v, l. 21, fhee fings. IV, v, l. 96, A noife within. IV, v, l. 109, A noife within. IV, v, l. 151, A noyfe within. IV, vi, IV, vii, Enter a Messenger with Letters. V, i, l. 240, Enter K. Q. Laertes and the corse. V, ii, l. 235, A table prepard, Trumpets, Drums and Officers with Cushion, King, Queene, and all the state, Foiles, daggers, and Laertes. V, ii, l. 289, Trumpets the while. V, ii, l. 292. Drum, trumpets and shot. Florish, a peece goes off. V, ii, l. 359. A march afarre off.
Printer and Publisher: The initials I. R. and N. L. are those of Iames Roberts and Nicholas Ling.

Second Edition.—Second Issue (see Facsimile)

The sheets of this edition were reissued in the following year, with no other alteration than that of the date on the titlepage from 1601 to 1605. Or perhaps, more probably, the play was issued towards the end of 1604, and after a few copies had been printed off the date was altered to 1605 while the sheet was on the press.

Assignment from the estate of Nic. Ling to Smethwick:
1607.] 19 *Novembris. John Smythick. Entred for his copies vnder thandes of the wardens these bookes followinge whiche dyd belong to Nicolas Lynge.*

viz. . . . . . .

6 *A booke called Hamlett . . .*
9 *The taminge of A Shrewe*
10 *Romeo and Julett*
11 *Loues Labour Lost.*

The full entry is given under *Romeo and Juliet.*

Third Edition

THE | TRAGEDY | OF | HAMLET | Prince of Denmarke. | by | William Shakespeare. | Newly imprinted and enlarged to almoft as much | againe as it was according to the true | and perfeƈt Coppy. | [Smethwick's device] AT LONDON, | Printed for *Iohn Smethwick,* and are to be fold at

his fhoppe | in Saint *Dunftons* Church yeard in Fleetftreet. | Vnder the
Diall. 1611.

Collation: One leaf, B-N⁴ O².
Head-title: The Tragedie of | HAMLET | *Prince of Denmarke.*
Running-title: The Tragedy of Hamlet | *Prince of Denmarke.*

KING LEAR

Entry in Stationers' Register:

1607.] 26 *Novembris. Nathanael Butter, John Busby. Entred for their copie
under thandes of Sir George Buck knight ann Thwardens A booke called Master
William Shakespeare his historye of Kinge Lear, as yt was played before the Kinges
maiestie at Whitehall vppon Sainct Stephens night at Christmas Last, by his
maiesties servantes playinge vsually at the Globe on the Bankſyde.*

FIRST EDITION (see Facsimile)

Collation: One leaf, B-L⁴.
Head-title: M. William Shak-ſpeare | *HIS* | Hiſtorie of King Lear.
Running-title: The Hiſtorie of King Lear.
Division into Acts and Scenes: None.
Stage Directions: I, i. Sound a Sennet. Enter one bearing a Coronet, then Lear [&c.].
—I, ii. A letter.—II, ii. Enter Edmund with his rapier drawne [&c.] l. 180, ſleepes.—
III, i. Enter Kent and a Gentleman at feuerall doores.—III, iii. Enter Gloster and
the Baſtard with lights.—III, vii. Enter Gloſter brought in by two or three; l. 78,
draw and fight; l. 80, Shee takes a ſword and runs at him behind.—IV, i. Enter Gloſt.
led by an old man.—IV, vi. He kneeles; l. 82, Enter Lear mad; l. 207, Exit King
running; l. 248, they fight; l. 256, He dies; l. 291, A drum a farre off.—V, ii.
Alarum. Enter the powers of France ouer the ſtage, Cordelia with her father in her
hand; l. 4, Alarum and retreat; l. 116, Enter Edgar at the third found, a trumpet
before him.—V, iii. Enter one with a bloudie knife; l. 238, The bodies of Gonorill
and Regan are brought in; l. 256, Enter Lear with Cordelia in his arms.
Source of Text: An unusually illegible playhouse copy. While the edition was being
printed the proofs of several sheets seem to have been read with the manuscript,
and numerous corrections introduced. The copies of these sheets which had been
printed without correction were not, however, destroyed, but mixed promiscuously
with corrected copies, so that there are different combinations of corrected and uncorrected sheets in the different extant copies of this edition.
Relation to the First Folio: A copy of this quarto, containing sheets E, H and K
in their uncorrected state, having previously been read with an independent manuscript, seems to have been taken for the Folio text.
Printer: The device on the titlepage has been identified by Mr H. R. Plomer (*The
Library* 2nd series, vol. VII, p. 164) with one used in 1606 by George and Lionel
Snowden, who in 1608 transferred their business to Nicholas Okes. The play was
thus printed either by the Snowdens or Okes, probably the latter.

SECOND EDITION (see Facsimile)

Collation: A-L⁴.
Head-title: M. William Shake-ſpeare | *HIS* | Hiſtory, of King Lear. (Below Roberts-
Jaggard headpiece of Royal Arms.)
Running-title: The Hiſtory of King Lear.
Divisions into Acts and Scenes: The printer frequently leaves a space before a new
entrance, and many of these spaces occur where a new scene begins, but there are
others where there is no change.
Source of Text: A copy of the "Pide Bull" edition in which sheets E and K had
been corrected, some obvious misprints being here amended.
Printer: William Jaggard in 1619.

M. William Shak-speare:

HIS
True Chronicle Historie of the life and
death of King L E A R and his three
Daughters.

With the vnfortunate life of Edgar, *sonne*
and heire to the Earle of Gloster, and his
sullen and assumed humor of
T O M of Bedlam :

As it was played before the Kings Maiestie at Whitehall vpon
S. Stephans *night in Christmas Hollidayes.*

By his Maiesties seruants playing vsually at the Gloabe
on the Bancke-side.

LONDON,
Printed for *Nathaniel Butter*, and are to be sold at his shop in *Pauls*
Church-yard at the signe of the Pide Bull neere
S.*Austins* Gate. 1.6 0 8

TITLEPAGE OF THE FIRST EDITION OF
"KING LEAR"

M. VVilliam Shake-ſpeare,
HIS
True Chronicle Hiſtory of the life
and death of King *Lear*, and his
three Daughters.

With the vnfortunate life of E D G A R,
ſonne and heire to the Earle of *Gloceſter*, and
his ſullen and aſſumed humour of T O M
of Bedlam .

As it was plaid before the Kings Maieſty at White-Hall, vp-
pon S. Stephens night, in Chriſtmas Hollidaies.

By his Maieſties Seruants, playing vſually at the
Globe on the *Banck-ſide.*

Printed for *Nathaniel Butter.*
1608.

THE
Historie of Troylus
and Cresseida.

As it was acted by the Kings Maiesties
seruants at the Globe.

Written by William Shakespeare.

LONDON
Imprinted by *G. Eld* for *R Bonian* and *H. Walley*, and
are to be sold at the spred Eagle in Paules
Church-yeard, ouer againft the
great North doore.
1609.

TITLEPAGE OF THE FIRST EDITION OF
"TROILUS & CRESSIDA"

THE
Famous Historie of
Troylus *and* Cresseid.

Excellently expressing the beginning
of their loues, with the conceited wooing
of *Pandarus* Prince of *Licia.*

Written by William Shakespeare.

LONDON
Imprinted by *G. Eld* for *R. Bonian* and *H. Walley*, and
are to be sold at the spred Eagle in Paules
Church-yeard, ouer againſt the
great North doore.
1 6 0 9.

**TITLEPAGE OF THE SECOND EDITION OF
"TROILUS & CRESSIDA"**

TROILUS AND CRESSIDA

Entry in Stationers' Register:

1602/3] 7 *Februarii. Master Robertes. Entred for his copie in full Court holden this day to print when he hath gotten sufficient aucthority for yt, The booke of Troilus and Cresseda as it is acted by my lord Chamberlens Men.*

The possible object of this entry, other than that of immediate publication, and also the meaning of the words, "as it was acted by my lord Chamberlens Men," will be discussed in Chapter III, page 66. It may be noted here that the formal phrase "in full Court holden this day," is not very often used. In other cases when it occurs about this time it seems intended to give additional authority to entries of books in which the Company was itself pecuniarily interested, or of religious or historical works about which questions might arise.

Edition following on this entry: None known.

Second entry at Stationers' Hall:

1608/9.] 28ᵐᵒ *Ianuarii. Richard Bonion, Henry Walleys. Entred for their copy vnder thandes of Master Segar deputy to Sir George Bucke and Master Warden Lownes a booke called the history of Troylus and Cressida.* vjᵈ.

FIRST EDITION. First issue (see Facsimile)

Collation: A-L⁴ M², last blank?

FIRST EDITION. Second issue (see Facsimile)

Collation: ¶²A ₂₋₄ B-L⁴ M², last blank? i.e. the original titlepage has been cut away and replaced by a half sheet—two leaves, the second signed ¶²—containing a new titlepage and an address to the reader.

Head-title: The history of *Troylus* | and *Cresseida.*

Running-title: The history | of Troylus and Cresseida.

Stage Directions: I, i, l. 90. Sound alarum. ll. 107 and 115, alarum. l. 188 [a line and a half before it is alluded to:] Sound a retreate. I, iii, l. 260. Sound trumpet. II, ii, 96. Enter Cassandra rauing. III, i, 160. sound a retreat. IV, i. Enter at one doore Æneas, at another Paris, Deiphobus, Antenor, Diomed the Grecian with torches. IV, v. Enter Aiax armed, Achilles [etc.]. l. 63. Flowrish [:] enter all of Troy. l. 112. Alarum. l. 116. Trumpets cease. V, i, 73. Enter Agam: Vlisses, Nest: and Diomed with lights. V, iii, 94. Alarum. V, iv, 1. Enter Thersites: excursions. V, viii, l. 14. Retreat. V, ix. Enter Agam: Aiax, Mene: Nestor, Diom: and the rest marching.

Relations to Folio: Quarto text not used by Folio editors.

PERICLES

Entry in Stationers' Register:

1608] 20 *Maij. Edward Blount. Entred for his copie vnder thandes of Sir George Buck knight and Master Warden Seton A booke called the booke of Pericles prynce of Tyre.*

Edward Blount. Entred also for his copie by the like Aucthoritie A booke called Anthony and Cleopatra. vjᵈ

Editions following on these entries: None known.

FIRST EDITION (see Facsimile)

Collation: A-I⁴, the last blank.

Head-title: The Play of Pericles | Prince of Tyre, &c.

Running-title: Sometimes *Pericles, Prince of Tyre* on both pages, rather less often *The Play of Pericles, Prince of Tyre,* printed across the two.

THE LATE,

And much admired Play,

Called

Pericles, Prince
of Tyre.

With the true Relation of the whole Hiſtorie,
aduentures,and fortunes of the ſaid Prince :
As alſo,
The no leſſe ſtrange,and worthy accidents,
in the Birth and Life,of his Daughter
MARIANA.

As it hath been diuers and ſundry times acted by
his Maieſties Seruants,at the Globe on
the Banck-ſide.

By William  Shakeſpeare.

Imprinted at London for *Henry Goſſon*, and are
to be ſold at the ſigne of the Sunne in
Pater-noſter row, &c.
1 6 0 9.

TITLEPAGE OF THE FIRST EDITION OF "PERICLES,
PRINCE OF TYRE"

THE LATE,
And much admired Play,
CALLED,
Pericles, Prince of Tyre.

With the true Relation of the whole Hi-
ftory, aduentures, and fortunes of
the faide Prince.

Written by W. SHAKESPEARE.

Printed for *T. P.* 1619.

TITLEPAGE OF THE FOURTH EDITION OF "PERICLES,
PRINCE OF TYRE"

THE
Tragœdy of Othello,

The Moore of Venice.

As it hath beene diuerse times acted at the
Globe, and at the Black-Friers, by
his Maiesties Seruants.

Written by VVilliam Shakefpeare.

LONDON,
Printed by *N. O.* for *Thomas walkley,* and are to be fold at his
fhop, at the Eagle and Child, in Brittans Burffe.
1 6 2 2.

TITLEPAGE OF THE FIRST EDITION OF "THE TRAGEDY
OF OTHELLO"

Division into Acts and Scenes: Acts II and III marked off by a line across the page.

Stage Directions: II, i, Enter Pericles wette. l. 120, Enter the two Fiſher-men, drawing vp a Net. II, ii, 16, The firſt Knight paſſes by, l. 20, the ſecond Knight. l. 60, Great ſhoutes, and all cry, the meane Knight. II, iii, Enter the King and Knights from Tilting. ll. 98 and 108, They daunce. II, v, Enter the King reading of a letter at one doore, the Knightes meete him. III, i, Enter Pericles a ſhipboard. III, ii, 48, Enter two or three with a Cheſt. l. 85, Enter one with Napkins and Fire. l. 104, Shee moues. l. 110, They carry her away. Exeunt omnes. IV, 13, Enter Marina, with a Basket of flowers. v, i, 80, The Song.

Evidence as to source of Text: Full of mistakes, which can only be explained by the copy having been taken down by shorthand writers at the theatre.

Relation to subsequent editions: No later edition has any independent authority, all being, directly or indirectly, reprinted from this, with correction of some mistakes and introduction of others.

Printer: Identified by Mr H. R. Plomer from the headpiece on the first page of text as William White.

Second Edition

Same titlepage and collation. A careless reprint of the first, by the same printer.

In this edition the first stage direction is misprinted: *Eneer Gower.* The running title is throughout *The Play of | Pericles Prince of Tyre.*

Third Edition

THE LATE | And much admired Play, | Called | Pericles, Prince | of Tyre. | With the true Relation of the whole Hiſtory, | aduentures, and fortunes of the ſayd Prince: | *As alſo,* | The no leſſe ſtrange and worthy accidents, | in the Birth and Life, of his Daughter | *MARIANA.* | As it hath beene diuers and ſundry times acted by | his Maieſtyes Seruants, at the Globe on | the Banck-ſide. | By *William Shakeſpeare.* | [Three printer's ornaments.] Printed at London by *S. S.* | 1611.

Collation: A-I⁴, the last blank.
Head-title: The Play of *Pericles* Prince | of Tyre, &c.
Running-title: *The Play of | Pericles Prince of Tyre.*
Printer: The initials are those of Simon Stafford.

Fourth Edition (see Facsimile)

Collation: 1 leaf, R-Z Aa⁴ Bb². The first leaf bears the title, the last is blank [?]. The signatures are continuous with those of Pavier's undated edition of *The Whole Contention,* though the play is now more often found divorced from this.
Head-title: THE HISTORY OF | Pericles Prince of Tyre [below headpiece of Royal Arms as used by Roberts and Jaggard.]
Running-title: *Pericles Prince of Tyre.*
Printer and Publisher: Printed by William Jaggard for Thomas Pavier.

ANTONY AND CLEOPATRA

Entry in Stationers' Register:
1608] 20 *maij.* See *Pericles.*

OTHELLO

Entry in the Stationers' Register:
6° *Octobris,* 1621. *Thomas Walkley. Entred for his copie vnder the handes of Sir George Buck, and Master Swinhowe warden, The Tragedie of Othello, the Moore of Venice.* · *vj*ᵈ.

Collation: A² B-M⁴ N², Title [A¹]; The Stationer to the Reader, A²; text B-N².

Preface: [Headpiece]. The Stationer to the Reader. [5-line T]*O set forth a booke with-out an Epistle, | were like to the old English prouerbe, A | blew* coat without a badge, *& the Au | thor being dead, I thought good to take | that piece of worke vpon mee : To com | mend it, I will not, for that which is good, I hope euery | man will commend, without intreaty: and I am the bol | der, because the Authors name is sufficient to vent his | worke. Thus leauing euery one to the liberty of iudge- | ment I haue ventered to print this Play, and leaue it | to the generall censure. | Yours,* | Thomas Walkley.

Head-title: The Tragedy of Othello *the Moore | of* Venice.

Running-title: The Tragedy of Othello *| The Moore of* Venice.

Division into Acts and Scenes: After the first Act: *Actus* 2, *Scæna* 1. After the third Act, *Actus* 4. After the fourth Act: *Actus* 5.

Stage Directions: 1, i, 160. Enter Barbantio in his night gowne, and seruants with Torches. 1, ii, 1, Enter Othello, Iago, and attendants with Torches. l. 28, Enter Cassio with lights, Officers and torches. l. 33, Enters Brabantio, Roderigo, and others with lights and weapons. 1, iii, 1, Enter Duke and Senators, set at a table with lights and Attendants. 11, i, [within] A saile, a saile. l. 180, Trumpets within. l. 200, they kisse. 11, ii, 1, Enter a Gentleman reading a Proclamation. 11, iii, 140, Helpe, helpe, within. l. 156, they fight. l. 157, A bell rung. l. 163, Enter Othello, and Gentlemen with weapons. He kneeles. 1v, i, 37, He fals doune. v, i, 45, Enter Iago with a light. Enter Othello with a light. v, ii, 18, He kisses her. l. 83, he stifles her. l. 84, Emillia calls within. l. 233, The Moore runnes at Iago. Iago kils his wife. l. 281, Enter Cassio in a chaire. l. 356, He stabs himselfe. Oth. fals on the bed.

Relation to subsequent editions: A different copy was used for printing the First Folio.

Printer: N. O. are the initials of Nicholas Okes, and the device on the titlepage is that used by him in succession to G. and L. Snowden.

CHAPTER III. THE GOOD AND THE BAD QUARTOS

IN our first chapter we argued that since the printing rights in plays had clearly some commercial value in Shakespeare's days it is incredible that any body of Englishmen would have suffered themselves to be systematically plundered of this value without offering a strenuous resistance. On the other hand it was also pointed out that the extent to which the Crown had taken all matters concerning the press into its own hands threw a practically insuperable obstacle in the way of obtaining redress by an ordinary action at common law. The players might thus acquiesce in being plundered now and again, as long as they were generally able to protect themselves. Again it was fully conceded that while a play was at the height of its success the players might reasonably object to any printed edition of it being circulated, but it was urged that as soon as the theatrical fashion of the day changed and the play became useless for the stage, any fee which could be obtained from a printer or bookseller for a copy of it to print, would be so much extra profit, and that we cannot imagine that this source of profit was systematically rejected. We found, indeed, positive evidence that it was not so rejected in the fact that in 1593-94, when theatres were closed because of the plague, and in 1600, probably under fear of Puritan interference, plays were sent to be printed in such numbers as only the lawful owners of them can be supposed to have supplied.

In our second or bibliographical chapter all the evidence available from external sources, or which can be extracted from the plays themselves, has been brought together, and we have now to consider whether this evidence points to all the Shakespeare quartos being tainted more or less indiscriminately with piracy and surreptitiousness, or whether it is possible to distinguish between some quartos and others, and to offer any solid reason for treating some as piratical and surreptitious, and others as genuine and honestly obtained. The question is of great importance for Shakespeare's text, inasmuch as in the case of several plays it is generally acknowledged that the text of the First Folio was set up from one of the quartos, with corrections of varying importance. Thus, if we condemn these quartos as surreptitious and pirated, we are committing ourselves to the assertion that the editors of the First Folio set up their text in part from the very editions which they condemned in their preface.

Now if we take the quartos which can be proved to have been, directly or indirectly,* the source of the text of the First Folio, or those generally which are pronounced by independent authorities to have "good" texts obviously belonging to the same family as those of the First Folio, we find that with the single exception of *Love's Labors Lost*, which will be separately considered, they all agree in having been entered, before their first publication in print, in the Stationers' Registers. These quartos are *Titus Andronicus*, *Richard II*, *Richard III*, *Henry IV* (Part I), the Heyes-Roberts edition of *The Merchant of Venice*, *Much Ado about Nothing*, *Henry IV* (Part II), Fisher's

---

* Directly as in the case of the "Pide Bull" edition of *King Lear*, a copy of which with some corrections is believed to have been sent to be set up for the Folio; indirectly, as in the case of *Richard II* and *Richard III*, where each quarto was printed from its predecessor, and the Folio from the last of the series.

64

edition of the *Midsummer Night's Dream*, the Ling-Roberts edition of *Hamlet*, the "Pide Bull" edition of *King Lear*, *Troilus and Cressida* and *Othello*. To these must be added Burby's edition of *Romeo and Juliet*, of which there was no entry in the Register but which was put on the market to take the place of a "bad" text.

On the other hand, if we take the quartos which have "bad" texts, differing widely and for the worse from those of the First Folio, we shall find that they also agree in one point, that is in either not being entered prior to first publication in the Stationers' Registers at all, or in having an entry of an unusual nature, entitling us to suspect something wrong. These plays are (i) Danter's edition of *Romeo and Juliet*, and Busby and Millington's *Henry V*, of both of which there are no entries previous to publication; (ii) the first quarto of *Hamlet* and also *Pericles*, both of which were published without having been licensed to the firms publishing them; (iii) *The Merry Wives of Windsor*, transferred to another publisher on the day of entry.

Finding, then, as we do, that quartos which have good texts and agree with the First Folio are entered regularly in the Stationers' Registers, and that quartos which have bad texts, not agreeing at all with the First Folio, are entered in the Stationers' Registers either irregularly or not at all, we are surely justified in arguing, by what used to be called in Logic the method of Agreement and Difference, that there is some causal relation at work which connects a good text with regular entry prior to publication in the Stationers' Register. Such a causal relation would compel us to protest against the common estimate of the members of the Stationers' Company as men so lost to any consideration of honesty or prudence that on payment of 6d. they could, as a matter of routine, reward the theft of an author's manuscript, or a transcript of it, with a perpetual copyright, so that the author himself would be unable to find anyone who would dare to print for him an edition of his own book. We have already seen that an exception must be made in the case of men of fashion like Sir Philip Sidney, who were almost forbidden by social etiquette to send anything they wrote to be printed. To have offered Sidney money for his *Defence of Poesy* or his *Astrophel and Stella* would have been to run a serious risk of being thrown down stairs. Under these circumstances to pirate one of his works might be impudent, but was scarcely dishonest. As to risk, whether it was dangerous or not to print a book without leave would depend on the real feelings of the author or his representatives. No one dared to print any work by Sidney during his life. When he had been dead some time, risks were taken, but with small profit to the venturers. In the case of the players, on the other hand, while the dishonesty and injury would be undeniable (for it must have been matter of common knowledge that authors were paid for their plays), the probable amount of risk in any particular case might be calculated on the basis of their presumable willingness or unwillingness to ask their patron to interfere. To an individual publisher, troubled with no scruples as to honesty, the risk may sometimes have seemed very well worth taking, and when it was accepted it may easily have seemed best to take it whole-heartedly. Whatever the proceedings which an author or owner of a manuscript through some influential channel might set in motion, they would probably be taken through the Stationers' Company, so that simultaneously to

65

incur from the Company a fine or threat of imprisonment for printing without entry or licence, would not greatly increase the risk. Whatever the increase may have been, the pirates, according to our evidence, seem to have preferred to take it, rather than to present themselves before the Company to ask that a play to which they had no right might be "entered for their copy." We know that the Company had a wholesome dread of authority, and this apparent unwillingness of those who must be admitted to have been the worst kind of play-stealers to appeal to it is surely not surprising.

This seems the best place to examine those interesting cases of plays being only conditionally allowed or actually "stayed" which have been quoted in the course of our bibliography. Even the addition to an entry of the words, "saluo jure cuiuscunque," such as we find in the attempted assignment of *Titus Andronicus* from Millington to Pavier, though undoubtedly intended only to protect the interests of members of the company, is yet of importance as showing that some other questions than that of the producibility of the sixpence might be asked when a book was brought for registration. But other conditions appear to conduce directly to the interest of the players. Thus, when James Roberts in 1598 made an application in respect to *The Merchant of Venice*, the entry contains a stipulation that it should not be printed by the said "James Roberts or anye other whatsoever, without lycence first had from the Ryght honorable the lorde Chamberlen," i.e., from the patron of Shakespeare's company. So again on May 27, 1600, Roberts entered, "under the handes of the wardens, A morall of Clothe breches and velvet hose, As yt is Acted by my lord Chamberlens seruantes. Provided that he is not to putt it in prynte without further and better Aucthority," and two days later "A Larum to London" under a like restriction. Again in February, 1602/3 at the close of Elizabeth's reign we find Roberts obtaining a provisional licence to print *Troilus and Cressida*, "when he hath gotten sufficient authoritye for yt." In June, 1599, as a result of the Marprelate controversy and other troubles, it had been enacted not only that "all Nasshes bookes and Doctor Harvyes bookes be taken whensoever they maye be found," and that restrictions be placed on satires, epigrams and English histories, but that "noe playes be printed excepte they bee allowed by suche as have aucthorytie." It is thus probable that at least some of these cautionary entries and others of a similar nature originated with the officials of the Stationers' Company, anxious to obey the wishes of the government. But the entry of *The Merchant of Venice*, with its notable reference to the Lord Chamberlain, the patron of Shakespeare's company, is earlier than the ordinance of June, 1599, and it is obvious that if an applicant could obtain "provisional protection" merely by mentioning the name of a play and promising that he would produce subsequently sufficient authority for printing it, then here was a way in which an obstacle could be raised against piracy without any need for going to press inconveniently early.

If there is any weight in the suggestion made in the last sentence, the current view of James Roberts as the most audacious of the "pirates" may possibly be an exact reversal of the facts. After many years of subordinate printing, Roberts, who had taken up his freedom as early as 1569, suddenly increased his importance in 1594 by marrying the widow of John Charlwood. According to the custom of the City of London he was thereby entitled to take up his livery, which he did in 1596, and he was presumably at this time a man of some means and respectability. Among the privileged work to which he would become entitled by marrying Charlwood's widow would be that of printing for the players " all manner of billes," and he would thus be brought into frequent communication with the theatre. It is certainly not impossible that he was employed by the Chamberlain's men to enter plays in this way on purpose to throw an obstacle in the way of pirates. If so, the manœuvre was not always successful, as, although he entered *Hamlet* in July, 1602, this did not prevent a pirated edition being printed the next year by Valentine Sims for Ling and Trundell, but in the case of the other plays it would seem to have answered its purpose.

That the Chamberlain's men may have had some hand in these entries may be considered possible on account not only of the conditional entry of *The Merchant of Venice* before the ordinance of 1599, but also by the "staying" of four of their plays on 4th August [1600], viz., *As You Like It, Henry the Fifth, Every Man in his Humour* and *Much Ado about Nothing*. The subsequent history of these plays is curiously different. *As You Like It*, as far as we know, was never printed in quarto form, being published for the first time in the Folio of 1623. *Henry V* was printed in the same year, without licence, by Thomas Creed for Thomas Millington, whether before or after the notice that it was to be stayed we have no means of saying. The notorious badness of the text and the absence of entry, according to the view here taken, combine in showing that it was not in any way authorized by the Chamberlain's men. Two years later it formed part of a batch of twelve books entered to Thomas Pavier on August 14, 1632, the entry running with very suspicious vagueness: " Entred for his Copyes by direction of Master White warden vnder his hand wrytinge These copyes followinge beinge thinges formerlye printed and sett over to the sayd Thomas Pavyer." This entry is thoroughly characteristic of the way things were done in the Stationers' Company. Master Warden White was the printer, William White, and Pavier was contracting with him for some of his " copyes," e.g. the *Spanish Tragedy* and Peele's *Edward Longshanke*, both of which are named in the list. White, being Warden, could make the entry in any form he chose, and so Pavier slipped into the list *The historye of Henry the V*th *with the battell of Agincourt*, thus obviating the necessity for mentioning that he was obtaining it from persons who had omitted to apply for a licence for it, and who could probably show no shadow of a claim to its possession. It seems clear that in this instance the piracy was successful. Apparently the staying notice came too late. The book may have been already published before the Chamberlain's men could get the Stationers' Company to declare that it should be stayed, and rather than be troubled to put the machinery in motion afresh, they acquiesced in their loss. Owing to the deal between Pavier and a Warden of the Stationers' Company in 1602, the book was " made an honest woman," much in the sense in which that phrase is generally used. For, however regular its position in the eyes of the Stationers' Company, after the entry of August 14, 1602, its disreputable past continues evident in the badness of the text. Pavier had set things right with the Stationers, but he never set them right as regards this book with the

67

players, and he therefore had no other text to print than the thoroughly bad one which the original pirate had been able to obtain.

As regards the first and second of the four books stayed in August, 1600, each side, on the view here taken, had gained a victory and suffered a defeat. The players had stopped altogether the publication of *As You Like It*. Pirates had put *Henry V* on the market in the teeth of their opposition, and they could only revenge themselves by abstaining from setting right the text, a form of vengeance which seems to show that Shakespeare cared more for his business relations with the Chamberlain's men than for his literary reputation. The remaining two plays, Ben Jonson's *Every Man in his Humor* and Shakespeare's *Much Ado about Nothing*, appear to have been published with the players' consent and at their convenience. Within ten days of the "staying" notice, on August 14, we find in the Stationers' Register an entry of Jonson's *Every Man in his Humor* to [Cuthbert] Burby and Walter Burre, and the following year (the interval being very probably arranged in the interest of the theatre, the play having been new in 1598) we find it published by Burre "as it hath beene sundry times publikely acted by the right honorable the Lord Chamberlaine his seruants." Nine days after the entry of *Every Man in his Humor* to Burby and Burre, on August 23, we get this double entry:

Andrewe Wyse, William Aspley. Entred for their copies vnder the handes of the wardens two bookes. the one called Muche a Doo about nothinge. Thother the second parte of the history of Kinge Henry the iiij^{th} with the humours of Sir John ffalstaff: wrytten by Master Shakespere. xij^{d}.

That the manuscripts of these two plays were obtained from the Chamberlain's men and printed with their full authority is as certain as anything can make it save the discovery of a statement to that effect in Shakespeare's autograph. The respectful mention of Shakespeare by name (previous entries in the Register had been anonymous) would indeed have been a pretty stroke of humour on the part of a pirate, but it is inconceivable that within three weeks of their "staying" order a pirate would have come near the Stationers' Company with the manuscripts of two plays which could be proved to have been stolen. For there is no question here of texts taken down in shorthand at the theatre. Both plays can be proved to have been printed from playhouse copies, which must either have been stolen from the players or published with their consent. In Act ii, sc. 3 of *Much Ado about Nothing* the name of the performer "Jack Wilson" is substituted for the stage-direction *Music*, and in Act iv, sc. 2, the names of the actors Kemp and Cowley are substituted for those of the characters Dogberry and Verges, whose parts they had to play. In the case of the second part of *King Henry IV* we find a similar substitution of the name of an actor "Sincklo" for that of the officer in Act v, sc. 4. Moreover, in this play, when the omission of the first scene of Act iii, was discovered, copy for it was forthcoming, and quire E was reprinted on six leaves instead of four to contain the additional matter.*

We have seen that in the case of *Henry V*, the first edition of which we regard as pirated, the old bad text went on being reprinted, even after the play, according to the ideas of the day, had become the legitimate property

---

*As compared with the Folio version there was still an omission of 171 lines, but these presumably had been cut out of the acting version.

of Pavier. It may now be worth while to go back in order to consider the history of the two other Shakespeare quartos which up to this time had been, one almost certainly, another possibly, surreptitiously published. The first of these is the edition of *Romeo and Juliet* printed and published by John Danter in 1597. That this was a piracy, and that the copy was obtained, in whole or part, by sending reporters to performances of the play, can hardly be doubted. Although it probably follows the same version as the authentic text, over seven hundred lines are omitted, and in place of the usual meagre stage-directions we find a number of descriptive notes such as a reporter might naturally jot down in order to supplement his version of the text:—"Enter Nurse wringing her hands, with the ladder of cordes in her lap.—He offers to stab himselfe and Nurse snatches the dagger away.—They all but the Nurse goe forth, casting Rosemary on her and shutting the Curtens.—Fryer stoops and looks on the blood and the weapons." Stage-directions of this kind are rarely found in any play by Shakespeare of which we have a trustworthy text. In the second place, we have evidence that the play was printed in a hurry, two presses being employed, no doubt simultaneously. Thus the first sixteen leaves (sheets A–D) are printed in a larger type than the remaining 24 (sheets E–K). Besides this change of type there is another difference which, despite the assertion of those who argue from their own sense of the fitness of things as to what a text derived from the players ought or ought not to contain, is pretty certainly an indication of a text due to reporters describing what they saw. Up to Act III, sc. 4, there is, as usual in the quartos, no divisions into acts and scenes, but from this point onwards the scenes are marked, not by words and numbers, but by the insertion of a printer's ornament where each new scene begins. Taken together, these features of Danter's quarto offer fairly conclusive evidence of piracy, and no editor, as far as I am aware, has ever regarded the edition as anything else. That Danter should be the first of the Shakespeare pirates was only in accordance with the beginning and end of his career. Before he was out of his apprenticeship he was in most serious trouble with the Company for helping to print at a secret press two school-books, a Grammar and Accidence, which formed one of its most profitable monopolies. After printing *Romeo and Juliet* he had the hardihood to meddle again with the same sacred volumes, and, as Mr H. R. Plomer puts it, "disappears in a whirlwind of official indignation and Star-Chamber shrieks," and shortly afterwards died.*

Danter had never had a shadow of a claim to any legal or customary right in *Romeo and Juliet*, and his disappearance made it easy to ignore him. The fact, however, remained that the book had been printed, and to get a licence for it would have necessitated explanations. But, as we have already noted, in substituting an authorized edition for a piracy ordinary precautions could be disregarded. That the second edition of *Romeo and Juliet*, printed in 1599 by Thomas Creed for Cuthbert Burby, was an authorized edition, printed with the goodwill of the players, there is good evidence. We have already met with Burby as one of the two men to whom Jonson's *Every Man in his Humor* was entered in August, 1600, a few days after the notice that it was

*Article on the Printers of Shakespeare's Plays and Poems, *The Library*, N.S. vol. VII, 149–166.

to be "stayed." In 1595 he had already entered and published the play of *Edward III*, which, whether Shakespeare had a hand in it or not, belonged to the Chamberlain's men. We shall have soon to speak of his edition of *Loves Labors Lost*. The editions with which he is connected all have good texts, and this second edition of *Romeo and Juliet* is no exception to the statement. According to Mr Daniel, the editor of the Facsimile, it contains 3,007 lines as against 2,232 in Danter's edition. It has been proved by Mr Daniel that it must have been printed from a written copy, the first four lines of Act II, sc. 3, and ll. 37-43 of Act III, sc. 3 having obviously taken their present form from a misunderstanding of manuscript corrections. In Act IV, sc. 5, we have a tell-tale substitution of the name of an actor, Will Kemp, for the character he was playing, and the form of the stage direction "Whistle boy" in V, 3, is also suggestive of a playhouse copy. Lastly, we have the facts that the play was regularly transferred from Burby to Nicholas Ling in January 1606/7, and from Ling to John Smethwick in November, 1607, that Smethwick's edition of 1609 is a reprint of Burby's, and that this 1609 edition in its turn was reprinted in the Folio of 1623.

We come now to the consideration of the edition of *Loves Labors Lost*, printed in 1598 by W. W. (the initials of William White) for Cuthbert (or, as the imprint calls him, "Cutbert") Burby, without any previous entry in the Stationers' Register. According to the theory on which we have strongly insisted, this absence of any previous entry offers grave cause for a suspicion of piracy. But there is absolutely nothing in the text by which such a suspicion can be supported. Like the other "good" quartos, it has no division into acts and scenes and very scanty stage directions. It was reprinted in the Folio of 1623, having in the interval been transferred from Burby to Ling and from Ling to Smethwick by the same entries as *Romeo and Juliet*. It is quite possible that, so far as this play is concerned, our theory breaks down, and, if so, if any one contends that its value is proportionately weakened, he will be absolutely within his rights. There is, however, considerable ground for believing that the 1598 edition is not really the *editio princeps*, but is an authorized edition superseding a pirated one now lost, and thus precisely on all fours with the (as I believe) authorized *Romeo and Juliet* of 1599, which superseded Danter's edition of 1597. Holding this view, it would be absurd self-denial to pass by the words, "Newly corrected and augmented," on the titlepage, as if they must necessarily refer either to nothing in particular, or to improvements made at the time that the play "was presented before her Highnes this last Christmas."

It may save turning back to repeat the title: "A Pleasant Conceited Comedie called Loues Labors lost. As it was presented before her Highnes this last Christmas. Newly corrected and augmented By W. Shakespeare. Imprinted at London by W. W. for Cuthbert Burby. 1598."

We may well wish here for a little more precision. In the earliest extant edition of *The Spanish Tragedie* it is said to be "Newly corrected, and amended of such grosse faults as passed in the first impression," leaving no doubt that the corrections and amendments refer only to different versions of the same text as compared with an edition now entirely lost, not to changes made by the author.

Equally explicit, on the other side, is the titlepage of *The Devil's Charter*, by Barnabe Barnes (1607): "The Divil's Charter: A Tragædie Conteining the Life and Death of Pope Alexander the sixt. As it was plaide before the Kings Maiestie, vpon Candlemasse night last: by his Maiesties Seruants. But more exactly renewed, corrected, and augmented since by the Author, for the more pleasure and profit of the Reader." Here there can be no doubt that the corrections are author's corrections, not merely a restoration of his original text. But in *Loves Labors Lost* the words, "Newly corrected and amended," standing in a line by themselves, are and must remain ambiguous. If any of our cocksure critics of Shakespeare can demonstrate to the conviction of anyone beside himself exactly where authorial corrections and amendments were made towards the end of 1597 in a play which must, as a whole, be considerably earlier, no doubt the demonstration will carry great weight. On the other hand, we have a right to insist that these words " Newly corrected and amended " occur (with the addition of " augmented ") on the titlepage of only one other play of Shakespeare's, and that is, " The most excellent and lamentable Tragedie, of Romeo and Iuliet. Newly corrected, augmented, and amended: As it hath bene sundry times publiquely acted by the right Honourable the Lord Chamberlaine his Seruants," printed the year after this for the same publisher, Cuthbert Burby, and, as has been shown, printed in succession to a piracy. In another instance which we shall soon have to consider, that of *Hamlet*, we again find that on the titlepage of the " good " edition* there is a reference to the imperfections of its predecessor. It is said to be " Newly imprinted and enlarged to almost as much againe as it was, according to the true and perfect Coppie." In this case we know that the improvements were both authorial and editorial. It is possible that this is true also, though to a far less degree, of *Romeo and Juliet*. It is not impossible that it may be true also of *Loves Labors Lost*. But having regard to the close parallel in the case of *Romeo and Juliet*, it would seem unreasonable to deny any likelihood to the theory that the words " Newly corrected and amended " on the titlepage of *Loves Labors Lost* do point to the existence at one time of an earlier and less correct edition which, like the earlier and less correct edition of *The Spanish Tragedye*, has entirely disappeared.

Besides *Henry V*, the Second Part of *Henry IV* and *Much Ado about Nothing*, two other plays by Shakespeare were published in 1600, *The Merchant of Venice* and *A Midsummer Night's Dream*. Of each of these there are two editions bearing the date of this year, but for the present we need only concern ourselves with one of each pair, leaving the other to be considered in our next chapter. As we have seen, James Roberts took out a conditional licence for *The Merchant of Venice* in July, 1598, but the permission of the "Right honorable the lord Chamberlen" for its publication was not forthcoming for over two years. On October 28, 1600, the book was re-entered by Thomas Haies " by Consent of master Robertes," this course being taken, in preference to an ordinary transfer, most probably because the terms of the previous entry had never been complied with. If Roberts had produced a written authority

---

* In the case of both *Loves Labors Lost* and *Hamlet* the same or similar words are found also in subsequent editions. A claim of this kind was not easily allowed to drop.

from the Lord Chamberlain, the fact would almost certainly have been mentioned. It was simpler, now that a bogey was no longer needed, to enter the book afresh, the mention of Roberts in the new entry being a sufficient compliment to the old, while it helped to secure for him the printing of the book. The edition has all the usual characteristics of a good quarto.

Twenty days before Hayes entered *The Merchant of Venice* in the Stationers' Registers, *A Midsummer Night's Dream* had been entered (8 Octobris 1600) by Thomas Fyssher. The resultant edition appeared in 1600, probably from the press of Valentine Sims. This again has all the usual characteristics of a good quarto. Moreover the imperative form of the stage directions, "Ly doune" (III, ii, 85) and "Winde hornes" (IV, i, 138) may be taken as indicating its origin from a playhouse copy.

Passing on to 1602 we reach *The Merry Wives of Windsor*, which was entered to John Busby on January 18, 1601/2, and assigned to Arthur Johnson on the same day. The name of John Busby we have already met on the titlepage of the pirated edition of *Henry V* printed for him and Millington in 1600. Arthur Johnson was just beginning business as a publisher in a small way, bringing out another book, *The Touch-stone of Prayer*, by a certain Tho. S. in this same year 1602, and thereafter publishing a dozen or more respectable and rather serious books, of which *A Closet for Ladies and Gentlewomen, or The Art of preserving, conseruing and Candying*, is the most mundane. The printer of the book was Thomas Creed, who had printed the pirated *Henry V* for Millington and Busby in 1600. The text leaves us in no sort of doubt that this edition of *The Merry Wives of Windsor* was also a piracy. Like Danter's *Romeo and Juliet* it is obviously, to a large extent, if not entirely, based upon the report of writers sent to the theatre to take down as much of the play as they could. As in the case of *Romeo and Juliet*, moreover, the substitution of descriptions for stage-directions is very noticeable, e.g., III, 10: "Sir John goes into the basket, they put cloathes over him, the two men carries it away. Foord meetes it, and all the rest, Page, Doctor, Priest, Slender, Shallow"; and v, 5: "Here they pinch him, and sing about him, & the Doctor comes one way & steales away a boy in red. And Slender another way he takes a boy in greene: And Fenton steales misteris Anne, being in white. And a noyse of hunting is made within: and all the Fairies runne away. Falstaffe pulles of his bucks head and rises up. And enters M. Page, M. Ford and their wiues, M. Shallow, Sir Hugh." Even more strongly than in the case of *Romeo and Juliet* we can say that stage directions such as these are rarely found in any edition of a play undoubtedly by Shakespeare which offers a satisfactory text.*

Here, then, we have a patently piratical edition of a play, printed by a printer who had already produced one piracy, but had also at an earlier date (1599) been employed to print a " good " quarto *(Loves Labors Lost)*, entered on the Stationers' Register by John Busby, who, like Creed, had been concerned in the pirated *Henry V*, and transferred on the same day to Arthur Johnson, a small publisher just starting on an eminently respectable line of business. The transference on the same day is a great puzzle. Dr Arber, in his tran-

---

*In addition to *Titus Andronicus* (which is not "undoubtedly by Shakespeare") the only possible parallel appears to be in parts of 1 *Henry IV*.

script of the Stationers' Register, expressed his opinion that the play must have been already once printed " by [for ?] Busby before this date, but not entered in the Registers until he came to assign it to A. Johnson." This is quite possible, but is certainly not the only explanation that can be entertained. If Arthur Johnson were at all a cautious young stationer and Busby, as was probably the case, brought him his piratical prize and offered to sell him the copy for a small price, he might very well have insisted that Busby should take the onus of entering it on the Stationers' Register before he would complete the bargain. It must be remembered that in the middle of January 1601/2 the credit of the Chamberlain's men was probably too low to enable them to defend their interests with any vigour. For it was they who, the previous year, had performed Shakespeare's *Richard II* (including, we may safely say on strong negative evidence, the deposition scene) in connexion with the abortive conspiracy of the Earl of Essex. This certainly very questionable performance was made much of at the trial of Essex. The Chamberlain's men found it convenient to go travelling in Scotland, and are heard of as acting at Aberdeen as late as October, and, if Fleay was right in maintaining that they performed no plays at Court this Christmas it is evident that they were either still absent from London or in very deep disgrace. In either case they would be less able to defend themselves against piracy than at any other time.

If *The Merry Wives of Windsor* was, as is probable, successfully pirated, another successful piracy soon followed, and this despite what looks like a definite attempt to prevent it. On July 26, 1602, that is quite shortly after the entry and (as we may suppose) publication of *The Merry Wives*, we find James Roberts entering for his copy " a booke called the Revenge of Hamlett Prince [of] Denmarke, as yt was latelie Acted by the Lord Chamberleyne his servantes." No edition followed immediately upon this entry, which, in my belief, was intended solely to place an obstacle in the way of the book being licensed to any one else. But at some date in 1603, not earlier than May 19,* there appeared, printed for N. L. (i.e. Nicholas Ling) and John Trundell " The Tragicall Historie of Hamlet Prince of Denmarke. By William Shakespeare. As it hath beene diuerse times acted by his Highnesse Seruants in the Cittie of London : as also in the two Vniuersities of Cambridge and Oxford and elsewhere." This edition does not bear the name of any printer, but following, as it does, upon the entry of James Roberts in the Register it has quite naturally been supposed to have been his work. This, however, is not the case. The clumsy headpiece at the beginning of 1603 text gives us a useful clue to its true typographical authorship. Bad as it is, the design of this headpiece was apparently much admired by Elizabethan printers, for variants of it are found in the possession of many different firms, so that fantastic people have been tempted to see in it a Rosicrucian emblem, introducing twice the letter *A*. The peculiarity of the variety of this headpiece here used is that it is heavily shaded or " azured " by means of horizontal lines. In this form it had already appeared in the quarto of *Richard III*, printed by Valentine Sims for Andrew Wise in 1597, and in

*The date of the licence in virtue of which the Chamberlain's company became the King's players.

that of *Henry IV*, Part II, printed by Sims for Wise and Aspley in 1600. It is also found in several other books printed by Sims, e.g. in Chapman's *An Humerous Dayes Myrth* (1599), in *Pasquils Passe and Passeth Not* (1600), in the *Historie of England* (1602), and *The Earle of Gowries Conspiracie* (1603). On the other hand, no instance of it can be found in books from any other press, and it certainly does not appear in any book printed by Roberts in the British Museum. There is really no room for doubt that the quarto of 1603 was the work of Sims, and that Roberts had no hand in the printing of it. This being so, we can be equally sure that he had also no hand in its publication, as it would certainly never have entered his head to allow Ling to act on his licence while giving the job to another printer. We must therefore conclude that Ling and Trundle brought out the *Hamlet* of 1603 in the teeth of Roberts's entry in the Stationers' Register and without making any entry of the book on their own account. That the quarto of 1603 is a bad piracy is generally admitted, as also that it represents the play in an intermediate stage between the lost *Hamlet* [of Kyd?] and the fully Shakespearian *Hamlet* of the Folio and the second and subsequent quartos. There being no authentic text of the play in this transitional stage, it is difficult to form any very clear idea as to how the pirated text was got into such shape as it possesses. Some passages appear to have been written down from memory, while blunders seem also to have been introduced in the course of putting together the different reports. The stage directions are much less descriptive than in *Romeo and Juliet* and *The Merry Wives*. The longest of them is in the fencing scene (v, ii, 82): "They catch one another's Rapiers and both are wounded. Leartes falles downe, the Queene falles downe and dies." But there is nothing strikingly unusual about this.

From about July, 1603, to March, 1604, the London theatres were closed on account of the plague, and the performance of the partly Shakespearian *Hamlet* was thus interrupted. It was presumably during this interval of eight or nine months that Shakespeare rewrote the play in its present form. It was published rather surprisingly early, an easy explanation of the alternative dates 1604 and 1605 found on copies of the first edition being that it was printed so near to the end of the former year that while the titlepage was on the press the idea of giving it the later date presented itself.

The imprint tells us that the play was "printed by I.R. for N.L.," the former pair of initials being proved to belong to James Roberts by the occurrence at the beginning of the text of his headpiece of the Royal Arms, while that N. L. was Nicholas Ling is shown both by his device and by the address "Under Saint Dunstan's Church in Fleetstreet," Ling having a shop there, in close proximity to his fellow-pirate John Busby. That Roberts should be the printer of the "good" quarto of *Hamlet* is quite right and regular, for his licence of 1602 would of course still hold good. But that Ling, who had joined with Trundle in bringing out the quarto of 1603, was its publisher may well amaze us. This also, however, was, in its way, quite in accordance with precedent. In 1599 Roberts had himself got into trouble about an edition of Markham's *Horsemanship*, the copyright in which apparently belonged to William Wood. He was obliged to hand over the stock to Wood, but received some payment for it, and it was amicably agreed that he should be employed to print any future edition. The situation was now reversed, and if the matter could be settled quietly neither Roberts nor the players had any temptation to bring it before the Stationers' Company.

The *Hamlet* of 1604-5 was the last Shakespeare quarto printed by James Roberts, but we have still to mention another of his conditional entries. On February 7, 1602/3 he entered for his copy, "to print when he hath gotten sufficient authority for yt, The booke of *Troilus and Cresseda* as yt is acted by my Lord Chamberlayns men." Queen Elizabeth died on March 24, and the plague, which reduced James I's coronation to a private ceremony and delayed his progress through London for a year, naturally caused the closing of the theatres. It is rather surprising under these circumstances to find that Roberts never put the book in print at all. After his retirement from business (1606) we find it entered a second time (January, 1608) without any reference to the earlier entry, which had clearly been forgotten.

The piratical *Hamlet* of 1603 very probably appeared after James had ascended the throne, and the first legitimate edition not till 1604, but the entry in the Stationers' Register in accordance with which the legitimate edition appeared was made in Elizabeth's reign, and the play is for this and other reasons most profitably considered with the Elizabethan first quartos of Shakespeare's plays, of which it makes the thirteenth in order of publication. As to four of the first five of these, *Titus Andronicus, Richard II, Richard III* and *Henry IV*, Part I, nothing special has been said, because they are perfectly regular from start to finish,* entry in the Stationers' Register being followed by the publication of several editions, and a quarto being ultimately handed to the compositors in 1623 as the basis of the Folio text. We should note, however, in passing the ability of the copyholder in 1608 to obtain "the additions to the Parliament sceane and the deposing of King Richard" as suggesting probable friendly relations with the players. The rest of these Elizabethan quartos have been separately considered. Twelve out of the total of the thirteen fall within the seven years 1597-1603. After the two quartos of the different versions of *Hamlet* only four other Shakespeare first editions were published in the nineteen years before the appearance of the First Folio. The striking disproportion between these numbers is undoubtedly due to the custom which grew up early in the reign of James for all plays to be entered in the Stationers' Registers "under the hand of" Sir George Buck, the Master of the Revels, or his deputy, Mr Segar, i.e., as a preliminary to getting a play registered a certificate of some sort had to be obtained from one or other of these officials. The payments which the Master of the Revels received from the players were considerable, the fee for each play he read for acting (not printing) as a preliminary to its performance, being seven shillings, in addition to a monthly propitiation of £2, and during the next thirty years the fees did not remain unaugmented. That sacred bond "a cash nexus" was thus established between the players and the censor, and Sir George Buck and his successor appear to have been content to plunder the players themselves without encouraging piratical publishers to do so.

---

* The only point to be noted is the exceptional fullness of the stage directions to *Titus Andronicus*, which may be taken, for what it is worth, as an addition to the usual arguments against the play being wholly by Shakespeare.

The risk of piracy being thus much diminished, the players were freed from any temptation to permit early publication in order to forestall it, and to a large extent now resumed their old policy of withholding plays from publication.

The first play of Shakespeare's to be printed under the new régime was his *King Lear*, which on November 26, 1607, was entered to Nathaniel Butter and John Busby under the hands of Sir George Buck and the Wardens as "A booke called Master William Shakespeare his historye of Kinge Leare, as yt was played before the kinges maiestie at Whitehall vppon Sainct Stephens night at Christmas Last, by his maiesties servantes playinge vsually at the Globe on the Banksyde." The St Stephen's night which preceded November, 1607, would be December 26, 1606, so, when the play appeared in print with 1608 as the date on the titlepage, the inference was made a little vaguer by the substitution of "S. Stephans night in Christmas Hollidayes" for "Sainct Stephens night at Christmas Last." The device on the titlepage has been identified by Mr Plomer (and also by Mr Sayle) with one used in 1606 by George and Lionel Snowden, who in 1608 transferred their business to Nicholas Okes, and both this and the headpiece are subsequently found in the possession of Okes. The book was thus clearly printed either by the Snowdens or by Okes. The text is one of the best known instances of the correction of a book while it was on the press, so that there is an uncorrected and a corrected edition of several of the sheets, which were bound up, however, at haphazard, so that scarce any two copies agree. Save for the mistakes in the uncorrected sheets the text is satisfactory, and was used as a basis for the Folio of 1623, in which, however, nearly three hundred of its lines disappear and over a hundred others are added. These changes may have been made in the playhouse version after 1608, though if two slightly differing transcripts were available when printing was contemplated in November, 1607, there is no probability that any anxious care was spent on deciding which should be published. There is no division into acts and scenes, and the stage directions are brief and very slightly descriptive. Thus everything about the book is normal and regular—entry, text, subsequent use by Folio editors—and the suspicions which the name of John Busby may have aroused are groundless. He was obviously the provider of the copy, as his name disappears from the imprint, but no doubt if he could not pirate a book he was ready to pay for it, if need be, and no one seems to have cherished long memories in these matters.

As far as essentials are concerned, the history of *Troilus and Cressida* is as simple as that of *King Lear*. It was entered to "Richard Bonion and Henry Walleys" on January 28, 1608/9, and an edition was printed the same year "by G. Eld for R. Bonian and H. Walley." There is nothing to excite suspicion in the stage directions, nor any division into acts and scenes, and the text is in general agreement with that of the First Folio, though somewhat less accurate.

This solid normal kernel is surrounded by several puzzling abnormalities which do not greatly concern us, but yet can hardly be passed over in silence. In the first place, the play, as we have seen, had already, on February 7, 1602/3, been entered conditionally to "Master Roberts . . . to print when he hath gotten sufficient aucthority for it," and in this conditional entry, which Roberts never acted on and which every one seems to have forgotten, it is described as "The booke of Troilus and Cressida as yt is acted by my lord Chamberlens Men." In the second place, the book is found in two different states, with a titlepage forming part of the first quire, and with a titlepage and preface on a separate half-sheet, substituted for the original titlepage only, the irregularity in the making-up leaving no room for doubt as to what has been done. Now, on the first titlepage the play is described as "The Historie of Troylus and Cresseida. As it was acted by the Kings Maiesties servants at the Globe." On the second titlepage all mention of its having been acted at the Globe disappears; the title now reads: "The Famous Historie of Troylus and Cresseid excellently expressing the beginning of their loues, with the conceited wooing of Pandarus Prince of Licia." Lastly, in the following admirably prophetic preface it is distinctly called "a new play, neuer stal'd with the Stage":

A neuer writer, to an euer reader. Newes.

Eternall reader, you haue heere a new play, neuer stal'd with the Stage, neuer clapper-clawd with the palmes of the vulger, and yet passing full of the palme comicall; for it is a birth of your braine, that neuer vnder-tooke any thing commicall, vainely: And were but the vaine names of commedies changde for the titles of Commodities, or of Playes for Pleas; you should see all those grand censors, that now stile them such vanities, flock to them for the maine grace of their grauities: especially this authors Commedies, that are so fram'd to the life, that they serue for the most common Commentaries, of all the actions of our liues, shewing such a dexteritie, and power of witte, that the most displeased with Playes, are pleasd with his Commedies. And all such dull and heauy-witted worldlings, as were neuer capable of the witte of a Commedie, comming by report of them to his representations, haue found that witte there, that they neuer found in themselues, and haue parted better wittied then they came: feeling an edge of witte set upon them, more then euer they dreamd they had braine to grinde it on. So much and such sauored salt of witte is in his Commedies, that they seeme (for their height of pleasure) to be borne in that sea that brought forth Venus. Amongst all there is none more witty then this: And had I time I would comment upon it, though I know it needs not, (for so much as will make you thinke your testerne well bestowd) but for so much worth, as euen poore I know to be stuft in it. It deserues such a labour, as well as the best Commedy in Terence or Plautus. And beleeue this, that when hee is gone, and his Commedies out of sale, you will scramble for them, and set up a new English Inquisition. Take this for a warning, and at the perill of your pleasures losse, and Iudgements, refuse not, nor like this the lesse, for not being sullied, with the smoaky breath of the multitude; but thanke fortune for the scape it hath made amongst you. Since by the grand possessors wills I beleeue you should haue prayd for them rather than beene prayd. And so I leaue all such to bee prayd for (for the states of their wits healths) that will not praise it. Vale.

The flat contradiction between this preface and the form of the entry by Roberts in February, 1603, does not greatly concern us, except that we are bound to protest against the theory once held by Mr Fleay and others that the preface formed part of the first issue and was withdrawn as incorrect. No printer can be imagined to have originally set up a titlepage and a preface on a half-sheet signed ¶, and to have begun the text with an imperfect sheet of three leaves. It is clear that such an arrangement can only have been produced by the need for cancelling a titlepage which formed the first leaf of a sheet. Thus it is the statement that the play was " acted by the King's Maiesties servants at the Globe" which was cancelled, and we can only imagine that all preparations for acting the play were made in February, 1603, that Roberts made his entry in the Stationers' Register on the eve of an intended performance which for some reason never took place, and that Bonian and Walley, when they bought the play, took it for granted that it had been performed, were subsequently informed of their mistake and used the information as an advertisement. If we believe that Roberts intended to print the play at an early date himself, it would be natural for him, in making his entry, to quote the usual phrase about its being acted from his projected titlepage. If he was merely putting down a "blocking motion," to make it more difficult to pirate the play, the acting was probably mentioned only for the sake of bringing in the name of the Lord Chamberlain. Why the play was never acted is an even higher matter, with which it is dangerous for bibliography to meddle. There is something to be said for the theory that it may have originally been written as a cooling commentary on Chapman's incomplete *Iliad* of 1598, and was now allowed to be published in anticipation of the completed translation, which is usually attributed to the year 1610. It is less dangerous to point out that soon after February, 1603, the theatres were closed by the Queen's death and the plague, and that some time before this arrangements had been disturbed and the company sent travelling on account of the performance of *Richard II* before the Essex conspirators. A little procrastination might thus easily have caused the play to be postponed, possibly twice rather than once. With all this, however, we have really nothing to do. Our thesis is that the entry of a play on the Stationers' Register is normally followed by an edition with as good a text as could be expected without the personal supervision of the author, or of some disinterested editor with some care for his reputation. The text published by Bonian and Walley, in pursuance of their entry, fulfils this requirement, and it is, perhaps, wiser not to spin theories about matters as to which some of Shakespeare's contemporaries were clearly mistaken.

We are entitled to take the same course in the case of *Pericles*, where the counterpart of our thesis holds good. This play was entered in the Stationers' Register on May 20, 1608, by Edward Blount, one of the chief promoters of the Folio of 1623, under the hands of Sir George Buck and Master Warden Seton. At the same time and by the same authority Blount entered Shakespeare's *Antony and Cleopatra*. In neither case did he take any further action, so that, on the face of them, these seem to have been of the nature of "blocking" entries rather than inspired with any intention of early publication. *Antony and Cleopatra* remained unprinted till 1623, but in 1609, without any transfer from Blount, a scandalously bad text of *Pericles* was printed (according to the typographical evidence, by William White) for Henry Gosson, and carelessly reprinted for him within the year. Then, in 1611, without any transfer either from Blount or from Gosson, the play was again "printed at London by S. S.," the initials of Simon Stafford. Finally, in 1619, again without any transfer either from Blount, Gosson or Stafford, it was "printed for T. P.", i.e., Thomas Pavier, the typographical evidence showing that it was the work of William Jaggard, who had acquired the stock of James Roberts, some of which was used in its production. The play seems to have been treated as a derelict, in which no one had any rights. And the text is as bad as any upholder of our thesis could desire, so bad that it has been likened to that of the pirated *Romeo and Juliet*, like which it was almost certainly taken down in shorthand at the theatre, only, unhappily, in this case it was never replaced by any respectable edition.

The last case which we shall have to examine is that of *Othello*, which was entered to Thomas Walkley, "under the handes of Sir George Buck and Master Swinhowe warden," on October 6, 1621, and printed for Walkley by N. O., i.e., Nicholas Okes, the following year. Walkley thought it necessary to contribute a preface headed "The Stationer to the Reader," which can only be described as a wasted leaf. He also marked off the beginnings of the second, fourth and fifth acts, but not that of the third. The stage directions are normal. The text has been described as "very respectable," though not so good as that of the Folio, to which it forms a useful supplement. It must certainly be ranked with the "good" quartos.

Looking back over our whole field, we find that before the appearance of the First Folio seventeen of Shakespeare's plays had been published in quarto, and two of these, *Romeo and Juliet* and *Hamlet,* in two widely differing texts, giving us nineteen texts altogether. Of these nineteen texts five are by universal consent thoroughly bad, viz., Danter's *Romeo and Juliet*, *Henry V*, *The Merry Wives*, the first *Hamlet* and *Pericles*, three at least of these being demonstrably derived from shorthand copies taken down at the theatre or from quotations from memory. Two of these five were never entered on the Stationers' Register at all, two others were not entered by the firm that printed them, *The Merry Wives* was entered and transferred on the same day. On the other hand, of the fourteen "good" texts, twelve were regularly entered on the Stationers' Register, and of the other two one (the second *Romeo and Juliet*) was certainly, and another (Burby's *Loves Labors Lost*) at least not impossibly, printed to take the place of a "bad" text. As a result of our examination of these plays, the precedent entries and the subsequent transfers, it is submitted with some confidence that sufficient attention has not been paid to the fact that they clearly form a class distinct from that of the five bad cases of piracy, and that it is very doubtful indeed whether we have any reason to condemn them as "stolne and surreptitious." It is not suggested for a moment that entry on the Stationers' Register is always and in all cases to be taken as a proof that the copy was honestly obtained by gift or purchase. It is believed that the prevalence of piracy has been somewhat exaggerated, but it is part of our case that it existed, and that when they thought that they could safely do so the pirates would naturally be glad to secure themselves in the possession of their booty by entering it on the Register. Without such entry it is clear from the cases of *Romeo and Juliet* and *Pericles* that the original pirate had no kind of copyright, though he might after a little time act as though he had, witness the later history of *Henry V* and also of *Pericles*. But, whatever the inducement to obtain registration, it is clear from the notes of *saluo jure cujuscunque* and reference to "sufficient authority," or specifically to the authority of the Lord Chamberlain, that registration could not always be obtained by the offer of sixpence. Under these circumstances to steal from a body of men who had business reasons for protecting their property and some influence, direct or indirect, at Court to enable them to do so, and not only to steal, but to steal, as it were, by the sound of a trumpet, this surely was not a method of procedure which would commend itself to any reasonably prudent pirate. Moreover, the theory which limits the number of the piratical editions to five (or six, if we favour the theory of a pirated *editio princeps* of *Loves Labors Lost*) is certainly not out of harmony with the statement of the editors of the First Folio from which this discussion started. "Where before," they tell their readers, "you were abus'd with diuerse stolne and surreptitious copies, maim'd and deform'd by the frauds and stealthes of injurious impostors, that expos'd them, even those are now offer'd to your view cur'd and perfect of their limbes." The exuberant tone of the address in which these words occur does not lead us to expect any understatements. If all the nineteen quarto texts had been surreptitiously obtained and piratically published, we might well expect a more sweeping condemnation. As it is, the "diuerse stol'n and surreptitious copies" are represented* by the quartos of *Henry V* and *The Merry Wives*, for mending and curing which the Folio editors must have the entire credit, and by the first quartos of *Romeo and Juliet* and *Hamlet*, in the case of which the credit must be shared with the second quartos. This is surely ample for the explanation of the passage, and for editors to allow the other quartos to be involved in the same condemnation, while relying on them largely for their texts, is mere helplessness. We must no longer look at these fourteen quartos individually as surprising examples of good qualities surviving in this or that member of a disreputable family. We must acknowledge that the family has no single black sheep in it, but that every member of it is of good average morals and utility. We do not claim more than this. There is not one jot of reason for believing that Shakespeare himself had anything to do with the quartos. That he can have corrected the proofs is absolutely out of the question. But the texts of these fourteen quartos are not worse than we should expect to result from hastily written playhouse transcripts placed in the hands of second- and third-rate printers in that far from flourishing typographical period 1594-1622, and there seems no reason for denying to this group of fourteen editions some such humble but not disreputable origin. If this be so, the epithets "stolne and surreptitious" may be applied with any desirable amount of scorn and contempt to the five plays already specified. But they should surely not be applied to any other. Moreover, we can read our First Folio—in the original if we are millionaires, in facsimile if we are students—with all the more confidence because we need no longer believe that its editors in their preface were publicly casting stones at earlier editions which they were privately using, often with no very substantial modification, in constructing their own text.

* *Pericles* they left on one side.

CHAPTER IV. THE QUARTOS OF 1619

BOTH in the Bibliography of the Quartos and in the last chapter consideration of four editions, one each of four different plays, has been as far as possible postponed. These four editions are that of *A Midsummer Night's Dream* with the imprint *Printed by Iames Roberts, 1600*; that of *The Merchant of Venice* with the imprint *Printed by I. Roberts, 1600*; that of *Henry V* with the imprint *Printed for T. P., 1608*; and that of *King Lear* with the imprint *Printed for Nathaniel Butter, 1608*. Starting from a discovery of my own the significance of which I at first misunderstood, a theory has been put forward by Mr W. W. Greg as to these four quartos which revolutionizes both their position in the bibliography of Shakespeare and (to a less extent) their literary value, and which leads up in an interesting manner to the preparations for publishing the Folio of 1623.

Some years ago a letter was received at the British Museum from a German gentleman stating that he was bringing over to England, with some other early books, a volume containing nine Shakespearian (or pseudo-Shakespearian) plays, which he had been advised in Germany were of considerable value. He offered the British Museum the refusal of any that it might want, and stated that he proposed to bring the volume to the Museum immediately on his arrival at Charing Cross, probably about 6 p.m. The hour proposed was a little late, but an assignation with a volume of Shakespearian quartos was not to be missed, and, being given the privilege of keeping it, I was rewarded with the sight of a charming fat little volume in plain brown calf with the name of a well-known seventeenth century book-buyer, EDWARD GWYNN, stamped in gold on the covers, a businesslike method of claiming ownership which he frequently adopted. On examination the volume was found to contain, bound in the following order,

> The Whole Contention between the two famous houses. *For T.P.*
> A Midsommer nights dreame. *Printed by Iames Roberts.* 1600.
> The first part of the Life of Sir John Old-castle. *London Printed for T.P.* 1600
> The Merchant of Venice. *Printed for I. Roberts.* 1600.
> Henry the fift. *Printed for T.P.* 1608.
> King Lear. *Printed for Nathaniel Butter.* 1608.
> Pericles Prince of Tyre. *Printed for T.P.* 1619.
> The Merry Wiues of Windsor. *Printed for Arthur Johnson.* 1619.
> A Yorkshire Tragedie. *Printed for T.P.* 1619.

All these plays were already in the British Museum, but the volume was in such admirable condition and generally such an attractive purchase that some pains were taken, but unavailingly, to find it an English home. It crossed the Atlantic, and now forms part of the Shakespeare Library gathered by Mr Marsden Perry at Providence, Rhode Island, where, while these pages were being put into type, I had the privilege of seeing it a second time.

Three or four years later, in 1906, owing to a chance conversation with a visitor while I was arranging a Shakespeare exhibition in the King's Library, another charming little fat volume of Shakespearian quartos was brought for me to see. This contained in the following order:

> The Whole Contention. *Pavier.*
> A Yorkshire Tragedy. *Pavier.* 1619.
> Henry the fift. *Pavier.* 1608.

Pericles. *Pavier.* 1619.
King Lear. *Butter.* 1608.
Midsommer night's dreame. *Roberts.* 1600.
Merchant of Venice. *Roberts.* 1600.
Merry Wives of Windsor. *Johnson.* 1619.
Sir John Oldcastle. *Pavier.* 1600.

The calf binding, as far as I could judge from the back, which alone was ornamented, was of about the middle of the eighteenth century, but everything else reminded me vividly of the Edward Gwynn volume, and sent me searching for the note of its contents which I remembered to have taken. When the note was found, it became evident that each volume contained the same editions of the same plays, though in a different order. The coincidence was so remarkable that I could not believe it to be accidental, and I was bitterly disappointed when on writing to the owner, Mr Hussey, I found that the volume had already been sent to Messrs Sotheby and by them to a bookbinder to be broken up, in order that the plays might be sold separately.

There was no bound volume containing these nine plays at the British Museum; was there any other in existence elsewhere? The most obvious person to have possessed one was Edward Capell, who in 1768 published his edition of Shakespeare's *Comedies, Histories and Tragedies set out by himself, in quarto, or by the players (his fellows) in folio,* and by this (alas! untenable) claim that the quartos were "set out" by Shakespeare himself, first drew public attention to their importance. Capell, unhappily, was one of the first collectors to revolt against the time-honoured and eminently preservative, though very inconvenient, practice of binding up bundles of plays or pamphlets into thick volumes. His collection, as preserved at Trinity College, Cambridge, did not contain these nine plays in a single volume, but, thanks to the minute care and accuracy with which the collection had recently been catalogued by Mr W. W. Greg, within a few minutes of beginning my search I felt as sure that Capell had at one time possessed such a volume as if I had seen it in his hand.

Most of Capell's quartos seem to be fairly good copies, but among them all there are nine, and nine only, which attain the measurements $7\frac{1}{2} \times 5\frac{5}{8}$ inches, and these nine are the same nine as I had found in the Gwynn volume and that belonging to Mr Hussey, which had since been broken up. Capell had not reduced his copies to mere units; they are now bound in two volumes, which stand side by side with the pressmarks Q 11 and Q 12, so that despite rebinding they may still be said to be kept together, the order of contents being:

[Q 11.] Yorkshire Tragedy.
       Merry Wives.
       Midsommer nights dreame.
       King Lear.
       Merchant of Venice.
[Q 12.] Sir John Oldcastle.
       Henry V.
       Pericles.
       The whole Contention.

The discovery that Capell's copies of these nine plays were all of a size, and that an unusual one, sent me very early the next morning to the Garrick Plays at the British Museum, and with the clue already given me I had no need to look for their titles on their backs. Within a couple of minutes I had picked out all nine plays from among their fellows simply by their height, and I think that there can be no doubt that David Garrick, like Edward Capell, purchased them in a volume and broke them up to suit his own convenience, the division in this case being carried as far as it could lawfully go.

The evidence, then, which I had gathered for these nine plays having once formed a single volume was:

(*a*) One copy, still united, with the name of a seventeenth century collector on the cover.

(*b*) One copy in a binding of about the middle of the eighteenth century, only recently broken up.

(*c*) Two sets of the nine plays, of uniform and unusual size, traceable to the possession of eighteenth century collectors, both of them known to have been in the habit of breaking up volumes and rebinding.

From the nature of the case it was hopeless to expect any large body of evidence. Until Capell drew attention to them the quartos were altogether neglected. After 1768 a volume containing all nine plays would have very little chance of remaining unbroken unless it fell into the hands of a quiet owner who made no speciality of plays. Auctioneers, booksellers and collectors would all have every temptation to break it up, and except a strange connexion between *The True Contention* and *Pericles*, as to which more will be said, there was nothing that we know of in the appearance of the volume to stay their hands.

Having carried my inquiry thus far I published (June 2, 1906) an article in *The Academy*, immediately after the sale of the Hussey quartos, in order to put my discovery on record and obtain, if possible, further evidence for it. By the kindness of Mr Luther Livingston, of New York, an important piece of new evidence was brought to my notice almost immediately. Mr Livingston wrote to me on June 14 (with a kind compliment on " a lovely bit of literary or bibliographical detective work "): " The Library of the University of Virginia has another such volume, I do not doubt. It is a volume presented to them by Thomas Mason Randolph, nearly a hundred years ago I suppose. It contains the seven Shakespeare plays of your list, and, I presume, though I do not know, it has the *Yorkshire Tragedy* and the *Sir John Oldcastle*. I am writing to the Librarian, and will let you know as soon as I have definite information."

Five days later Mr Livingston fulfilled his promise in the following at once mournful and satisfactory letter:

I have heard from the Librarian of the University of Virginia, Mr John S. Patton. The volume of plays which formerly belonged to the Library is no more! It was destroyed by fire in 1895. At least, it has not been found since that date, when a fire destroyed a large part of the Library.

Mr Patton was not librarian at the time and has never seen the book. He has no positive record of the order in which the players were arranged, but in an old manuscript catalogue he has found the following entry:

" A volume containing the following plays, small 4to:
> The Contention of the Two Famous Houses, York and Lancaster.
> A Yorkshire Tragedie. 1619.
> The Excellent History of the Merchant of Venice. 1600.
> Pericles, Prince of Tyre. 1619.
> The Chronicle History of Henry 5th. 1608.
> Sir John Old-Castle. 1600.
> The History of King Lear. 1608.
> A Pleasant Conceited Comedy of Sir John Falstaffe. 1619.
> A Mid-Sommers Nights Dreame. 1600."

There is little doubt but that this old list actually shows the arrangement of the plays in the volume. If this is the case, it is different from both of the volumes which you record.

There are only two Public Libraries in the U.S., I believe, which contain even nine quartos, and it is a great pity that the old volume, given by Thomas Jefferson's nephew, should have been burned.

With Mr Livingston's regrets for the fate of the book I cordially sympathized. None the less, it was a great satisfaction to receive information of the existence of yet another set of these nine plays. As the information at first came to me, it looked as if the Virginia set must be put on a level with the two in seventeenth and eighteenth century bindings which first roused my interest, for Thomas Jefferson was a considerable collector for many years, and this volume might well have been in an early binding. According, however, to a later discovery by Mr Patton, which, no doubt by an inadvertence, he omitted to mention to his original inquirer, this was not the case, for in a letter in *The Athenæum*, No. 4238 (January 16, 1909), Mr Sidney Lee was able to state on his authority that "the nine Shakespeare quartos in question" came to the library in 1853, each in a separate binding, and were bound together by a bookseller in Charlottesville in 1853 or soon afterwards. They may, of course, originally have been in a volume, have been broken up in the eighteenth century and reunited in 1853, but they must be ranked now with the Garrick or Capell sets rather than with the Gwynn or Hussey volumes. Their corroborative value, however, is still considerable, as they came to the library unaccompanied by any other Shakespeare quartos, and there is thus a strong probability that they represent a single purchase, either by Governor Randolph or Jefferson. With the addition of the Randolph copies our evidence for the theory that sets of these nine plays were on sale together at one time, i.e., in 1619, now consists in the discovery of five such sets (Gwynn, Hussey, Capell, Garrick, Randolph) as still, or quite recently, in existence. Considering how easily nine plays, without any obvious connexion, would be separated to suit the convenience of buyers, it is not a little remarkable that so many witnesses for our case should have survived. In his admirable introduction to the Clarendon Press facsimile of *Pericles* Mr Lee stated the number of copies of the 1619 edition of *Pericles* in known ownership as 17, while there are also six unlocated copies, " one or two of which may possibly be identifiable with some already enumerated." Without a copy of the 1619 *Pericles* no set of our quartos would be complete, and the maximum number of sets which could have remained united is thus something between seventeen and twenty-three. Taking the mean between these numbers, we may say that five out of about twenty sets have remained complete and

84

unmixed, and this is surely as high a proportion as any one who knows the manners and customs of the auction room could possibly expect.

Two other points are worth mentioning. In the first place, the height of the copies of these nine quartos, even when we put on one side those which can be *proved* to have been preserved as sets, is certainly rather higher than the average of the Shakespeare quarto as a class, which would naturally be the case if for the first century and a half of their existence they had been kept in volumes. Secondly, they are certainly more common than Shakepeare quartos taken generally. In his census of the surviving copies, located and unlocated, of all the quarto editions of *Pericles*, Mr Lee has been able to trace only nine of the first (*Enter**) of the two 1609 editions, and five of the second (*Eneer**); only two of the Gosson edition of 1611; from seventeen to twenty-three, as we have seen, of the 1619 edition with which we are specially concerned; seven and nine, respectively, of the two issues of 1630 (shorter and longer imprints) and nineteen of that of 1635. Our 1619 quarto is thus distinctly the commonest, there being more copies of it extant than of the three preceding editions put together. When a complete census of all the known Shakespeare quartos is produced, similar, if not quite so striking, results will probably emerge in the case of all the quartos of the volume. Mr Luther Livingston, who, as the author of *American Book-Prices Current*, is an expert in these matters, in his first letter to me expressed his agreement with my conclusions on the ground that they explained "why several quarto Shakespeares are so (comparatively) common in the market." In *The Library* for April, 1908, in reviewing Mr Slater's (English) *Book-Prices Current* for 1907, I was able to point out that "under his numbers 3010-12 and 3014-17 and 5339-45 he had recorded two nearly complete sets, the one only lacking *Henry V* and *The Merry Wives*, the other only *The Merchant of Venice* and the *Yorkshire Tragedy*. The first set, which had previously been sold at the Birket Foster sale in 1894, might possibly have come from a single source (possibly George Daniel's library), the second, the property of Mr Van Antwerp, were known to have come from several different collections. Thus their occurrence together in the auction room offers no direct evidence of the existence of simultaneous sale in 1619, but is worth mentioning as a proof that these editions are the ones which it is easiest to pick up in a hurry, as would naturally be the case if they had been preserved in volumes until the eighteenth century.†

On all these various grounds I hope I am not unreasonable in taking it as proved that copies of these nine quartos in their original condition were put on the market at the same time, either in a publisher's binding or as an unbound set which cried aloud to buyers to bind it up speedily into a volume. In his account of the Stratford copies of *The Merchant of Venice, Midsummer Night's Dream, King Lear*, and *Merry Wives*, Mr Sidney Lee wrote in February, 1908:‡ "It is worth the bibliographer's notice that the four

*The first word in the first stage direction in the play, by the correct or incorrect printing of which the two editions of 1609 are distinguished.

† See also the note to p. 98, and Mr G. W. Cole's Census of the Quartos of 1619 on p. 165.

‡ The Quarto Editions of Plays by Shakespeare, the Property of the Trustees and Guardians of Shakespeare's Birthplace, Described by Sidney Lee. Stratford on Avon. Printed for the Trustees and Guardians of Shakespeare's Birthplace. 1908. pp. 8, 9.

85

Shakespearean quartos which are described in this pamphlet are sometimes met bound together, with early quarto editions of five other plays, in a plain brown calf cover dating from early in the seventeenth century," going on to mention "the other contents of this old bound volume" as "invariably" the plays with whose names the reader must by this time be familiar. As I had myself only been able to find *one* extant example of such a volume "with a plain brown calf cover dating from early in the seventeenth century," Mr Lee's phrase "are *sometimes* met" was a good deal more sweeping than I should care to use myself, but his acceptance of my discovery of the "volume" was a great pleasure to me. I regret that subsequent developments appear to have caused him rather to recede from this his first position.

Facts are one thing, theories another. The facts in my *Academy* article formed a nucleus to which others, in pleasant agreement with them, have since been added. My theories, or explanations of the facts, have had to be laid aside. After noting that five of the plays belong to the year 1619, and that it seemed difficult at first to see why three plays of 1600 and two of 1608 should come thus cheek by jowl with others of such much later date, what I wrote was:

There is, however, a striking point common to four out of five of these earlier issues—each of them is one of two editions printed in the same year. Besides the " Roberts" edition of the *Midsummer Night's Dream* and *The Merchant of Venice*, there are those which bear the names also of their respective publishers, Fisher and Heyes; besides the "Pavier" edition of *Sir John Oldcastle*, there is that with the initials of V. S., i.e. Valentine Sims, as its printer on Pavier's behalf; besides the "Butter" edition of *King Lear*, there is that known to students as the "Pide Bull " edition, because in addition to Butter's name it gives the sign of his shop, the Pied Bull. Now, every publisher knows by sad experience that a first edition of a book may be exhausted so rapidly that to refuse to print a second seems a mere turning away good money ; and yet, when a second is printed, only a few copies are sold. The demand which seemed so vigorous was really for only another hundred or two hundred copies, and if a second thousand, or even five hundred, are printed, the bulk of them become at once dead stock. It is dispiriting to think that this was the fate which befell the *Merchant of Venice*, the *Midsummer Night's Dream* and *King Lear*, and that Jacobean readers were so much less appreciative of *Henry V* than their Elizabethan predecessors. But, if we are to account for these editions of 1600 and 1608 being bound up with other editions printed in 1619 otherwise than as an accident, we can only do so by supposing that they belonged to unsold stock, and that the news of the forthcoming folio of 1623 caused them to be thrown on the market as what we now call a "remainder."

So I wrote with an amiable and conservative desire to cause the minimum of disturbance to accepted views on the relation of the quartos in question to other editions of the same plays. According to my present view I had at least this excuse, that I was believing exactly what it is highly probable I was intended to believe. If so, what I was intended to believe was not in accordance with the facts. In any case, my theory of the remainder market left one or two points, which were lying, not hidden away, but on the very surface, quite unexplained.

For instance, there is the very striking point of the imprints. The normal imprint on a Shakespeare quarto is that of the first edition of *Richard II :* " London Printed by Valentine Simmes for Andrew Wise, and are to be

sold at his shop in Paules church-yard at the signe of the Angel. 1597."
More often perhaps than not the printer was only represented by his
initials, but this was, doubtless, with no idea of making a mystery of his
name, but to emphasize the greater importance of the publisher. This normal imprint, with the printer's name or initials, the publisher's name and
the publisher's address, is found in the following thirty Shakespeare quartos
printed before 1623.

PRINTER, PUBLISHER, ADDRESS.

Titus Andronicus. 1594, 1600.
Richard II. 1597, 1598, 1608 (2 issues).
Richard III. 1597, 1598, 1602, 1605, 1612, 1622.
Romeo and Juliet. 1599.
Henry IV, Pt I, 1598, 1599, 1604, 1613, 1622.
Love's Labors Lost. 1598.
Merchant of Venice. 1600 (Heyes).
Henry V. 1600, 1602.
Henry IV, Pt II, 1600 (same title for both issues).
Much Ado about Nothing. 1600.
Merry Wives of Windsor. 1602.
Hamlet. 1604, 1605.
Troilus and Cressida, 1609 (both issues).
Othello. 1622.

If for any reason the publisher chose to ignore the printer, we get the
publisher's name and address, as on the titlepages of the following nine
quartos.

PUBLISHER AND ADDRESS.

Titus Andronicus. 1611.
Richard II. 1615.
Romeo and Juliet. 1609.
Henry IV, Pt I. 1608.
Midsummer Night's Dream. 1600 (Fisher).
Hamlet. 1611.
King Lear. 1608 (Pide Bull).
Pericles. 1609 (both issues).

Now let us look at the imprints of our nine titlepages of the volume.
We will take them in the order of their dates.

Midsummer Night's Dream. Printed by Iames Roberts, 1600.
Merchant of Venice. Printed by I. Roberts. 1600.
Sir John Oldcastle. London. Printed for T. P. 1600.
Henry V. Printed for T. P. 1608.
King Lear. Printed for Nathaniel Butter. 1608.
Merry Wives. Printed for Arthur Johnson. 1619.
A Yorkshire Tragedy. Printed for T. P. 1619.
Pericles. Printed for T. P. 1619.
Whole Contention. Printed at London for T. P.

In all these nine imprints there is not a single example of the normal variety
which specifies the printer, publisher and publisher's address, or even of the
less common form which gives the publisher and his address only. Two of
the nine imprints mention the printer only, and among all the other Shakespeare quartos but two parallels can be produced to match them, (i) the

pirated edition of *Romeo and Juliet*, of which the imprint reads: " London. Printed by John Danter. 1597," and (ii) the third edition, obtained without a transfer, of the pirated *Pericles*, which reads: " Printed at London by S. S. 1611." The other seven titlepages in our volume give in two cases the name, in five only the initials, of the publisher, without mentioning his address. There is exactly one parallel to this form in other Shakespeare quartos, and as it has to dance *vis-à-vis* to two varieties it obligingly itself comprises both. This is the pirated edition of *Hamlet*, of which the imprint reads: " At London printed for N. L. and Iohn Trundell. 1603."

The combined abnormality and disreputability of the only Shakespearian parallels which can be found to match these imprints is really startling.* Only three out of the forty-two other titlepages possess the characteristics which we find on every one of the nine titlepages of the set, and these three parallels all belong to pirated editions. Until the connexion of these nine volumes with one another was discovered, their imprints might pass unremarked. Each one could be quoted as a parallel to any other. But now that the existence of some connexion between them has been established, to find that they offer nine examples of a form of imprint to which only three parallels can be found out of the forty-two other titlepages with which they are most naturally compared demands explanation. When Pavier published *Henry V* in 1602, he placed his address on the title in the usual form, " and are to be sold at his shop in Cornhill, at the sign of the Cat and Parrets neare the Exchange." When Arthur Johnson published *The Merry Wives* in the same year, the imprint contains the like information—" and are to be sold at his shop in Powles Churchyard, at the signe of the Flower de Luce and the Crowne." Why did both Pavier and Johnson omit their addresses in these reprints of 1608 and 1619? Why do we find addresses on the other " 1600 " editions of *Sir John Oldcastle*, *The Merchant of Venice*, and the *Midsummer Night's Dream* and not on these? Why did Pavier drop his in all his 1619 editions? It is no answer to say that all these books were printed by James Roberts and his successor, William Jaggard. Roberts printed addresses on other quartos. Why were they omitted from these nine? Moreover, the inclusion or omission of the publisher's address was surely a question for the publisher to decide, and we are asked to believe that Roberts in 1600, Pavier in the same year, Pavier and Butter in 1608, and Pavier and Johnson in 1619 all took this course, either by mere coincidence or (on my timid original theory) because they foresaw that the books would be on the remainder market together at some future time. Surely we have here the height of improbability.

* If the inquiry were extended to plays by other dramatists the proportion of editions with no address in their imprints would certainly be much higher. But I think that there is every reason to believe that Shakespeare's company were more, not less, successful than the others in protecting themselves against piracy, and if piracy and the absence of a vendor's address are in any way connected, as would appear to be the case, it would be natural, therefore, that there should be more address-less editions in the case of other authors. It must be understood, of course, that the absence of an address in the imprint would only indirectly be connected with piracy or the absence of an entry in the Stationers' Register. The same cause which made a pirate shun the Stationers Company would make him fear lest his stock should be seized. Other causes might have a like effect. *Eastward Ho*, which bears no address, had been regularly entered on the Register, but its regularity in this respect did not alter the fact that a play, the authors of which had been imprisoned for it, might not be a very safe book to sell.

THE
Whole Contention
betweene the two Famous
Houses, LANCASTER and
YORKE.

With the Tragicall ends of the good Duke
Humfrey, Richard Duke of Yorke,
and King Henrie the
sixt.

Diuided into two Parts : And newly corrected and
enlarged. Written by *William Shake-*
speare, Gent.

Printed at LONDON, for T. P.

THE LATE,
And much admired Play,
CALLED,
Pericles, Prince of
Tyre.

With the true Relation of the whole Hi-
story, aduentures, and fortunes of
the saide Prince.

Written by W. SHAKESPEARE.

Printed for *T. P.* 1619.

A
YORKSHIRE
TRAGEDIE.

Not so New, as Lamentable
and True.

Written by W. SHAKESPEARE.

Printed for *T. P.* 1619:

A
Most pleasant and ex-
cellent conceited Comedy,
of Sir Iohn Falstaffe, and the
merry VViues of VVindsor.

VVith the swaggering vaine of Ancient *Pistoll,* and Corporall *Nym.*

Written by W. SHAKESPEARE.

Printed for *Arthur Johnson,* 1619.

FOUR PLAYS OF THE SET ADMITTEDLY PRINTED IN 1619.

The first part

Of the true & hono-
rable history, of the Life of
Sir Iohn. Old-castle, the good
Lord Cobham.

*As it hath bene lately acted by the Right
honorable the Earle of Notingham
Lord High Admirall of England,
his Seruants.*

Written by William Shakespeare.

London printed for T.P.
1600.

THE
Chronicle History
of Henry the fift, with his
battell fought at Agin Court in
France. Together with an-
cient Pistoll.

*As it hath bene sundry times playd by the Right Honou-
rable the Lord Chamberlaine his
Seruants.*

Printed for T.P. 1608.

THE
EXCELLENT
History of the Mer-
chant of Venice.

With the extreme cruelty of Shylocke
the Iew towards the saide Merchant, in cutting a iust pound of his flesh. And the obtaining
of Portia, by the choyse of
three Caskets.

Written by W. SHAKESPEARE.

Printed by J. Roberts, 1600.

M. VVilliam Shake-speare,
HIS
True Chronicle History of the life
and death of King Lear, and his
three Daughters.

With the vnfortunate life of EDGAR,
sonne and heire to the Earle of Glocester, and
his sullen and assumed humour of TOM
of Bedlam.

*As it was plaid before the Kings Maiesty at White-Hall, vp-
pon S. Stephens night, in Christmas Hollidaies.*

By his Maiesties Seruants, playing vsually at the
Globe on the Banck-side.

Printed for Nathaniel Butter.
1608.

FOUR PLAYS OF THE SET WITH DATES HERE CONTENDED
TO BE FICTITIOUS. ALL PRINTED IN 1619.

The moſt excellent

Hiſtorie of the *Merchant of Venice*.

VVith the extreame crueltie of *Shylocke* the Iewe towards the ſayd Merchant, in cutting a iuſt pound of his fleſh : and the obtayning of *Portia* by the choyſe of three cheſts.

As it hath beene diuers times aɛted by the Lord Chamberlaine his Seruants.

Written by William Shakeſpeare.

AT LONDON,
Printed by *I. R.* for Thomas Heyes, and are to be ſold in Paules Church-yard, at the ſigne of the Greene Dragon.
1 6 0 0.

M. William Shak-ſpeare:

HIS
True Chronicle Hiſtorie of the life and death of King L E A R and his three Daughters.

With the vnfortunate life of Edgar, *ſonne* and heire to the Earle of Gloſter, and his ſullen and aſſumed humor of T O M of Bedlam :

As it was played before the Kings Maieſtie at Whitehall vpon S. Stephans night in Chriſtmas Hollidayes.

By his Maieſties ſeruants playing vſually at the Gloabe on the Bancke-ſide.

LONDON,
Printed for *Nathaniel Butter,* and are to be ſold at his ſhop in *Pauls* Church-yard at the ſigne of the Pide Bull neere S*t.* *Auſtins* Gate. 1 6 0 8

The firſt part

Of the true and hono-

rable hiſtorie, of the life of Sir *John Old-caſtle,the good* Lord Cobham.

As it hath been lately aɛted by the right honorable the Earle of Notingham Lord high Admirall of England his ſeruants.

LONDON
Printed by V.S. for Thomas Pauier, and are to be ſolde at his ſhop at the ſigne of the Catte and Parrots neere the Exchange.
1 6 0 0.

THE
CRONICLE

Hiſtory of Henry the fift,
With his battell fought at *Agin Court* in *France.* Togither with *Auntient* Piſtoll.

As it hath bene ſundry times playd by the Right honorable the Lord Chamberlaine his ſeruants.

LONDON
Printed by *Thomas Creede,* for Tho. Milling-ton,and Iohn Busby. And are to be ſold at his houſe in Carter Lane, next the Powle head   1600.

TITLEPAGES OF THE ORIGINAL EDITIONS, COPIED, AS IS HERE CONTENDED, IN 1619.

A

Midſommer nights dreame.

As it hath beene ſundry times publikely acted, by the Right Honourable, the Lord Chamberlaine his
ſeruants.

VVritten by VVilliam Shakeſpeare.

Printed by Iames Roberts, 1600.

THE REPRINT OF 1619

A

Midſommer nights dreame.

As it hath beene ſundry times pub-
lickely acted, by the Right honourable, the Lord Chamberlaine his
ſeruants.

Written by William ShakeSpeare.

¶Imprinted at London, for *Thomas Fiſher,* and are to
be ſoulde at his ſhoppe, at the Signe of the White Hart,
in *Fleeteſtreete.* 1600.

ORIGINAL EDITION.

92

The striking uniformity of the nine unusual imprints on the titlepages of these plays might of itself have suggested that they must all have been printed at the same time under the same direction. Moreover, soon after my *Academy* article had appeared, I discovered that William Jaggard was using both the *Heb Ddim Heb Ddieu*, and the *Post Tenebras Lux* (or Half Eagle and Key) device in other books both before and after 1619, and that the stock of James Roberts had passed into his possession some years before this. Mr Greg, in conversation with me, threw out the idea that the whole volume might have been printed by Jaggard in 1619, and I went so far as to place all the nine titlepages in a row, and admitted to myself that their general resemblance certainly made the suggestion plausible. But the typography and arrangement of the texts presented differences as well as resemblances. They *might* all have been printed at the same time, but it would certainly be very difficult, if not impossible, I thought, to prove it, and having no leisure for the task I let it alone.

Shortly before Christmas, 1907, Mr Greg convinced my conservative mind that the whole set not merely might have been but *was* printed at the same time by working out with extraordinary care and skill a very intricate but very pretty method of proof. Not only do these plays possess nine imprints all of the same pattern and that pattern quite abnormal among Shakespearian quartos, but they also possess twenty-seven watermarks distributed over the eight sections into which the volume is divided by its signatures (those of *The Whole Contention* and *Pericles* being continuous) in such a way as to link all the sections closely together. The greatest work on watermarks ever published, or ever likely to be, is that by M. Charles Briquet, entitled, *Les Filigranes: dictionnaire historique des marques du papier dès leur apparition vers 1282 jusqu'en 1600*, in which reproductions are given of 16,112 marks, together with numerous references to books and documents, which can be dated and placed, in which each mark is found. As a result of the experience gained in compiling this monumental work, M. Briquet is convinced that the device of twisted wire tied to the paper frame to make a watermark had a life of about two years before it lost its shape altogether, and that it is unusual to find any given "make" of paper still in existence unused after ten years, and very unusual indeed to find it surviving after fifteen. Now, what Mr Greg demonstrated was that no fewer than five of the watermarks used in the paper of *The Merchant of Venice* or *Midsummer Night's Dream* dated 1600 are found also in identically the same forms in the *Lear* dated 1608 and again in the *Pericles* of 1619, in addition to minor connexions between pairs of plays in different groups.* On the theory that the dates 1600 and 1608 are authentic, we have to suppose that Roberts in 1600, in print-

* The following summary is compiled from Mr Greg's table of the watermarks occurring in the four sets of these plays belonging respectively to Capell (T.C.C.), Garrick (B.M.), Mr Huth and Malone (Bodley). The number of watermarks assigned to a play is thus sometimes greater than would be found in any single copy. The three groups into which the plays are divided are those suggested by the connexion of their marks and offer some clue to the probable order of printing:

(1) *The Whole Contention* (sixteen sheets) has only one watermark, and this is found again only in *Pericles*.

Pericles (nine sheets) has six watermarks, sharing five each with *M.V.* and *Lear*, four each with *Y.T.*, *M.W.*, *M.N.D.*, and one with *The Contention*.

ing two plays for himself and a third for Pavier, used a job lot of paper bearing some fifteen different watermarks; that what was left of this job lot was preserved for eight years and then handed over to Jaggard, who added a few other kinds and printed two plays for different publishers; lastly, that the remnants of the job lot were again carefully saved for eleven more years and then again added to and used to print four more plays. Since the theory that rocks were created with ready-made fossils in them in order to tempt proud geologists to unbelief, so staggering a proposition has hardly been set forth.

Mr Greg also pointed out the unusual size of the numerals used for the dates in the imprints, of which no other instance can be found while Roberts was at work, and also that the *Heb Ddim Heb Ddieu* device was found in no other book bearing his name. As it is impossible to prove a negative, this evidence can never be complete, but after personal examination of all the books, over thirty in number, printed by Roberts, which I have been able to find at the British Museum, I can testify that as far as these are concerned it is entirely accurate. Between 1593 and 1606 (inclusive) Roberts used numerals of several different sizes to date his titlepages, but never any nearly as large as those which appear uniformly on all the nine of the volume. During the same period he appears once to have used the *Post Tenebras Lux* device which appears on the *Midsummer Night's Dream*. On some three or four other books there is found the device of a serpent with mottos, *Nosce te ipsum* and *Ne quid nimis*, derived through Charlwood from W. Baldwin. On no book of his at the British Museum can I find the *Heb Ddim Heb Ddieu* device which appears on eight of the nine titlepages of the volume, or any other besides the two already mentioned.*

Of numerals that could be used for dating imprints a printer might easily possess several founts. As a rule at this period both printers and publishers were fairly faithful to one device, but we have found Roberts using two, and there is no reason why he should not have added a third. As regards his stock in these respects we can only state what we find. A handful of figures or an old device would cost but a few pence. We cannot argue that it is unreasonable to imagine that he possessed more varieties than he would be likely to need. A fount of type, however, could by no means be bought for

The *Yorkshire Tragedy* (four sheets) has four watermarks, all of which it shares with *Pericles*, and three each with *M.W.*, *M.V.*, *M.N.D.* and *Lear*.

(2) The *Merry Wives* (seven sheets) has eight watermarks, sharing six each with *M.V.* and *M.N.D.*, four each with *Pericles* and *Lear*, three with *Y.T.*, one each with H^5 and *O*.

The *Merchant of Venice* (eight sheets) has nine watermarks, sharing six each with *M.W.* and *M.N.D.*, five each with *Pericles* and *Lear*, three with *Y.T.*, one with H^5.

The *Midsummer Night's Dream* (ten sheets) has ten watermarks and one sheet unmarked, sharing six each of these points with *M.W.* and *M.V.*, five with *Lear*, four with *Pericles*, three with *Y.T.*, two with H^5 and one with *Oldcastle*.

Lear (eleven sheets) has fourteen watermarks and some paper unmarked, sharing six of these fifteen points with H^5, five each with *Pericles*, four with *M.W.*, *M.V.* and *M.N.D.*, three with *Y.T.*, two with *Oldcastle*.

(3) *Henry V* (seven sheets) has eight watermarks and some unmarked paper, sharing six of these nine points with *Lear*, four with *Oldcastle*, two with *M.N.D.*, one with *M.W.*

Sir John Oldcastle (ten sheets) has six watermarks, sharing four of these with *Henry V*, two with *Lear*, and one each with *M.W.*, *M.V.*, *M.N.D.*

*As to this use of the two devices, see appendix at end of chapter.

94

a few pence. If a printer had money to spare, he might procure a new one in order to have a greater variety of kinds and sizes, but for a small printer, as Roberts remained from first to last (even after he married Charlwood's widow), to procure a fount of roman type of exactly the same size as one which he had been using for seven years, to use this in printing three plays, and then never to use it again, would be an amazing piece of extravagance. Yet, if we credit James Roberts with having printed both editions of *The Merchant of Venice*, which bear the date 1600, this extravagance must be attributed to him. Both the "Heyes" edition and the "Roberts" edition are printed in roman types (interspersed with italics of the same size) of which twenty lines measure about 82 mm. But the type used in the "Roberts" edition is from a fount which was only just coming into use in 1600, and which continued in use for many years, being identical with that found in the folio of 1623, a fact hitherto curiously overlooked. The type used for the "Heyes" quarto, on the other hand, belonged to a very old fount, used by several printers towards the end of the sixteenth century, Charlwood, from whom Roberts obtained his stock of it, having employed it for several books in the 'eighties. The upper case letters in it are larger than those in the newer type, and the general effect is that of slightly greater height and less roundness.

Now in the two quarto editions which Roberts undoubtedly printed in 1600, that of *The Merchant of Venice*, which he printed for Thomas Heyes, and that of *Titus Andronicus*, which he printed for Edward White, he used his old "82" roman type despite the fact that the upper case of it was running very short, so that on some pages of *The Merchant of Venice* hardly one in four of the lines begin with a capital. He could not go on like this, and so he was obviously obliged to buy some more capitals, and the old fount apparently being quite exhausted he had to buy them of the new kind; but except the suspected quartos no book or portion of a book printed in the new fount can be traced to his press. He went on using his old fount with a handful of new capitals to it until he gave up his business, when it passed into the possession of Jaggard, who used it in reprinting one or two small books which he had taken over from Roberts. Jaggard himself, when he started in business, had bought a good supply of the new fount, which other printers also were now using, and when the old fount was useless for anything else he used some of the old capitals with the new fount, just as Roberts had used some of the new capitals with the old fount. And this slight admixture is found in about the same degree in all the quartos of the set which it is here claimed were printed by Jaggard in 1619, though some of them bear Roberts's name or initials and the date 1600. On this theory the presence of these wrong fount letters is neatly explained; on the theory which accepts the dates 1600 and James Roberts as the actual printer of these quartos of the set so dated his use and disuse of the new type are hopelessly tangled.

According to the theory of those who cling to the correctness of the dates 1600 the quarto of *The Merchant of Venice* "Printed by I. Roberts 1600" is earlier than that which Roberts printed for Heyes. That is to say, he first used his new type and then printed another edition for Heyes with the defective old type and page after page showing a pitiful lack of capitals. In the same year

95

hee feekes my life, his reafon well *I* know;
I oft deliuerd from his forfeytures
many that haue at times made mone to me,
therefore he hates me.

  Sal. I am fure the Duke will neuer grant
      this forfaiture to hold.

  An. The Duke cannot denie the courfe of law:
for the commoditie that ftrangers haue
vvith vs in Venice, if it be denyed,
will much impeach the iuftice of the ftate,
fince that the trade and profit of the citty
confifteth of all Nations. Therefore goe,
thefe griefes and loffes haue fo bated me
that *I* fhall hardly fpare a pound of flefh
to morrow, to my bloody Creditor.
Well *Iaylor* on, pray God *Baffanio* come
to fee me pay his debt, and then *I* care not.   *Exeunt.*

      Enter *Portia, Nerriffa, Lorenzo, Ieffica,* and a
           man of *Portias.*

  Lor. Maddam, although I fpeake it in your prefence,
you haue a noble and a true conceite
of god-like amitie, which appeares moft ftrongly
in bearing thus the abfence of your Lord.
But if you knew to whom you fhow this honour,
how true a gentleman you fend releefe,
how deere a louer of my Lord your husband,
I know you would be prouder of the worke
then cuftomarie bountie can enforce you.

  Por. I neuer did repent for dooing good,
nor fhall not now : for in companions
that doe conuerfe and wait the time together,
vvhofe foules doe beare an egall yoke of loue,
there muft be needes a like proportion
of lyniaments, of manners, and of fpiritʒ
vvhich makes me thinke that this *Anthonio*
beeing the bofome louer of my Lord,
muft needes be like my Lord. If it be fo,

                           how

FROM THE HEYES QUARTO OF 1600

Ile not be made a ſoft and dull ey'd foole,
To ſhake the head, relent, and ſigh, and yeeld
To Chriſtian interceſſors : follow not,
Ile haue no ſpeaking, I will haue my bond.

Exit Iew.

   Sol. It is the moſt impenetrable curre
That euer kept with men.
   Ant. Let him alone,
Ile follow him no more with bootleſſe prayers.
He ſeekes my life, his reaſon well I know :
I oft deliuer'd from his forfeitures
Many that haue at times made mone to mee,
Therefore he hates me.
   Sal. I am ſure the Duke will neuer grant
This forfeyture to hold.
   An. The Duke cannot deny the courſe of Law :
For the commodity that ſtrangers haue
With vs in Venice, if it be denied,
Will much impeach the iuſtice of his ſtate,
Since that the trade and profit of the City
Conſiſteth of all Nations. Therefore goe,
Theſe greefes and loſſes haue ſo bated me,
That I ſhall hardly ſpare a pound of fleſh
To morrow, to my bloody Creditor.
VVell Iaylor on, pray God *Baſſanio* come
To ſee me pay his debt, and then I care not.   *Exeunt.*

    Enter Portia, Nerriſſa, Lorenzo, Ieſſica, and a
           man of Portias.

   Lor. Madam, although I ſpeake it in your preſence,
You haue a noble and a true conceite
Of God-like amity, which appeares moſt ſtrongly,
In bearing thus the abſence of your Lord.
But if you knew to whom you ſhew this honour,
*Ho*w true a Gentleman you ſend releeſe,

                       Ho w

he must also be supposed to have printed *Titus Andronicus* in his old type and *Sir John Oldcastle* and *A Midsummer Night's Dream* in his new, and after this to have laid aside his new type altogether, and have gone on for another six years with his old. Few students who know anything of the ways of printers will find it easy to believe this. A page from each quarto of *The Merchant of Venice* is here shown in "facsimile," about two-thirds of the text being the same in each case, and even under the disadvantages of photographic reproduction it should suffice to convince any one that the "Heyes" quarto is not merely earlier than that "Printed for I. Roberts 1600" but belongs typographically to an earlier generation. Short, moreover, as is the text common to both pages, it will suffice also to suggest that this is true not only of the forms of the letters but also of the spelling, which in the suspected quartos, when a balance is struck, will be found distinctly more modern than that which Roberts used in 1600. In setting up Jaggard's reprint, as I think they undoubtedly did, from a copy of the Heyes edition,* his compositors as a rule would follow the spellings they found before them. When they varied from them, they would do so, more or less unconsciously, according to their own practice, which would certainly not itself be either scientific or even uniform. But just as from one folio to its successor we can trace, when a balance is struck, distinct progress towards a more modern spelling, so, though occasionally in *The Merchant of Venice* Jaggard's men revived an obsolescent form, for every such revival there are two, three or four words spelt in a more modern fashion than in the Heyes quarto, and this certainly makes it more difficult than ever to believe that the Heyes is the earlier of the two.

It may be well at this point to review the ground which we have so far covered. Accident directed the attention of the present writer to the possibility that these eight quartos, three of them dated 1619, two dated 1608, three dated 1600, formed for selling purposes a group by themselves, and this was confirmed by finding that while, if we may regard *Pericles* as typical of the rest, about twenty copies of them may be supposed to exist, in no fewer than five cases all nine have been found together in the same ownership in a way which justifies us in regarding them as having formed what may, at least loosely, be called a "set." On examining the members of these sets we have found that they are, edition for edition, distinctly more common, in some cases much more common, than other Shakespeare quartos purporting to be of the same dates;† that they all have similar imprints, marked off from the overwhelming majority of other Shakespeare quartos by the absence of addresses; that the dates in all these imprints are

---

*The view of the Cambridge editors is that the two texts were independently set up from the same manuscript. But the use of capitals for the name of GOD in the same passage, and in that passage only, Act II, sc. 2, l. 75, seems to prove that one printer must have copied the other. Roberts, like other printers of his day, used this typographical reverence in theological works, and a compositor accustomed to the practice followed it in a single, quite inappropriate place. It is easier to believe that a second compositor imitated him mechanically than that both took it from a manuscript, where, indeed, it is hardly conceivable that it could have occurred.

†Since writing the early part of this chapter I have extracted the following rather striking figures from Mr Livingston's *Auction Book-Prices*: Of the true 1600 *Merchant of Venice* Mr Livingston records 8 sales, of the reprint 13; of the true 1600 *Midsummer Night's Dream* 5 sales, of the reprint 15; of the true 1600 *Sir John Oldcastle* 4 sales, of the reprint 16; of the true 1608 *King Lear* 2 sales, of the reprint 14.

in large numerals, which cannot be found elsewhere in books printed in the
years 1600-1608; that seven of them bear a device not known to have been
used by Roberts, and which he could not have used in 1600 without en-
croaching on the rights of William White,* but which was frequently used
by William Jaggard after 1610; that the same watermarks are found in
plays bearing all three dates; that all but two of the plays (these two being
both dated 1619) are printed in the same type and in approximately the
same state of that type; that James Roberts not only cannot be shown to
have used this type, but that he possessed, from 1594 onward, a much older
type of precisely the same size, which from 1600 he eked out with new
capitals and went on using with a persistency which forbids us to believe
that he had all the time a new fount lying by him in reserve; that more
particularly is it difficult to believe that he printed the Heyes edition of
The Merchant of Venice in the old type, almost without line-capitals, after
having printed an earlier edition for himself in the new type, as the accepted
theory maintains; and, lastly, that the spelling of the quartos in question is
distinctly more modern than that used by Roberts in 1600. Thus, whether
we examine them in respect to publishing, printing, paper or spelling, we
find these quartos dated 1600 and 1608 agreeing closely with those dated
1619 and unlike other Shakespeare quartos of the years to which they
ostensibly belong, and, since dates other than those of actual production are
sometimes found in imprints, we are driven to believe that the dates 1600
on three of the quartos and 1608 on two others are not the dates of production, but that the whole set was printed by William Jaggard, the successor of James Roberts, in 1619.

As soon as a scientific hypothesis is formed in order to account for a
number of facts, we expect it to help in the explanation of other difficulties,
and the hypothesis that all these nine plays were printed in 1619 may certainly be used in this way. Students of the bibliography of Shakespeare have
been familiar for so long with the continuity of the signatures in the 1619
editions of the *Whole Contention between the two Famous Houses, Lancaster and
Yorke* and *The Late and much admired Play, called, Pericles, Prince of Tyre,*
that they have ceased to be surprised at it. The titlepage of the first occupies sig. A1, the text, A2-Q4. The titlepage of *Pericles* occupies a single
leaf, unsigned, and the text sigs. R-Z, 2A, 2B. Why these two very ill-matched
plays should have been thus joined together has never been explained. If
they formed the first and second pieces in a volume of nine Shakespeariana,
their connexion is more obvious. That they were originally intended to
occupy this position is strongly suggested by the facts (i) that the *Contention* stands first in the Gwynn and Garrick copies, two out of the three
whose order is known; (ii) that the same make of paper is used throughout
all the four copies of the *Contention* (Capell, Garrick, Malone, Huth) examined by Mr Greg, whereas no other variety is used consecutively for more
than two sheets. It was only natural for a printer to start with the kind of
paper of which he had the largest stock, and this Jaggard seems to have
done.

Another point with which the printing of these plays in 1619 is almost

* See the first appendix to this chapter.

99

certainly connected is the appearance in the Stationers' Register under date "8 Julij, 1619," of the entry:

Laurence Hayes. Entred for his copies by Consent of a full Court theis two Copies following which were the Copies of Thomas Haies his fathers, vizt
A play called The Marchant of Venice
And the Ethiopian History.

Thomas Hayes had been dead by this time at least fifteen years. Laurence Hayes did not reissue *The Merchant of Venice* until 1637. Why this sudden claim to it on July 8, 1619? If Laurence Hayes desired either to protect his right from infringement, or to vindicate it after an infringement had taken place, owing to the reprinting of *The Merchant of Venice* by Jaggard in 1619, his action becomes intelligible. It is interesting to note that two days after his entry there was a new master and new wardens of the Stationers' Company, and Jaggard, the printer of the plays, was one of the wardens. Did Hayes make his application on July 8 * in order to get it in before Jaggard was warden? That is not a question we can hope to answer.

When the extreme abnormality of the titlepages as compared with those of other Shakespeare quartos was first observed, two possible explanations had to be considered. The absence of addresses in the imprints might be taken as a confession of piracy, as in the case of the only three other Shakespeare quartos in which no addresses had been put. Or the absence of addresses might be due to another cause for which precedent could be found, the intention (in this case not carried out) of printing a general titlepage, thereby reducing the titlepages of the individual volumes to the rank of half-titles, in which the imprints would have a complimentary and bibliographical import rather than a strictly business one. Neither explanation by itself is satisfactory. From the standpoint of the Stationers' Company the volume could hardly be called piratical. Every play was a reprint, and with reprints the Company did not concern itself unless one of its members lodged a complaint for infringement of copyright. Among the plays were three derelicts, or plays which the setters-forth chose to consider so, *Pericles*, which might fairly be considered one, and *The Merchant of Venice* and *Midsummer Night's Dream*, neither of which had been printed for nineteen years. Roberts, Jaggard's predecessor, had been connected with *The Merchant of Venice*. From the titlepage of the *Midsummer Night's Dream*, as it appeared in the volume, it looked as if he had been connected with that also. Any wrong which the book might do could be explained as an inadvertence.

Of course, if the consent of Butter was not obtained to the publication of *King Lear*, or that of Arthur Johnson was not obtained for that of *The Merry Wives*, the case is entirely altered. Johnson and Butter were living members

*He himself may be thought to have been trying to steal a march on William Barrett by his entry of the *Ethiopian History*. This had been entered on September 6, 1602, to Thomas Hayes "by consent of master Coldocke" (publisher of the edition of 1587), but on May 21, 1604, Thomas Hayes's widow transferred it to William Cotton, who published an edition in 1606, and on February 16, 1617, it was found on a list of "all the copies which belonged to master Cotton" which were transferred "to master Barrett." Barrett published the edition in 1622, so this 1619 entry by Laur. Hayes was of no effect, and it is charitable to assume that he had forgotten, if he ever knew, what his mother had done in 1604. Both books had at one time belonged to Thomas Hayes, and in securing his interest to the one which he had really inherited Laurence Hayes may easily have thrown in the other without any bad faith.

of the Stationers' Company, fully able to protect their rights. They had co-operated within the last two years in bringing out a late edition of Lyly's *Euphues*. Their united forces would certainly have been arrayed against aggression. As we have noted, William Jaggard was either already or just about to become one of the Wardens of the Stationers' Company. It is not likely that he would have involved himself in a serious quarrel just before or during his year of office. As against Johnson or Butter he could not have had a shadow of a defence. The imprint which we find on *Lear* and *The Merry Wives*, " Printed for N. Butter," " Printed for Arthur Johnson," may thus safely be taken as implying consent, and if so no obvious piracy was committed.

The alternative theory, which explains the short imprint on the titlepages of the individual plays by an (unfulfilled) intention of issuing a general titlepage to the whole collection, is strongly supported by the continuous signatures which link *Pericles* to the whole *Contention*. Unless these are treated simply as a blunder, they compel us to believe that an intention of issuing a collection was at one time entertained. But by the same reasoning the abandon-ment of the continuous signatures suggests the abandonment of the intention, and this is emphasized by the change to a much larger type (twenty lines measuring 94 mm. instead of 82 mm.) in the *Yorkshire Tragedy* and *The Merry Wives*, the two plays which were probably printed immedi-ately after *Pericles*.* Yet in these plays and in all the five others we still have address-less imprints, and it is among the five other plays that we find the dates 1600 and 1608 substituted for 1619.

We are bound at this stage to supplement facts with theory and conjecture, and we may, perhaps, get some light on the history of the project if we remember that Pavier and Jaggard, who were presumably its chief promoters, Jaggard as the printer of the whole volume and Pavier as the publisher of most of the individual plays, had both shown their admiration for Shakespeare by affixing his name to publications with which he had had little or nothing to do. Pavier had already done this in regard to the *Yorkshire Tragedy*, and was now prepared to do it also for *Sir John Oldcastle*, in addition to the doubtful cases of *The Whole Contention* and *Pericles*. Jaggard, for his part, had put forth *The Passionate Pilgrim* as by Shakespeare, the only literary outrage which is known to have ruffled that tolerant person's equanimity. The start they made with their new volume showed that their fondness for these attri-butions had not diminished. *The Whole Contention* was a version, inferior to that in the players' hands, of two plays very doubtfully by Shakespeare; *Pericles* was much in the same class; the *Yorkshire Tragedy*, which was appa-rently to come next, was not by Shakespeare at all; *Sir John Oldcastle* and *Henry V*, the two other plays over which Pavier had rights, were the one spurious, the other a bad text discreditably obtained. Now Jaggard was con-nected with the players through his monopoly (derived from Roberts) for printing playbills, and if he chanced to mention a project for printing *The Whole Contention*, *Pericles*, the *Yorkshire Tragedy*, *Sir John Oldcastle* and *Henry V* with a collective titlepage as a volume of Shakespeare's plays, he may have heard enough plain-speaking to frighten him. If the plan were originally

* See note on pp. 93, 94.

Pavier's, Jaggard himself may have seen the necessity for modifying it. Hence the abandonment of the idea of a collective titlepage, because of the impossibility of inventing one which might not call down an effective protest; hence also, we may conjecture, an attempt to strengthen the volume by including more genuine plays. It is quite possible, of course, that the adhesion of Butter, who owned *King Lear*, and of Arthur Johnson, who owned the (pirated) text of *The Merry Wives*, had been given to the original scheme. Even when thus strengthened, however, the collection would have contained, in addition to *Lear*, two doubtful plays, two spurious plays and two tolerated piracies, and any attempt to put such a collection on the market as an imitation of Ben Jonson's *Works* (1616) or Sir William Alexander's *Monarchicke Tragedies* (3rd edition, 1616) might have raised a storm. Are we wrong in imagining that it was when the defects of their own "copies" were perceived that the appropriation of *The Merchant of Venice* and the *Midsummer Night's Dream* was resolved on? The inclusion of these would be no offence in the eyes of the players, since copyright in them had already been acquired by stationers. The risk of interference from Stationers' Hall, as already explained, was not great. But to give the volume or set a better chance of passing unquestioned from either quarter, it would be well to destroy all evidence of its having been intended as a collected edition, and to avoid making definite claims to the two plays which were being annexed. *Pericles* was separated from *The Whole Contention*, the other plays were given separate signatures, and uniformity of type was abandoned. But it was possible to do more than this. From quite early times in the history of printing we find cases of dates of original issues being reprinted in later editions rather by way of assuring a purchaser that no material changes had been made than for the sake of bibliographical deception. Proclamations, statutes and yearbooks were certainly thus reprinted, dates and all; Middleton's reprint of a volume of Pynson's *Froissart* is an early instance from lay literature, the reissue of Hobbes's *Leviathan* a much later one. By adopting this plan for some of the plays over which they possessed full rights, *Lear*, *Henry V* and *Sir John Oldcastle*, the promoters would destroy any excess of uniformity in the volume, suggest to careful purchasers that original issues had been reprinted unaltered, and to careless ones that here were the original issues themselves, and at the same time render possible the appropriation of *The Merchant of Venice* and the *Midsummer Night's Dream* without any definite claim to them being advanced. Since Roberts was no·longer in business, " Printed by James Roberts 1600 " as an imprint in a book printed in 1619 could be interpreted, at a pinch, as meaning a faithful reprint of an edition printed by Roberts in the year named. The same imprint when applied to the *Midsummer Night's Dream* could not be thus justified, since Fisher's edition was not from Roberts's press. It is rather significant that in this case some trouble was taken to make the reprint really look as if the statement on the titlepage might be true. In this one play the device of the Half Eagle and Key with the motto *Post Tenebras Lux*, which Roberts had owned, was placed on the titlepage, and the initial at the beginning of the text and the use of roman type for the headlines both suggest conscious imitation of the original issue.

As suggested in the note to page 93 the plays were very probably printed in the order: *Whole Contention, Pericles, Yorkshire Tragedy, Merry Wives, Merchant of Venice, Midsummer Night's Dream, Lear, Henry V, Sir John Oldcastle.* But, save that some trouble seems to have been taken in separating *Pericles* from the *Whole Contention,* no order was observed when the plays were bound. It is probable also that plays were sold singly, and that some purchasers bought sets unbound and bound them at their own pleasure. If it were not for the continuous signatures of the *Whole Contention* and *Pericles,* the theory of publication (accomplished or intended) of the nine plays in volume form might be abandoned, the proof that the plays were all printed at the same time being now stronger than the theory of their original inclusion in a publisher's volume from which it started. In the case of a petty fraud of this kind, which remained unsuspected by Shakespeare students for nearly two centuries after it was committed, we cannot expect to reconstruct with precision every step taken in Jaggard's printing office in 1619 and the motive which prompted it. I would rather emphasize than minimize the uncertainty of the suggestions thrown out in the last few pages.

Despite all that has been said, some students may still hunger for the good days when the "Roberts" edition of *The Merchant of Venice* was declared earlier than the Roberts-Heyes, and the "Printed for T.P." edition of *Oldcastle* earlier than that printed by Sims, when it was argued as to which of the two "1600" editions of *Lear* must be given the priority, and the delightful theory could be put forth that the "Roberts" *Midsummer Night's Dream* was piratically printed from Fisher's for the use of the players. But if such a student in his regret for these happy theories is led to imagine that all that has been written in this chapter may be swept aside as a fantastic dream built upon two or three chance coincidences, let him bethink him of the explanations which he must offer ere he can once more securely hold his ancient view.

He must explain not only why these nine quartos are in several cases found together, but why they are distinctly commoner than other quarto plays bearing the same dates, and more especially why the four plays which have doublets of the same year, whether they be considered the first edition or the second edition, are in each case considerably the commoner of the two. He may even be asked to explain why, when only five quartos attributed to Shakespeare have been believed to have gone through two distinct editions in a year, four out of these five cases should be found among our suspects.

Turning to the publishing and printing aspects of the question, he will doubtless consider as proofs of business ability the success with which Roberts superseded Sims in his job of printing *Sir John Oldcastle* for Pavier, either ousted the original printer of the *Midsummer Night's Dream* from Fisher's good graces in the same way or rushed out before the close of 1600 a piratical reprint on the heels of Fisher's (only licensed in October) without molestation, and finally persuaded Thomas Hayes to accept a worn out old type for his edition of *The Merchant of Venice,* when earlier in the year (*ex hypothesi*) a new one had been used for the same play. Some other explanation, however, will have to be found for Roberts having subsequently stowed away his new type and gone on using the old.

Business ability on the part of Jaggard, again, will be called in to explain his success in superseding Nicholas Okes in printing the second 1608 edition of *Lear*. Or, if Okes superseded Jaggard, then the business ability was his. Yet it may be thought a coincidence that in not one of these four doublets was the same type, and in only one of the four the same printer, employed for both editions of the same year.

Imprints are usually matters in which publishers take some concern, but the argument that Roberts sometimes liked to omit a publisher's address and that the tradition of the firm must be maintained, no doubt sufficed to persuade Butter and Johnson and Pavier that there was no object in stating where their quartos might be bought. The job lot of papers may have been saved up in the same spirit of affectionate loyalty to their original user. The continuous signatures of *The Whole Contention* and *Pericles* were just a compositor's freak, and Laurence Hayes no doubt looked in at the Stationers' Hall in July, 1619, and mentioned the little matter of his claim to *The Merchant of Venice* merely for the greater confusion of the present writer.

But, even if yet sounder explanations than these should be advanced, on the whole it may seem simpler to believe that Pavier and Jaggard indulged for business reasons in a small mystification, which was certainly very successful.

APPENDIX I. THE "HALF EAGLE AND KEY," AND "HEB DDIM" DEVICES

THE two devices which appear on the nine Shakespeare and pseudo-Shakespearian quartos of the volume of 1619 raise some very troublesome problems which for long seemed insoluble. That bearing the arms of the City of Geneva, a Half Eagle and Key, with the motto *Post Tenebras Lux*, which appears on the titlepage of *Midsummer Night's Dream*, was first used, by Rowland Hall, in 1562, and passed into the hands of John Charlwood, who lived at the sign of the Half Eagle and Key in Barbican. Charlwood died in 1593, and his widow, Alice Charlwood, married James Roberts, and thus put him in possession of the business. In 1606 Roberts sold his printing plant to William Jaggard, the formal transfer of the business taking place two years later, and that of the publishing stock not until 1615. As the address of William Jaggard was in Barbican, it is very probable that from 1606 onwards he occupied Roberts's house. Jaggard used the design of the Half Eagle and Key device as part of the ornamental border to Heywood's *Troia Brittanica* in 1609. The actual block has not been proved to have been used by him until 1617. At a much later date it is found in the possession of his successor, T. Cotes. As it appears on the titlepage of the *Midsummer Night's Dream*, this block has three cracks in it, visibly larger than the corresponding cracks in an impression in an edition of Dent's *Plain Man's Pathway* published in 1605 without printer's name. This seemed to offer a convenient ocular proof that the *Midsummer Night's Dream*, though dated 1600, must have been printed at least after 1605. But a subsequent discovery of an edition of R. Wimbledon's *Sermon*, with a colophon, "Printed by James Roberts, 1599" proved that the variations in the size of the cracks were due to varying degrees of dryness or pressure rather than to any permanent change in condition, and the comparison between the states of the block in "1600" and 1605 ceased to have any importance.

The other block, which represents a carnation, and bears the Welsh motto, *Heb Ddim heb Ddieu* (Without God without all) was the device of Richard Jones, who continued in business until 1602, but does not appear to have used it after 1596. From 1610 onwards it was used by William Jaggard. No example of the use of this block in any book printed by Roberts other than the two suspected quartos has yet been found. Nevertheless it seems probable that it was from Roberts that Jaggard obtained both this and the Half Eagle and Key block.

A subsidiary difficulty as regards this latter eventually suggested a solution of the problem as regards both devices. That Charlwood and Roberts should use a block which represented the sign of their house was only to be expected, but both in 1591, before Charlwood's death, and in 1594, after Roberts had succeeded to the business, this device is found in editions of the *Solace of Sion*, by Urbanus Regius, printed not by Charlwood or Roberts, but by Richard Jones. Another book by the same author, *A Homily or Sermon of Good and Evil Angels*, was licensed to Charlwood in 1584, and reprinted by him in 1590, but with the *Solace of Sion* the presence of his device on the titlepage seemed the only proof of his having had any connexion. Search, however, in the pages of Herbert's *Ames* revealed the names of six books as to which Jones and Charlwood were partners, and though the *Solace of Sion* is not one of them the fact of their working together over other books suggests a similar partnership as an easy explanation of the appearance of the Charlwood-Roberts device on Jones's titlepages of 1591 and 1594. It does a little more than this. On the rare occasions when Roberts used a device on a titlepage it was always that which Charlwood had derived from Wm Baldwin (1549) with the mottoes *Nosce teipsum* and *Ne quid Nimis*. It is not until 1599 that the Half Eagle and Key appears at the end of Wimbledon's *Sermon*. Now in 1598 Richard Jones, though continuing to trade as a publisher for a few years longer, sold his printing business to William White. It seems quite likely that it was only in this year, when clearing up, that Jones remembered to return to Roberts the Half Eagle and Key device which he had borrowed in 1594, and that at the same time he handed over to him (as a fellow Welshman?) the *Heb Ddim heb Ddieu* device also. If so, both devices were in Roberts's ownership in 1600, though we have no record of his having used the Half Eagle and Key more than once or the *Heb Ddim heb Ddieu* device at any time. As this latter mark had been frequently used by Jones, it would indeed have led to some confusion had Roberts begun using it within a couple of years of the transfer of Jones's business to William White. After a lapse of a dozen years no objection could be taken, and from 1610 onwards Jaggard seems to have used it fairly often.

APPENDIX II. ROBERTS'S ROMAN "82" TYPE

THE roman 82, which is found in the "Heyes" quarto of *The Merchant of Venice*, appears also in the following books:

In 1593 in Nashe's *Christs Teares over Jerusalem* ("To the reader") and Wimbledon's *Sermon* ("To the Christian reader").

In 1595 in *An Hospitall for the Diseased* (headings in text) and *The Widdowes Treasure* ("To the Curteous Reader" and headings in text).

In 1596 in Babington's *Notes upon Genesis* ("To the godly disposed Reader"), Drayton's *Robert Duke of Normandy* ("To the Reader"), Dering's *Sermon preached before the Queenes Maiestie 1569* (running-title and quotations) and Drayton's *Mortimeriados* (dedication).

In 1597 in *A Short Catechism for Householders* (headlines and questions).

In 1598 in *The Metamorphoses of Pigmalions Image* (text).

In 1599 in another edition of *The Widdowes Treasure*, and Markham's *How to chuse ride traine and diet both Hunting Horses and running Horses* ("To the Gentleman reader" and headings in text).

In 1600 in another edition of Dering's *Sermon* and in *The Treasurie of Hidden Secrets* (address "To All Women," verses, headings in text and table), and in the text of the "Heyes" *Merchant of Venice* and the *Titus Andronicus*, "Printed by I. R. for Edward White."

In 1601 in Lupton's *A Thousand Notable Things* (imprint) and Sir Thomas Smith's *Commonwealth of England* (part of title, also table).

In 1602 in Babington's *Briefe Conference betwixt Mans Frailty and Faith* (Speeches of Frailtie).

In 1603 in Harsnet's *Declaration of egregious Popish Impostures* (text).

In 1604 in *The Customers Replie* (note).

In 1605 in another edition of Harsnet's *Declaration;* and in 1604/05 in the *Hamlet* printed for Ling.

It is also found in the dedication to an undated edition of Lyly's *Euphues,* "Printed by I. Roberts for Gabriel Cawood."

Mainly used for prefaces, dedications and other minor parts of books chiefly printed in black letter, this "82" type was thus, both before and after 1600, employed also for texts. It was used, moreover, rather more after 1600 than before, and it will not be easy to suggest any reason why, according to the generally accepted theory of the order of the editions, Roberts should have obtained a new type of exactly the same size as one which he had long possessed to print a first edition of *The Merchant of Venice*, have then abandoned this new type to print the Heyes edition in the older fount, at the end of the year have reprinted the Fisher edition of the *Midsummer Night's Dream* (itself only licensed in October) in the new type, and then have never used this new type again.

Mr. WILLIAM ‖ SHAKESPEARES ‖ COMEDIES, ‖ HISTORIES, & ‖ TRAGEDIES ‖ Publiſhed according to the True Originall Copies. [Portrait signed: Martin Droeshout ſculpsit London.] *LONDON.* ‖ Printed by Iſaac Iaggard, and Ed. Blount. 1623.

Colophon (454ᵃ): *Printed at the Charges of W. Jaggard, Ed. Blount, I. Smith-weeke,* ‖ *and W. Aſpley,* 1623.

Head-title: The Workes of William Shakeſpeare, ‖ containing all his Comedies, Hiſt-ories and | Tragedies: Truely ſet forth, according to their firſt | *ORJGJNALL.*

Collation: A⁶⁺¹[B]², 9 unnumbered leaves; A-Z, Aa, Bb⁶ Cc², 152 leaves, paged 1-303, pp. [276] and [304] blank; a-g⁶ gg⁸ h-v⁶ x⁴, 132 leaves, mispaged 1-232; 2 unsigned leaves, ¶, ¶¶⁶, ¶¶¶¹, 15 leaves, the second paged 79, 80, the rest unpaged; aa-ff⁶ gg² Gg hh kk-zz aaa-bbb⁶, 146 leaves, mispaged 1-993 (for 399). Total 454 leaves.

Misprints in Signatures (some copies vary): Sig. V is misprinted as Vv; a₃ as Aa₃; m₃ as l₃, tt₂ as tt₃: xx, xx₂, xx₃ as x, x₂, x₃; yy₂, yy₃ as y₂,y₃.

Misprints in the pagination (some copies vary): First pagination: 50 misprinted as 58; 59 as 51; 86 as 88; 153 as 151; 161 as 163; 164, 165, as 162, 163; 189 as 187; 249, 250 as 251, 252; 265 as 273. Second pagination: 47, 48 omitted; 89, 90, misprinted as 91, 92; leaf following p. 100 unpaged; the numbers 69-100 repeated; 165, 166 misprinted as 167, 168. Last pagination: 77-80 misprinted as 79-82; leaf following p. 98 unpaged and the numbers up to 108 omitted; a hundred numbers omitted after p. 156; 279 misprinted as 259; 282 as 280; 308 as 38; 379 as 389; 399 as 993.

The text printed in two columns, separated by a rule, and with rules surrounding the text and running-title. Sixty-six lines to a column. The column of type measures about 268 mm. and the type-page, as enclosed by the rules, 282 × 171. Types: a roman type of which 20 lines measure 82 mm., with stage directions and proper names in italics of the same body. The "Verses on the Portrait" in large roman, of which 20 lines would measure about 180 mm. Dedications: large italics (20 lines = 140 mm.); address, "To the Great Variety of Readers," roman (20 lines = 116 mm.); the Verses by Digges in medium italics and roman (20 lines, slightly leaded = 118 mm.). The "Verses" by Ben Jonson mainly in italics, and those by Hugh Holland mainly in roman (20 lines in each case = 93 mm.)

Contents: *

PRELIMINARIES

Ben Jonson's verses on the portrait, headed "To the Reader" and signed B. I. (leaf 1ᵇ, recto blank.)

Titlepage and engraved portrait. (2ᵃ, verso blank: an insert.)

Dedicatory letter, "To the most noble and incomparable paire of brethren. William Earle of Pembrooke . . . and Philip Earle of Montgomery," signed "Iohn Heminge. Henry Condell." (leaf 3, Sig. A₂.)

Address "To the great Variety of Readers," signed "Iohn Heminge. Henry Con-dell." (4ᵃ, sig. A₃ recto, verso blank.)

Commendatory verses signed "Ben: Ionson" (leaf 5.)

Commendatory verses signed "Hugh Holland" (6ᵃ, verso blank.)

"A Catalogue of the ſeuerall Comedies, Hiſtories, and Tragedies contained in this Volume." (7ᵃ, verso blank).

Commendatory verses signed "L. Digges" and "I. M," probably the initials of Iames Mabbe. (8ᵃ, verso blank.)

Head-title, as quoted above, followed by "The Names of the Principall Actors in all these Playes." (9ᵃ, verso blank.)

⁎ For an explanation of the order here assigned to these preliminary leaves, see below, Chapter VIII, pages 137-140.

* No attempt is made in this section to represent the headings typographically.

COMEDIES

The Tempest. No quartos. Acts and Scenes. Epilogue. The Scene. Names of the Actors. (pp. 1-19. A-B₄ recto.)

The Two Gentlemen of Verona. No quartos. Acts and Scenes. Names of the Actors. (pp. 20-38. B₄ verso D₁.)

The Merry Wives of Windsor. Two (bad) earlier quartos. Printed from MS. Acts and Scenes. (pp. 39-60. D₂-E₆.)

Measure for Measure. No quartos. Acts and Scenes. The Scene. Names of the Actors (pp. 61-84. F-G₆.)

The Comedie of Errors. No quartos. Acts. (pp. 85-100. H-I₂.)

Much Adoe about Nothing. One earlier quarto. Printed from a copy of this used in the theatre. (pp. 101-121. I₃-L₁ recto.)

Loues Labors Lost. One earlier quarto (but see p. 70). Printed from this. Acts. (pp. 122-144. L₂ verso-M₆.)

A Midsommer Nights Dreame. Two earlier quartos. Printed from a copy of the second, used in the theatre. Acts. (pp. 145-162. N-O₄.)

The Merchant of Venice. Two earlier quartos. Printed from the first. Acts. (pp. 163-184. O₅-Q₂.)

As You Like It. No quartos. Acts and Scenes. (pp. 185-207, Q₃-S₂ recto.)

The Taming of the Shrew. No earlier quartos of Shakespeare's version. Acts. (pp. 208-229. S₂ verso-V₁ recto.)

All's Well that Ends Well. No quartos. Acts. (pp. 230-254. V₁ verso-Y₁.)

Twelfe Night, Or what you will. No quartos. Acts and Scenes. (pp. 255-275, followed by a blank page. Y₂-Z₆.)

The Winters Tale. No quartos. Acts and Scenes. Names of the Actors. (pp. 277-303, followed by a blank page. Aa-Cc₆.)

HISTORIES

The Life and Death of King John. No quartos of this version. Acts and Scenes. (pp. 1-22. a-b₅.)

The Life and Death of King Richard the Second. Four earlier quartos (two issues of the third). Printed from a corrected copy of the fourth. Acts and Scenes. (pp. 23-45. b₆-d₅ recto.)

The First Part of *Henry the Fourth*, with the Life and Death of Henry Sirnamed Hotspur. Six earlier quartos. Printed from a corrected copy of the fifth. Acts and Scenes. (pp. 46, 49-73. d₅ verso—f₆ recto.)

The Second Part of *Henry the Fourth*, Containing his Death and the Coronation of King Henry the Fift. One earlier quarto (two issues). Printed from MS. Acts and Scenes. Epilogue (whole page). Names of the Actors (whole page). (pp. 74-100+one leaf unpaged. g-gg₈.)

The Life of Henry the Fift. Three earlier quartos of a different version. Printed from MS. Acts. Prologue. (pp. 69-95. h-k₂ recto.)

The First Part of *Henry the Sixt*. No quartos. Acts (Scenes also in Acts III and IV). (pp. 96-119. k₂ verso-m₂ recto.)

The Second Part of *Henry the Sixt*, with the Death of the Good Duke Humfrey. Earlier quartos of a different version (The First Part of the Contention betwixt the two Famous Houses of York and Lancaster). Printed from MS. Undivided. (pp. 120-146. m₂ verso-o₃.)

The Third Part of *Henry the Sixt*, with the death of the Duke of Yorke. Earlier quartos of a different version (The True Tragedy of Richard Duke of York). Printed from MS. Undivided. (pp. 147-172. o₅-q₄.)

The Life and Death of Richard the Third, with the Landing of Earle Richmond, and the Battell at Bosworth Field. Six earlier quartos. Printed from MS. Acts and Scenes. (pp. 173-204. q₅-t₂.)

The Famous History of *The Life of King Henry the Eight*. No quartos. Acts and Scenes. Prologue and Epilogue. (pp. 205-232. t₃-x₄.)

The Tragedie of *Troylus and Cressida*. One earlier quarto (two issues). Printed from MS. Undivided. Prologue (whole page). Originally began on page 77. Omitted from Catalogue. (One leaf unpaged; pp. 79, 80; thirteen leaves unpaged; last page blank. ¶–¶¶¶$_2$.)

The Tragedy of *Coriolanus*. No quartos. Acts. (pp. 1–30. aa–cc$_3$.)

The Lamentable Tragedy of *Titus Andronicus*. Three earlier quartos. Printed from a corrected copy of the third, with the addition of a scene. Acts. (pp. 31–52. cc$_4$–ee$_2$.)

The Tragedy of *Romeo and Juliet*. Three (or four) earlier quartos. Printed from the third. Undivided. (pp. 53–79. ee$_3$–Gg recto.)

The Life of *Tymon of Athens*. No quartos. Undivided. Names of the Actors (whole leaf). (pp. 80–98 + one leaf unpaged. Gg verso–ii^6.)

The Tragedie of *Julius Cæsar*. No quartos. Acts. (pp. 109–130. kk$_6$–nn$_4$ recto.)

The Tragedie of *Macbeth*. No quartos. Acts and Scenes. (pp. 131–151. kk$_6$–nn$_4$ recto.)

The Tragedy of *Hamlet, Prince of Denmark*. Three (or four) previous quartos. Printed from MS. Acts and Scenes up to II, ii; the rest undivided. (pp. 152–165, 257–280. nn$_2$ verso–qq$_5$.)

The Tragedie of *King Lear*. Two earlier quartos. Printed from MS. Acts and Scenes. (pp. 283–309. qq$_2$–ss$_3$ recto.)

The Tragedie of *Othello, the Moore of Venice*. One earlier quarto. Printed from MS. Acts and Scenes. Names of the Actors. (pp. 310–339. ss$_3$ verso–tt$_6$ recto.)

The Tragedie of *Anthonie and Cleopatra*. No quartos. Undivided. pp. 340–368. tt6 verso–zz2.

The Tragedie of *Cymbeline*. No quartos. Acts and Scenes. (pp. 369–399, misprinted 993, followed by a blank page. zz$_3$–bbb$_6$.)

Size: The largest copy known is said to measure $13\frac{3}{8} \times 8\frac{1}{2}$ inches.

CHAPTER VI. THE FOLIO OF 1623:—II. THE COLLECTION OF THE COPY

THE publication of the First Folio edition of Shakespeare's plays was preluded by the following entry in the Stationers' Register under date "8º Nouembris 1623."

Mr. Blount: Isaak Jaggard. Entred for their copie under the hands of Mᵣ Doctor Worrall and Mᵣ Cole, Warden, Mᵣ William Shakspeers Comedyes, Histories and Tragedyes, soe manie of the said copyes as are not formerly entred to other men vizᵗ, Comedyes. The Tempest. The two gentlemen of Verona. Measure for Measure. The Comedy of Errors. As you like it. All's well that ends well. Twelft Night. The winters tale. Histories. The thirde parte of Henry the sixt. Henry the eight. Tragedies. Coriolanus. Timon of Athens. Julius Cæsar. Mackbeth. Anthonie and Cleopatra. Cymbeline.

It may be noted in passing that it has been very plausibly contended by Mr W. W. Greg* that the entry of "*The thirde part of Henry the sixt*" was an error for "the firste parte," as to which more will be said hereafter; also that on May 20, 1608, not only had "a boke called The booke of Perycles prynce of Tyre" (the absence of which from the First Folio needs explanation) been entered to Edw. Blount "under thandes of Sir George Buck, knight, and Mr. Warden Seton," but also "by the lyke aucthoritie, a booke called Anthony and Cleopatra," so that the penultimate item in the entry of November, 1623, was superfluous.

While the entry in the Stationers' Register was made only by Jaggard and Blount, the First Folio is stated in its colophon to have been "printed at the charges of W. Jaggard, Ed. Blount, I. Smithweeke, and W. Aspley." William Jaggard, as we have just seen, had been engaged as recently as 1619 in printing the quartos of that year, which included (besides *Pericles*, *Sir John Oldcastle* and the *Yorkshire Tragedy*) i, a (bad) text of *The Merry Wives of Windsor*, of which the "copy" was owned by Arthur Johnson; ii-iii, (good) texts of the *Midsummer Night's Dream*, the property of Thomas Fisher, whose rights, however, appear to have been absolutely ignored, and of *The Merchant of Venice*, whose copy-owner, Laurence Hayes, took steps to prevent (either at once or for the future) his interests being similarly treated; iv-v, two copies belonging to Thomas Pavier, viz., a (bad) text of *Henry V* and also the old plays, *The First Part of the Contention of the Two Famous Houses of York and Lancaster* and *the True Tragedy of Richard Duke of York* (now linked together as *The Whole Contention*), the variant versions of Parts II and III of *King Henry VI*; and, finally, vi, *King Lear*, which belonged to N. Butter. Whether William Jaggard himself or (as seems less likely) Pavier had been the promoter of this venture of 1619, Jaggard would be in a good position† for negotiating with the copy-owners of all these plays, and it seems pro-

---

*In an article on "The Bibliographical History of the First Folio," contributed to *The Library*, N.S., IV, 258-285, to which throughout this chapter I am very greatly indebted.

†The form of the entry by Laurence Hayes suggests that an agreement had been already reached, or was in view, as to *The Merchant of Venice*. As to *The Midsummer Night's Dream*, Jaggard had successfully stepped into Fisher's shoes. It has already been argued at length that *The Merry Wives* and *Lear* could not have been printed in 1619 without the consent of Arthur Johnson and Butter. It thus seems reasonable to believe that what Jaggard could do in 1619 he could do again in 1623.

bable that he was a prime mover in making the arrangements for the publication of the First Folio, the contract for printing which was given to his son Isaac Jaggard, who had recently succeeded to this side of the business.

The name of the second partner in the venture on its publishing side, Edward Blount, occurs also in the imprint on the titlepage, " Printed by Isaac Iaggard and Ed. Blount 1623." Its appearance there cannot be attributed to any scrupulous adherence to the facts of the case, for Blount was a stationer, not a printer, and the printing must be attributed solely to Jaggard. It is equally obvious that the prominence assigned to Blount was not due to his already owning numerous copyrights of Shakespeare's plays, for he had never yet published any play by Shakespeare, and his ownership of a single copyright, that of *Antony and Cleopatra*, had apparently, as we have seen, slipped his memory. The presumption thus arises that he must have taken a large share in the risk of the book, and we find that in 1630 he was able to transfer to Robert Allot the sixteen plays of Shakespeare copyrighted in 1623 as if they had been his sole property. We must not, however, argue from this that his importance in the partnership was greater than that of the Jaggards, for it is certain that behind the entries in the Stationers' Register there were often (as must have been the case with Ben Jonson's *Works*) supplementary agreements between the venturers. When a printer appears in association with a publisher, his main object was usually to obtain the contract for printing; and when we find that the Second Folio, of 1632, was printed for Allot by Thomas Cotes, Isaac Jaggard's successor, it seems probable that the firm had some claim on the printing contract. Edward Blount, however, may have had a further importance as probably possessed of more literary feeling than the other partners, and thus not impossibly the editor of the volume. He had served an apprenticeship with William Ponsonby, the authorized publisher of works by Sir Philip Sidney and Edmund Spenser, had himself been a friend of Christopher Marlowe and shown a loyal respect for his memory, had been recognized, half-quizzingly, as a patron of letters and had himself written dedications and prefaces which go to prove a personal interest in the books he published.*

The third partner in the venture, John Smithweeke, or rather Smethwick, had acquired by transference from Nicholas Ling the copyrights of three " good " Shakespeare texts, those of *Loves Labors Lost*, *Romeo and Juliet* and *Hamlet*. By the same means and at the same time he had also acquired the older play, *The Taming of A Shrew*, which Shakespeare had developed into *The Taming of The Shrew*, without doing much to redeem its brutality. The fact that one sixpence had already been paid for registration seems to have dispensed the owner of the " copy " of the original from any need to register the later play based on it, though it had not apparently availed to prevent Shakespeare from making what use he pleased of his predecessor's work.†

* See Mr Lee's excellent article, "An Elizabethan Bookseller," in *Bibliographica*, ii, pp. 474-498.

† I cannot quote any non-Shakespearian play withheld from registration for this reason, but when we find that, besides *The Shrew*, two parts of *Henry VI* and *King John* were not considered to need registration in 1623, and that these were all (granting the mistake of numeration in the case of *Henry VI*, already mentioned) based on older plays, we seem fully justified in assuming a causal connexion. See next page.

William Aspley, the last of the four venturers, had in 1600 obtained copyright and brought out "good" editions of *Much Ado about Nothing* and the Second Part of *Henry IV* in association with Andrew Wise. At that time Wise was already in possession of three "copies," those of *Richard II*, *Richard III* and 1 *Henry IV*, but these he transferred in 1603 to Matthew Law. It seems hardly reasonable to suggest that because twenty years earlier Law had obtained these plays from a former partner of Aspley's, therefore Aspley would now be in an advantageous position to negotiate for the use of them. Nevertheless, the suggestion has been made, and may be recorded as a possible line of connexion, though not one on which we can look with satisfaction.

Only a very few cases remain for special mention. As to *Othello*, which was printed in quarto for Walkley, after the Folio must have been already in contemplation, if not actually begun, we may assume that any consent granted by the players to its appearance as a separate play would have been subject to their own right of printing it in a collected edition. Shakespeare's text of *King John* and (saluo jure cuiuscunque) of 2 and 3 *Henry VI* had not yet been printed, but the old plays out of which they grew had enjoyed some popularity, partly due no doubt to the perhaps not altogether unfair revenge by which they had been passed off as Shakespeare's. *The Trouble-some Raigne of John, King of England, with the discouerie of King Richard Cordelions Base sonne (vulgarly named the Bastard Fawconbridge); also the death of King John at Swinstead Abbey*, had been published by Sampson Clarke in 1591, reprinted by Valentine Simmes for John Helme in 1611, when it was stated to be "Written by W. Sh.," and reprinted again by Aug[ustine] Mathewes for Thomas Dewe in 1622, with the bolder lie, "Written by W. Shakespeare." It had apparently never been entered in the Stationers' Register, and Dewe had merely picked it up as a derelict. He could thus be safely ignored, while the existence of the old play was a sufficient pre-text for saving sixpence off the registration fee.

The case of 2 and 3 *Henry VI* was equally simple to deal with, though a good deal more complicated to narrate. 2 *Henry VI* is another version of

The First Part of the Contention betwixt the two famous Houses of Yorke and Lancaster, with the death of the good Duke Humphrey: And the banishment and death of the Duke of Suffolke, and the Tragicall end of the proud Cardinall of Winchester with the notable Rebellion of Iack Cade: And the Duke of Yorkes first claime vnto the crowne.

This was registered by Thomas Millington on March 12, 1594, and printed for him by Creed in the same year. In 1595, without troubling to pay another registration fee, Millington had printed for him by P[eter] S[hort],

The True Tragedie of Richard Duke of Yorke, and the Death of good King Henrie the Sixt, with the whole contention between the two Houses Lancaster and Yorke, as it was sundrie times acted by the Right Honourable the Earle of Pembroke his seruants.

Both plays were reprinted for Millington in 1600, the latter by W[illiam] W[hite], the former by Valentine Simmes.* In April, 1602, he transferred

*And, according to Hazlitt and Lowndes, by W. W. also.

them both to Pavier, not under their own names, but, as has been shown by Mr Greg in the article in *The Library* (N.S. IV) already quoted, as *The first and second Parts of Henry VI*, a title which might naturally be given them, since the earlier was called *The first part of the Contention*, etc., and the second was a continuation of it. In giving them this name Pavier, it can hardly be doubted, had already in contemplation the fraud which he subsequently committed in the undated quarto edition of 1619, the title of which reads:

The Whole Contention betweene the two Famous Houses, Lancaster and Yorke. With the Tragicall ends of the good Duke Humfrey, Richard Duke of Yorke, and King Henrie the sixt. Diuided into two Parts: And newly corrected and enlarged. Written by William Shakespeare, Gent.

What would have happened in 1623 if Pavier, instead of being an ally of Jaggard, had really been, as Mr Lee imagines, "perverse," is a matter of speculation. A debate before a full court of the Stationers' Company on the position in which the copyholder of the old plays stood to the owners of the manuscripts of the new ones would have been good to listen to. But between Stationers, when once anything had occurred out of the ordinary course, all restrictions seem to have disappeared (no unnatural result when the issue would have had to be fought out between two members of a trade union before a tribunal of their friends), and probably, if necessary, Pavier would have been ignored, just as Dewe was.

The only play in the "Catalogue" as to which copyright remains to be considered is that of *Titus Andronicus*, which Danter had registered and printed in 1594, selling it through Edward White and Thomas Millington. After Danter's death there is no note of any transfer, but in 1600 Edward White, either treating the play as a derelict, or by an unregistered agreement with Danter's widow, brought out a new edition. Two years later, April 19, 1602, *Titus and Andronicus* figures as the last of three works (1 and 2 *Henry VI* being the second) transferred from Thomas Millington to Pavier "by warrant vnder master Setons hand" (Master Seton being one of the Wardens), but "saluo jure cuiuscunque." Clearly, Millington, as one of the two sellers of Danter's edition of 1594, thought that he had some colourable claim on the book, and, for aught we know, his claim was as good, or as bad, as Edward White's. The latter, however, was first in the field, and Pavier (who did nothing with *Henry VI* for seventeen years) took no action. In 1611 Edward White brought out another edition, and Pavier did not include *Titus* in the quartos of 1619. What happens as regards the play in 1623 we have no means of determining. The venturers may have come to terms with Edward White, or they may have relied on Pavier's claim, or they may have taken the view that, as there had been no transfer from Danter either to White or to Millington, they had as good a right to reprint the play as any one else. Under the circumstances, if Edward White were consulted at all, it is not probable that he showed himself very difficult.

We can now reprint the "Catalogue" of the contents of the First Folio, indicating the owners of the "copies" of the several plays and, where necessary, the probable agents through whom their consent was secured.

COMEDIES

The Tempest.	Blount & I. Jaggard.
The two Gentlemen of Verona.	Blount & I. Jaggard.
The Merry Wives of Windsor.	Johnson (ally of W. Jaggard).
Measure for Measure.	Blount & I. Jaggard.
The Comedy of Errors.	Blount & I. Jaggard.
Much Ado about Nothing.	Aspley.
Love's Labour's Lost.	Smethwick.
Midsummer Night's Dream.	Fisher. (Appropriated by W. Jaggard.)
Merchant of Venice.	L. Hayes. (? Bargain with W. Jaggard.)
As You Like It.	Blount & I. Jaggard.
The Taming of the Shrew.	Smethwick (through old play).
All's Well that Ends Well.	Blount & I. Jaggard.
Twelfth Night.	Blount & I. Jaggard.
The Winter's Tale.	Blount & I. Jaggard.

HISTORIES

The Life and Death of King John.	(Old play derelict.)
The Life and Death of Richard II.	Law. (Aspley influence?)
The First Part of Henry IV.	Law. (Aspley influence?)
The Second Part of Henry IV.	Aspley.
The Life of Henry V.	Pavier (ally of W. Jaggard).
The First Part of Henry VI.	Blount & I. Jaggard. (Miscalled Part 3.)
The Second Part of Henry VI.	⎰ Pavier (ally of W. Jaggard. Through old
The Third Part of Henry VI.	⎱ plays for registration purposes).
The Life and Death of Richard III.	Law. (Aspley influence?)
The Life of Henry VIII.	Blount & I. Jaggard.

TRAGEDIES

Coriolanus.	Blount & I. Jaggard.
Titus Andronicus.	E. White. (Claimed also by Pavier.)
Romeo and Juliet.	Smethwick.
Timon of Athens.	Blount & I. Jaggard.
The Life and Death of Julius Cæsar.	Blount & I. Jaggard.
Macbeth.	Blount & I. Jaggard.
Hamlet.	Smethwick.
King Lear.	Butter (ally of W. Jaggard).
Othello.	Walkley (? on special terms).
Anthony and Cleopatra.	Blount & I. Jaggard.
Cymbeline.	Blount & I. Jaggard.

The names of two plays will be missed from the "Catalogue," *Pericles* and *Troilus and Cressida*, and both omissions are probably highly significant, though of different things. In the case of *Pericles* the play is omitted not only from the "Catalogue" but from the book altogether. Now, even if we grant, as we are almost bound to do, that Edward Blount had forgotten that the "copy" of this had been entered to him on the same day as that of *Antony and Cleopatra*, which certainly seems to have slipped his memory, yet the last printer and publisher of the play had been Jaggard and Pavier, and, although a theory has been set forth that Pavier chose in this case to be "perverse," and refused his consent to the incorporation of the play in the Folio, in the absence of any suggestion as to why he should make trouble over this derelict, on which he had laid hands, rather than over *Henry V* (and 2 and 3 *Henry VI*), on which he had a real claim, we are bound to believe that if *Pericles* had been wanted for the Folio it could have been obtained. In this case, therefore, we seem confronted with the deliberate classification of *Pericles*, along with *Sir John Oldcastle* and the *Yorkshire Tragedy* (which must certainly have been considered owing to the Jaggard-Pavier editions of them), as outside the Shakespeare canon. Its exclusion is not without importance for any critical estimate of Shakespeare's probable share in the play. It is also not without importance for any critical estimate of the degree of care exercised by the editors of the First Folio, and on the whole it is more likely to raise than to lower them in the eyes of good critics.

The second play left unmentioned in the "Catalogue," *Troilus and Cressida*, is omitted from that only, not from the book, but there is evidence that it was taken up from the position at first assigned to it, immediately after *Romeo and Juliet*, and plumped down at the last moment, after the "Catalogue" leaf was printed off, between *Henry VIII* and the original beginning of the tragedies, *Coriolanus*. More will be said of this hereafter in discussing the "make-up" of the Folio, but in the present connexion it is important to note that *Troilus and Cressida* is precisely the play over the right to reprint which we might expect trouble to arise. It is this play which has the prophetic preface in which not only is there the prediction of how Shakespeare's comedies would be scrambled for, but also a reference to "the grand possessors" as apparently opposed to its publication. Any explanation of this reference, in the existing state of our knowledge, must be mere guesswork, but it is at least possible to see that if the "grand possessors" had made themselves disagreeable when Bonian and Walley wished to print a quarto, Bonian and Walley, or rather Henry Walley, the surviving member of the firm, might be the more inclined to be disagreeable when the "grand possessors" wished to print a folio. But as to this we know nothing.

In the foregoing section it has been taken for granted that the holder of a separate copyright could, if he chose, prevent or render difficult the inclusion of the work in question in a collected edition. It has been suggested, however, as an alternate theory, that the right acquired by the previous publication of a work was not of a nature to enable the holder to oppose its being reprinted in this particular way. It is probably true, indeed, as has been claimed, that no single instance can be quoted in which, where a work had been published separately and was then included in a collected edition by a different stationer, a transfer of copyright was obtained. But what we must suppose to have been assigned in the present case was clearly not the full copyright (in which case there would not have been, as there were, any quarto editions by separate copyholders after the appearance of the First Folio), but a right to reprint in a particular form, and there is no difficulty in believing that such minor assignments were made, and paid for, although they were not registered at Stationers' Hall. It seems reasonably certain from the subsequent dealings of the parties that William Stansby had an arrangement of this kind with Walter Burre, the holder of the copyrights of most of the plays included in the 1616 edition of Ben Jonson's *Works*. The same volume, moreover, which does not contain "Ben Jonson His Case is Alter'd," printed for Bartholomew Sutton in 1609, and the "second

116

volume" of 1640, which does not contain *The New Inn*, printed by Thomas Harper for Thomas Alchorne in 1631, seem to offer at least possible instances of the exclusion of a work from a collected edition owing to the publisher of such edition failing to come to terms with the holder of the copyright, though in the absence of any record of such bargainings we cannot be certain that this was the real cause. Stronger arguments than these seem to be (i) the inherent unreasonableness of permitting this particular form of breach of copyright, and (ii) the strong presumption that if it had been possible to print collected editions in defiance of copyright many more such editions would have been published. Moreover, the table of the plays in the First Folio and the owners of the copyrights in them of itself suggests that the four venturers who took the risks came together just because between them they were able to overcome any difficulty created by the existing copyrights, and thus leads us to believe that such a difficulty was at least anticipated.

Having now done our best to show the relations of the promoters of the First Folio to the owners of existing copyrights, we may pass on to the question of how other materials were obtained. It is obvious that by enlisting the help of Heminge and Condell, Shakespeare's fellows, the publisher secured the use of whatever manuscripts, or printed editions with manuscript corrections or additions, were in the possession of the King's Players. We have, therefore, to inquire what these materials amounted to, and whether it is probable that they were supplemented from any other source. As usual, Mr Sidney Lee offers a detailed and confident account of everything that was done. Thus he informs us (i) that it was contrary to the custom of the day for dramatists to preserve their manuscripts; (ii) that after the dramatic author's original draft had been freely edited by the managers for whom he wrote, the "corrected autograph was copied by the playhouse scrivener, this transcript became the official 'prompt-copy,' and the original was set aside and destroyed, its uses being exhausted"; and (iii) that, "even it were the ultimate hope of the publishers of the First Folio to print all Shakespeare's plays, in the inevitable absence of his autograph MSS. from the finished theatrical transcripts or official 'prompt-copies,' their purpose was again destined to defeat by accidents on which they had not reckoned." Mr Lee's sources of information enable him to state that "the 'prompt-copies' of old pieces that had ceased to appeal to the public were quickly discarded," and he alludes, of course, to the fire by which the Globe Theatre had been destroyed in 1613. He proceeds:

The publishers of the First Folio had, therefore, to depend on other sources than the playhouse in their task of collecting "copy." Fortunately, it was the habit of actors occasionally to secure a more or less perfect transcript of a successful piece either for themselves or for a sympathetic friend. Though some private owners easily mislaid dramatic MSS., others carefully preserved them, and it was clearly through the good offices of private owners that the publishers of the First Folio were able to supplement the defects of the playhouse archives. By such means transcripts, occasionally even "prompt-copies" of plays that had passed out of the actors' repertory, reached the printer's hands. Private transcripts were, as a rule, characterized to a greater degree than official transcripts by copyists' carelessness and by general imperfections; they rarely embodied the latest theatrical revisions; they omitted stage directions. But in 1623 they filled, so far as Shakespere's work was concerned, an important gap in the playhouse resources.

It is greatly to be regretted that Mr Lee has not indicated the evidence on which all these positive and detailed statements are based. He may have sources of information of which the present writer is discreditably ignorant, but even at the risk of this being the case it seems legitimate to suggest that there is here surely a good deal of overstatement. Our chief, if not our only, source of information about transcripts of plays in private hands is the preface of the publisher, Humphrey Mosely, of the first folio edition of Beaumont and Fletcher's plays. This contains so many points of interest for students of the Shakespeare Folio that it may be as well to print all the first part of it for reference:

The Stationer to the Readers.

Gentlemen, BEfore you engage farther, be pleased to take notice of these Particulars. You have here a New *Booke;* I can speake it clearly; for of all this large Uolume of *Comedies* and *Tragedies,* not one, till now, was ever printed before. A *Collection of Playes* is commonly but a *New Impression,* the scattered pieces which were printed single, being then onely Republished together: 'Tis otherwise here.

Next, as it is all New, so here is not anything *Spurious* or *impos'd;* I had the Originalls from such as received them from the *Authours* themselves; by Those, and none other, I publish this Edition.

And as here's nothing but what is genuine and Theirs, so you will finde here are no *Omissions;* you have not onely All I could get, but All that you must ever expect. For (besides those which were formerly printed) there is not any Piece written by these *Authours,* either Joyntly or Severally, but what are now publish'd to the World in this Volume. One only play I must except (for I meane to deale openly) tis a *COMEDY* called the *Wilde-goose Chase,* which hath beene long lost, and I feere irrecoverable; for a *Person of Quality* borrowed it from the *Actours* many yeares since, and (by the negligence of a *Servant*) it was never return'd; therefore now I put up this *Si quis,* that whosoever hereafter happily meetes with it, shall be thankfully satisfied if he please to send it home.

Some *Playes* (you know) written by these *Authors* were heretofore Printed: I thought not convenient to mixe them with this *Volume,* which of it selfe is entirely New. And indeed it would have rendred the Booke so Voluminous, that *Ladies* and *Gentlewomen* would have found it scarce manageable, who in Workes of this nature must first be remembred. Besides, I considered those former Pieces had been so long printed and re-printed, that many Gentlemen were already furnished; and I would have none say, they pay twice for the same Booke.

One thing I must answer before it bee objected; 'tis this: When these *Comedies* and *Tragedies* were presented on the Stage, the *Actours* omitted some *Scenes* and Passages (with the *Authours'* consent) as occasion led them; and when private friends desir'd a Copy, they then (and justly too) transcribed what they *Acted.* But now you have both All that was *Acted,* and all that was not; even the perfect full Originalls without the least mutilation; So that were the *Authours* living, (and sure they can never dye) they themselves would challenge neither more nor lesse then what is here published; this Volume being now so complete and finish'd, that the Reader must expect no future Alterations.

For *literall Errours* committed by the Printer, 'tis the fashion to aske pardon, and as much in fashion to take no notice of him that asks it; but in this also I have done my endeavour. 'Twere vaine to mention the *Chargeablenesse* of this Work; for those who own'd the *Manuscripts,* too well knew their value to make a cheap estimate of any of these Pieces, and though another joyn'd with me in the *Purchase* and Printing, yet the *Care & Pains* was wholly mine, which I found to be more then you'l easily imagine, unless you knew into how many hands the Originalls were dispersed. They are all now happily met in this Book, having escaped these *Publike Troubles*, free and unmangled. Heretofore when Gentlemen desired but a Copy of any of these *Playes*, the meanest piece here (if any may be called Meane where every one is Best) cost them more then foure times the price you pay for the whole *Volume*.

Now the first point that we have to note as to the evidential value of this preface is that it appeared twenty-four years after the publication of the Shakespeare Folio, and more than thirty after Shakespeare's death. In an interval as long as this there was room for many changes of practice both among playwrights and among their rich supporters, and because complimentary fees were obtained from Beaumont and Fletcher's admirers in return for transcripts of their plays, we have no right to assume that Shakespeare's were copied for the same purpose. In the period before the rule that every play had to be licensed for publication by the Master of the Revels the making of such transcripts would have indefinitely increased the risk of piracy, and this, so far as it goes, is a reason for declining to believe, without contemporary evidence, that they were made. It must also be remembered, when we find Mosely drawing attention to the "many hands" into which "the originalls were dispersed," that at the time of the publication of the Beaumont and Fletcher folio the theatres had been closed for several years, and for aught we know the players for whom they were written might have divided them among themselves, so that the copies had to be obtained from all the ten who signed this dedication. So far as Mosely may be trusted, it is clear that no use was made in 1647 of private transcripts, as he claims most positively to have "had the Originalls from such as received them from the Authours themselves" (i.e., from the players), and "by those and none other" to have published his edition.

A second point which may be taken in considering the sources of the previously unprinted plays is that it was not in 1623, but in 1613, that the inquisition for true copies of Shakespeare's works must have been keenest, always supposing, that is, that it be really necessary to assume that all or many of the copies in the possession of the players perished at the destruction of the Globe Theatre. Whether or no, the play about Henry VIII, which was being performed when the thatch of the roof caught fire, was that in which Shakespeare had a hand, the great dramatist of the Globe had only recently retired to Stratford, where he lived for nearly three years after the catastrophe, and the stock of his plays must have been an asset of considerable value to his former company. Mr Sidney Lee himself gives a list of no fewer than eighteen, or with *Pericles* nineteen, of his dramas that remained as late as 1623 in the repertory of the theatre, and for which prompt-copies must therefore have been in the players' hands. Nine of these (*The Tempest*, *The Taming of the Shrew*, *Twelfth Night*, *The Winter's Tale*, *Henry VIII*, *Julius Cæsar*, *Macbeth*, *Othello* and *Cymbeline*) supplement the fifteen which had appeared in print in Shakespeare's life, while two others (*Merry Wives* and *Henry V*) were urgently needed for the sake of replacing bad texts by good ones. This gives us a total of twenty-four out of thirty-six plays for which there was no obligation to seek for private transcripts, although, as a matter of fact, only a very few of the printed texts were used without corrections from other sources. The twelve plays neither already in print nor still being acted in 1623 were *The Two Gentlemen of Verona*, *Measure for Measure*, *The Comedy of Errors*, *As You Like It*, *All's Well that Ends Well*, *King John*, the three Parts of *Henry VI*, *Coriolanus*, *Timon*, and *Antony and Cleopatra*. Some of these, the last for instance, it is highly improbable that the players would have been willing to do without in 1613; in the case of others, such as *The Comedy of Errors*, *All's Well that Ends Well*, and the three Parts of *Henry VI*, it is hardly blasphemous to suggest a doubt whether there would have been any competition among playgoers to possess transcripts of them after their first freshness had worn off. In the case of 2 and 3 *Henry VI* there is no need to argue the question, because it is absolutely certain that prompt-copies were used. The theory of recourse being had in 1623 to transcripts in private hands thus seems wholly superfluous. Even granting that all the "archives" of the Globe were destroyed in 1613, it is surely quite possible that some of the partners in the company had kept some of those "original drafts" as to which Mr Lee is so confident that they were "set aside and destroyed," their "uses being exhausted,"* and despite Mr Lee's equally confident assertion that "it was contrary to custom for dramatists to preserve their manuscripts," the idea that these trifles might one day "come in useful" is one which might surely have occurred to the thrifty nature of Shakespeare himself, quite apart from any question of parental pride. "Wee haue scarse receiued from him a blot in his papers," Heminge and Condell remarked, or were made to remark, in the "Address To the Great Variety of Readers," to which their names are appended in the First Folio. It may be absurdly credulous to base upon this statement a belief that some "papers" of Shakespeare's may have been in existence after the fire at the Globe, and have served, directly or indirectly, to complete the copy for the First Folio; but it is possible also to go to rather absurd lengths in substituting a very doubtful theory, based on the practice of a later generation, for the evidence of contemporaries. We have no right whatever to assert that a single line of the Folio was set up from Shakespeare's autograph; but neither have we any right to exclude altogether the possibility of use having been made of his drafts. On the other hand, while we have no right to deny that transcripts of some of his plays may have existed in private hands and that recourse may have been had to some of these, it is surely not unreasonable to ask Mr Lee to produce the evidence on which he makes his definite and unqualified statement that "in 1623" such transcripts "filled, as far as Shakespeare's work was concerned, an important gap in the playhouse resources."

If instead of building theories upon fragments of evidence a whole generation out of date we let the Folio of 1623 speak for itself, we shall reach the conclusion that manuscript copies of the plays must have been easily pro-

---

* In so far as reliance can be placed in Humphrey Mosely's truthfulness, it is abundantly clear that in the case of Beaumont and Fletcher's plays there had not been any such destruction of original drafts as Mr Lee takes for granted, but that these were available to restore the full text of passages which had been abridged in acting. Mr Lee, of course, accepts the preface as evidence for the omission of "scenes and passages," while scouting altogether Mosely's own claims. It is noteworthy that in the case of Massinger's *Believe as You List*, the prompt-copy, which has come down to us, is in the author's autograph.

curable. As we have already seen, sixteen out of the thirty-six plays in the Folio were in print in earlier editions in quarto. Of exactly half of these no use whatever was made, the Folio editors preferring to print from manuscripts. In five other cases the quartos were used with additions, corrections or alterations. Only in three cases out of the possible sixteen was the text of a quarto taken without amendment, or at least authentication, by later use in the theatre. It is worth while to note what these three plays were: the "corrected and augmented" *Loves Labors Lost* of 1598, the 1600 quarto of *The Merchant of Venice*, the publication of which had been entrusted to Thomas Heyes after the book had been carefully "stayed," and the 1609 reprint of the "corrected, augmented and amended" 1599 quarto of *Romeo and Juliet*. No start could possibly give more confidence that the Folio editors exercised some real discrimination and care than to find that it was for these three plays, and these only, that they relied exclusively upon existing printed texts. In one respect they might have done a little better still. They might —if they had anticipated by intuition what modern editors have learnt by sad experience—have used the 1599 *Romeo and Juliet* itself instead of the reprint of it. But in this matter of the selection of their copy they did very well indeed, and their well-doing deserves ten times more recognition than it has received.

Turning now to the five printed quartos used with additions, corrections or alterations we find that these were the 1600 *Much Ado about Nothing* in a copy corrected for the stage, the 1619 reprint of the *Midsummer Night's Dream* in a copy which must have been used by the prompter, the 1615 reprint of *Richard II*, the 1613 reprint of *Henry IV*, and the 1611 reprint of *Titus Andronicus*, this last with the addition of a previously unprinted scene (Act III, sc. 2). Here again, modern editors who know that a reprint usually introduced many more errors than it corrected, would have preferred original editions. But in the case of *Richard II* the "new additions of the Parliament Sceane and the deposing of King Richard" were not introduced till 1608, so that there would have been no wisdom in taking an edition earlier than this, while the restoration of a scene in *Titus Andronicus* was very distinctly to the venturers' credit.

But the most notable fact of all in any estimate of the care exercised by the editors of 1623 and of the sources at their command is their total rejection of eight out of sixteen of the already printed texts. In two cases the need for the substitution of a better text was urgent, for the quartos of *The Merry Wives of Windsor* and *Henry V* are so bad that it is disputable whether they merely mutilate and distort the same version that appears in the Folio or represent an earlier stage of it. There was an obvious duty to substitute good texts for these bad ones, if it could possibly be done, and the editors did it. But they did much more than this. Of the other six plays, 2 *Henry IV*, *Richard III*, *Troilus and Cressida*, *Hamlet*, *King Lear*, *Othello*, the already printed texts are on an altogether higher level than those of *The Merry Wives* and *Henry V*. Some of them are at least very fairly good, and yet, when these were (presumably) procurable for sixpence apiece, and when printed texts must have been much easier to set up afresh than those carelessly interlineated transcripts of whose defects Mr Lee has so much to say, the editors preferred to have recourse to independent manuscripts. If these independent manuscripts were hard to procure and had to be paid for, how highly should we rate the zeal and the disinterestedness of the editors who took, and the publishers who sanctioned, the more difficult and expensive course! If on the other hand the manuscripts were easy to procure and had not to be paid for, the inference is obvious that they must have been in the possession of the players themselves, and the theory of "private transcripts" becomes more superfluous than ever.

As to the procurement of the copy for the preliminary leaves there is more than one dubious point. Save as to their connexion with the Globe Theatre we know little or nothing of Heminge and Condell, but despite the undisproved possibility of their having been endowed with all the requisite gifts of editorship, there is an inclination to assume that they did nothing but hand over all the copy they could collect (curiosity is keen to know what was paid for it!) and sign their names to the dedication and Address to the Readers. It has been suggested that the Address was written for them by Ben Jonson, but in view of his well-known comment on the alleged absence of blotted lines in Shakespeare's manuscript he can hardly have himself written the phrase which gave rise to it. The combination of the tradesmanlike proem with real enthusiasm suggests the hand of Blount, and of all the men connected with the Folio whose names we know Blount seems by far the most likely to have taken an active share in the editorial work, though some anonymous press-corrector in Jaggard's office may have been still more influential. That Ben Jonson had aught to do with the Folio beyond writing his two sets of verses there is no shred of evidence. If his lines on Droeshout's portrait are compared with their subject, we may well be inclined to wonder whether he had seen that very doubtful masterpiece at the time that he wrote them, and if the suspicion be just it disposes at once of any theory of his having been intimately connected with the work of publication. As to his verses our sense of fitness leads us to believe that he was called in by Blount to do poetical honour to Shakespeare as sufficient in himself to represent all the wits and all the poets of the day. The other verses were probably spontaneous offerings, which the publishers had not the courage to refuse, though their acceptance has raised the question why if these were printed there were not more.

CHAPTER VII. THE FOLIO OF 1623:—III. THE EDITING

IN the previous chapter, relying on the evidence of independent editors quoted in our Bibliography of the quartos (Chapter II), we have seen how the Folio editors selected from the printed material at their disposal. Some printed texts they put on one side altogether and made no use of. Three, which they had especially good reason to trust as having been issued under circumstances which gave them, in an exceptional degree, the express sanction of the players, they followed without any changes in the text that can be regarded as editorial. In a third group, printed texts were handed to the compositors, but texts which had either themselves been used for theatrical purposes, or to which some of the peculiarities of manuscript prompt-copies had been transferred. These additions are mostly of little importance, but the probability that these quartos had been used in the theatre certainly increases our confidence in the text.

In considering the plays for which no printed copy was used, while not venturing to deny the existence of manuscript copies in private hands and the possible use of these for the Folio, we found that the existence of such private transcripts in the case of Shakespeare's plays had not been proved and that there was no necessity for postulating it. In any case, save for its effect in depreciating the Folio text by taking it one step further away from the author's autograph, the theory of private transcripts has little interest, since it appears to be admitted that, if obtained at all, they were obtained from the players, and we are thus either dealing with the playhouse copies themselves or with authorized transcripts from them.

Thus the whole of the copy for the First Folio was derived either immediately or ultimately from the players, but while some of it had already appeared in print, a greater amount was printed from manuscripts of which, to our infinite loss, no single specimen has come down to us. In the case of the plays set up from printed texts we can see with some approach to exactness the kind of alterations and improvements which the Folio editors introduced and how far they were consistent in making them. It is quite certain, however, that these were not the plays in which the editors took the greatest interest. A generation later, when the Beaumont and Fletcher folio was being put together, all plays which had previously been printed were rejected *en bloc*. Fortunately, Shakespeare's editors did not go as far as this, but they left clear evidence of the value at which they rated their printed and unprinted materials by the respective positions which they assigned them. In this respect they seem to have anticipated the doctrine of William Morris, who, in his fine Kelmscott edition of Chaucer, put the *Canterbury Tales* at the beginning and *Troilus and Cressida* at the end for no other reason than that he liked a book to begin and end strongly. The key to the inner arrangement of the plays in the Folio of 1623, which Mr Sidney Lee seems to consider merely haphazard, is that, so far as history and the accidents of the press allowed them, the editors placed unprinted plays in all the important positions and hid away those already printed in the middle of them.

Of the five comedies with which the volume opens, four had never been printed before, and one, *The Merry Wives of Windsor*, which is placed between the two pairs of absolute novelties, only in a piratical version so bad that no

123

use was made of it in setting up the Folio. At the opposite end of the section we find the four new and one nearly new comedies of the beginning neatly balanced by four new and one nearly new* comedies at the end. Hidden away in the middle are four successive plays which had already been printed.

When we pass from the comedies to the histories we are confronted with the fact that the chronological order of the kings offered such an obvious principle of arrangement that there was no excuse for manipulating it. It is thus merely a chance that the first play, *King John*, had never previously been printed in Shakespeare's version, and the last, *King Henry VIII*, had never previously been printed at all.

In the tragedies we must put on one side *Troilus and Cressida*, which, we know, originally held the place now scantily occupied by *Timon*, was subsequently (even as late as the time when the "Catalogue of the seuerall Comedies, Histories and Tragedies contained in this Volume" was printed) intended to be omitted altogether, and at the last moment was inserted in front of *Coriolanus*, with which the section properly begins. We must note also that *Romeo and Juliet* interrupts what would otherwise be an unbroken succession of classical plays, and that *Antony and Cleopatra*, which should naturally have followed *Julius Cæsar*, in the same way interrupts what would otherwise be an unbroken succession of post-classical ones. Taking the sections as they stand, we find that each begins with one and ends with two unprinted plays, while plays already printed are, as in the case of the comedies, hidden away in the middle.†

There is so much appearance of deliberation in all this that the discovery that unprinted plays are placed at the beginnings and ends of sections emphasizes at once the importance placed on unprinted plays as compared with printed ones, and on plays at the beginnings and ends of sections as compared with those hidden away in the middle. This twofold evidence gives us a valuable clue to the editorial ideals of the promoters of the First Folio, and carries us a little further than we could get by a simple comparison of Quarto and Folio texts where these are available for contrast.

Let us take first the matter of division into acts and scenes, which was certainly considered desirable by the editors, although only incompletely carried out. With one or two partial exceptions the quartos printed before 1623 were wholly undivided. In the Folio of the plays which had already appeared in print *Troilus and Cressida* and *Romeo and Juliet* are left in this state; *Hamlet* is fully divided as far as Act II, sc. 2, and then left untouched; *Much Ado*, *Loves Labors Lost*, *A Midsummer Night's Dream*, *The Merchant of Venice*, *Henry V*, and *Titus Andronicus* are divided into acts but not into scenes; *Richard II*, the two Parts of *Henry IV*, *Richard III*, *Lear* and *Othello* are fully divided. The coexistence of such various stages of development at first sight seems merely haphazard; but it is not so. *Troilus*, which was turned out of the Folio and replaced at the last moment, suffers the fate of an outcast; *Romeo and Juliet* and the six plays only divided into acts all occur where the zeal which can be traced at the beginning of each section had spent itself, and before the rally which marks the end. The five plays fully divided, on the other hand, all come at points to which we can see, from other evidence, that importance was attached.

If we look at the plays previously unprinted, the point comes out even more clearly. The comedies open with four and close with two plays fully divided into acts and scenes. The histories do the same. The classical tragedies have had but small pains spent on them; in these the outer plays are divided into acts only, the inner not at all. In the post-classical tragedies, on the other hand, which bring the volume to a close, five (printed and unprinted) in succession are fully divided, the series being only broken by the wholly undivided *Anthony and Cleopatra*, which, as already noted, is so clearly out of place between *Othello* and *Cymbeline* that we must imagine it to have been overlooked and inserted in the only position available at the eleventh hour.

It is worth noting, as a proof that all this was a matter of editing in 1623, that while there is not a single comedy left wholly undivided, among the histories there are two (2 and 3 *Henry VI*), and among the tragedies four and a half (*Troilus, Romeo and Juliet, Timon*, part of *Hamlet* and *Anthony and Cleopatra*). It would seem as if the plays which it was known would occupy important positions were edited in advance, and that on the others the editor worked with the compositors pressing on his heels, so that he was more hurried over the histories than over the comedies, and more so still over the tragedies. If so, we have here a point of some importance as against the theory, which has been maintained, that the three sections were set up simultaneously and printed at different presses.

Looking at the treatment of the plays as a whole, we find that full division into acts and scenes was a primary editorial ideal, carried out completely in seven comedies, six and a half histories, and four and a half tragedies; compromised in seven comedies, one and a half histories, and three tragedies; neglected altogether in two histories and four and a half tragedies.

A second editorial ideal which can be clearly traced, though it has not yet been worked upon sufficiently to permit of statistics, was the substitution of literary for theatrical stage directions, i.e. of notes helping a reader to understand the play for memoranda reminding the prompter and actors of what had to be done. This process has not been completed even at the present day, for "directions" retained in editions intended for general readers still require some technical knowledge of the Elizabethan stage, as, for instance, in the retention of the word "within" in its theatrical sense of the room behind the stage, where for literary purposes we should substitute "without."* But if we look at the plays occupying important positions in the First Folio we shall find that the stage directions, though usually not so numerous as in modern editions, in their form bear few or no traces of the old theatrical phraseology. On the other hand, in plays occupying less important positions (the distinction is not quite so uniform here as in the case

---

*E.g., "Knocking within" means knocking on the outer side of the door; "tumult within" means that an angry crowd outside is preparing to burst in. In each case the noise was to be made in the actors' room, but in reading Shakespeare we hardly desire to be reminded of this, and to young students the phrase may even be confusing.

of divisions into acts and scenes) we find that stage directions of quite a markedly theatrical nature have been allowed to stand. A good instance of such a direction is the note, "Bed put forth," in 2 *Henry VI*, Act III, 2, 146, in preparation for the speech of Warwick, three lines lower down, "Come hither, gracious sovereign, view this body." In modern editions Warwick is made to leave the stage after l. 135, and after l. 148 we have the direction, "Re-enter Warwick and Others, bearing Gloucester's body on a bed." In the Folio there are no directions for Warwick's exit and re-entrance, or for the bed to be ceremonially brought in. The spectators were expected to be satisfied with the actor standing aside while the king soliloquizes, the bed being thrust forth when it was wanted, and the actor pointing to it when his cue came. In order that this might be done, warning had to be given for the bed to be thrust forth some seconds before it had to be pointed at, and for this reason the direction comes at l. 146 instead of at 148.

Two interesting instances of directions of this kind in *The Midsummer Night's Dream* were pointed out by Dr Furness in his Variorum Edition, vol. x, 1905, p. xv. "In v, 1, 134, before Pyramus and the others appear, we have the stage direction, '*Tawyer with a trumpet before them.*' In 'Tawyer' we have the name of one of the company, be it Trumpeter or Presenter, just as in *Romeo and Juliet* we find '*Enter Will Kempe.*' The second trace of the prompter's hand is to be found, I think, in III, 1, 116, where Pyramus [i.e., Bottom], according to the stage direction of the Folio, enters '*with the Asse head.*' In all modern editions this is, of course, changed to 'an Ass's head,' but the prompter of Shakespeare's stage, knowing well enough that there was but one Ass-head, inserted in the text, 'with *the* Assehead,' the only one they had."

The interesting thing about these particular directions is that they do not occur in the "Roberts, 1600" (i.e., Jaggard, 1619) quarto from which the Folio text was set up, and the Folio is thus more theatrical and less literary than the quarto.* But the quarto itself, like that of Fisher, which it reprinted, bears traces of its theatrical origin. For instance, when Oberon and Titania meet in the wood near Athens, the direction reads: "*Enter the King of Fairies at one doore with his traine, and the Queene at another with hers.*" We do not expect to find doors in a wood, and the allusion is, of course, to those leading from the actors' room on to the stage. Thus, the text of *Midsummer Night's Dream*, as printed in the quartos and Folio, bears evidence of having first been printed from a theatrical source and subsequently reprinted from an example of this first text, which had either itself been used in the theatre or had been brought afresh into accordance with a theatrical manuscript.

It can be shown that another of the comedies had the same fate. In the case of *Much Ado about Nothing* the names of the actors Kemp and Cowley are substituted in the quarto of 1600 (Act IV, sc. 2) for those of Dogberry and Verges. This trace of the theatrical origin of the quarto is reproduced in the Folio, with the additional substitution of the name of Jack Wilson†

---

* According to Dr Furness, there are about fifty-six stage directions in Fisher's quarto, about seventy-four in "Roberts," and in the Folio about ninty-seven, not counting the divisions into acts.

†"*Enter Prince, Leonato, Claudio and Iacke Wilson.*"

for the word *Musicke* to cover the singer of the song in Act II, sc. 3. In this
case also, then, it appears that not only was the quarto printed from a prompt-
copy, but that a copy of the quarto, marked as a prompt-copy, was used in
printing the Folio, and no editorial care was taken to remove the " directions " which were solely intended for use in the theatre.

Other instances of theatrical notes being allowed to remain in the Folio
text are in *The Taming of the Shrew*, Induction, scene 2, where the name of
the actor Sincklo is used instead of an impersonal " 1 [or 2] Player"; and
again, in 3 *Henry VI*, Act III, sc. 1, where, instead of the modern stage-direction, " *Enter two Keepers*," we find, " *Enter Sinklo and Humfrey*" (i.e., Humphrey
Jeffes). So, again, it has been plausibly conjectured that the mysterious *G* and
E found tacked on to the names of the First and Second Lord in *All's Well
that Ends Well*, Act II, sc. 1, found again in the *French E* and *French G* in
Act III, sc. 2, and once more on their reappearance as *Cap. E* and *Cap. G*
in scene 6 of the same Act, stand for two of the minor actors in Shakespeare's company, Robert Gough and William Ecclestone.

There are no such survivals from the prompt-copy as these in *The Tempest*
or *The Two Gentlemen of Verona*, save, indeed, the inevitable " *within* " (" A
confused noyse within ") on the very first page of the former. Against this we
have to set a number of purely literary notes not easy to parallel in the authentic quartos,* or, indeed, in the Folio itself. The very first of all is remarkable
for its literary form:

*A tempestuous noise of Thunder and Lightning heard : Enter a Ship-master and a Botes-
waine.*

Later in the play we have:

Enter Caliban with a burthen of Wood (a noyse of Thunder heard).
Ariell plaies the tune on a Tabor and Pipe.
*Solemne and strange Musicke: and Prosper on the top (inuisible:) Enter seuerall strange
shapes bringing in a Banket; and dance about it with gentle actions and salutations, and
inuiting the King &c. to eate they departe.*
*A noyse of Hunters heard. Enter diuers Spirits in shape of Dogs and Hounds hunting them
about: Prospero and Ariel setting them on.*
Here Prospero discouers Ferdinand and Mirandah playing at Chesse.

The affinity of *The Tempest* to the Masques, in the books of which elaborate
literary descriptions were a feature, helps to explain these notes, which enable the reader to follow the action of the play in imagination and are far
removed from the " noise within " of the prompt-books. But, although the
more the action resembles that of a masque the fuller the notes, yet from
the very outset the tendency to substitute descriptions for ordinary " directions " is marked. In subsequent comedies, in important positions, a negative
rather than a positive influence is found at work. The exits and entrances of
the characters are recorded with care, but hardly anything else is noted. Towards the end of *Measure for Measure* vigilance begins to slacken, and we
have not only the technical use of " within," but " Enter Duke, Varrius,
Lords, Angelo, Esculus, Lucio, Citizens at seuerall doores " for what is
plainly a scene in the open air; so also some of the directions in the later

---

* For elaborate descriptive notes to supply lacunæ in the text in a pirated quarto, see the " stage
directions " quoted in the 1602 *Merry Wives of Windsor*, Chapter II, p. 45.

scenes of the *Comedie of Errors* are slightly descriptive. But, except in *Henry VIII* and, to a less extent, in *Coriolanus*, the promise of *The Tempest* was only to a very small extent carried out in later plays, and the addition of the descriptive notes necessary for understanding the action has been almost entirely the work of modern editors.

Another feature which is prominent in the case of the early comedies was only fitfully continued, in two cases at least with the obvious purpose of filling an inconvenient blank page. To three out of the four first plays are appended Lists of the Actors, or, as we should call them, Dramatis Personæ, the omission of this in *The Merry Wives of Windsor* being probably due to the fact that there was no room for it at the foot of the page, and no wish, in this instance, to give it a page to itself, as it was found convenient to do in the case of the second Part of *Henry IV* and *Timon of Athens*. There are some other plays where the inclusion of the names of the actors might have been as inconvenient as at the end of *The Merry Wives*, but in numerous instances there was ample room for them, and their omission must be assigned to failing energy. The appearance of an epilogue when wanted at the end of 2 *Henry IV* to fill a whole page may cause us to wonder whether more of these addenda could have been produced had it been found convenient. But the fact remains that after *The Tempest* very few plays are furnished with these additions.

Enquiries into the division of the different plays into acts and scenes, into the nature of their stage directions and the provision of epilogues have already taken us somewhat beyond the usual limits of bibliography. Into a purely literary examination of the treatment of the text by the promoters of the First Folio we are forbidden to enter, partly by a wholesome fear of losing ourselves in a mass of details, partly because bibliographical prepossessions might also lead us astray. It is better and safer to continue to lean, as we have done in the matter of the relations of the quartos and the Folio, on the opinions of independent specialists. These leave us no room for doubt that very varying degrees of care were bestowed on different plays, and they certainly do not forbid us to believe that the position which a play occupies in the volume offers a very fair index to the amount of care which will be found to have been bestowed on it. Thus Dr Furness does not hesitate to hold up *The Tempest* as the very best in the way of text, and elsewhere we find *The Two Gentlemen of Verona*, which immediately follows it, contrasted with *All's Well that Ends Well* as examples of good and bad texts. So again at the opposite end of the comedies the "excellent state of the text" of *Twelfth Night* is taken by Dr Furness as a commonplace of Shakespearian criticism, while, contrary to what we might have expected (see below, page 135), over *The Winter's Tale* even the compositors appear to have taken special trouble.

When a quarto was thought good enough to print from, though it is a clear gain (despite some groans to the contrary from editors weary of collating) to have the Folio text as well as the quarto, it is almost always the latter that wins support. Thus as to *Much Ado about Nothing, Loves Labors Lost*, the *Midsummer Night's Dream, Richard II* and *Henry IV*, Part I, there is an editorial consensus that quarto readings are mostly to be preferred to those of the Folio. Perhaps the points to which Dr Furness thought it worth while to call special attention as regards the *Midsummer Night's Dream* will give as good an idea as can be obtained of the relations of the Folio and quarto in such cases as these. On the one hand a line (III, ii, 164) which occurs in both quartos is accidentally omitted and another line of text is turned into a stage direction. On the other hand we have the substitution of "petty" for "pelting" as an epithet of river in II, i, 95, which may or may not be right; Hermia's line (III, ii, 127), "I am amazed at your words," is restored to its proper length and rhythm by the insertion of the epithet "passionate," and in III, i, 90, the speech incorrectly assigned by the quartos to Quince is rightly given to Puck.

These examples of mistakes and corrections which Dr Furness has selected as specially worthy of note in the case of the *Midsummer Night's Dream* do nothing to lessen the high probability that there was no editorial meddling with the text of the plays, as contrasted with such matters of form as their division into acts and scenes and the supply of additional stage directions. The new mistakes must obviously be debited to the printers; the corrections were almost equally certainly made in the theatre. There seems every likelihood that when the copy, whether in manuscript or printed, was once obtained, it was sent to the printer untouched, as far as the text was concerned, and that he was left to reproduce it as accurately as he could. This is exactly what any one imbued with the methods of modern scholarship would wish to have been done. As far as the imperfections of Jaggard's compositors and reader permitted, the texts at the editors' disposal appear to have been reproduced untampered with for the use of posterity. Nor is there any reason to take any very gloomy view of the result. To omit one line of text and turn another into a stage-direction are, of course, high crimes when the author whose work is thus maltreated is Shakespeare, but when these are the worst defects that can be found in a reprint of some length, it is nonsense to pile up epithets in depreciation of the poor journeymen. We may take comfort also from our knowledge that although it is more difficult to print from manuscript than from type, the difficulty in our own day is always met by giving the work to experienced compositors instead of prentice hands, so that it is a commonplace among authors that the worst copy often yields the best proof. We have no positive evidence that this compensatory system was already at work in 1623, but as it rests on common sense we are fairly safe in assuming that it was, and there is no reason to believe that the plays printed for the first time in 1623 were more incorrectly set up than those which were reprinted. The probability is slightly on the other side.

Two quotations from recent prefaces by Dr Howard Furness may fitly bring this section to a close. The first is from his edition of *Anthony and Cleopatra* (1907), where, on page vi, he writes:

It is not generally realized, I think, to what an extent this First Folio survives in all our texts, and how little, how very little, it varies, save in spelling, and in stage-directions, from the most popular texts of the present day. We have heard so much of the 'corruption of the old texts,' of the labour expended and of the eminent critical ability demanded, to render them intelligible, that these original texts are come to be regarded as sealed books to all but the most learned eyes; and should they be divested of the emendations of the critics, it would be labour lost to attempt to understand them. It may be, perhaps, worth the while to examine how far editors and critics have amended Shakespeare's language so as to fit it for our comprehension. The present is the longest of Shakespeare's Plays—it lacks but thirty-six lines of four thousand. Taking as a guide the *Cambridge Shakespeare*, edited by Dr W. Aldis Wright, which is accepted the world over as the standard modernised text, and examining its footnotes, we shall find that after omitting stage-directions, metrical divisions of lines, mere punctuation, and immoment changes of spelling, the original text of this play in the Four Folios has been set aside and emendations by editors or critics adopted in sixty instances. I am aware that there is not in this calculation the nice accuracy of an astronomical problem, in that the omission of punctuation, which at times makes the difference between sense and nonsense, may be censured as ill-advised; yet, making all allowances, nay, doubling sixty and calling it a hundred and twenty, there still remain three thousand eight hundred and odd lines of this play which come to us exactly as Shakespeare's printers have transmitted them, excepting a difference in spelling, which would not trouble a schoolboy withal.

In our second quotation, taken from the preface to *Loves Labors Lost* (1904), we find Dr Furness appraising the value of the Folio, not by taking a single play as a sample, but by a survey of the whole field. On page vi he writes:

Ever since the appearance, forty years ago, of *The Cambridge Edition* of Shakespeare, followed by its offspring, *The Globe Edition*, this whole question of texts, with their varying degrees of excellence, which had endlessly vexed the Shakespearean world, has gradually subsided, until now it is fairly lulled to a sleep as grateful as it is deep. . . For this refreshing repose we are mainly indebted to the excellent conservative text adopted by *The Globe Edition*, and also to the device of its editors which places an obelus against every line, 'wherever the original text has been corrupted in such a way as to affect the sense, no admissible emendation having been proposed, or whenever a lacuna occurs too great to be filled up with any approach to certainty by conjecture.' Here, then, on the pages of *The Globe Edition*, we have ocular proof of the number of passages which, through the errors of compositors, have been in the past subjects of contention by our forbears. From the emphasis of the exclamations at defective passages, uttered by critics in years gone by, and from their insistence on the corrupt state of Shakespeare's text, it would be naturally inferred that these obeli are to be found freely scattered on every page. The number of lines in Shakespeare's Dramas and Poems as given in *The Globe Edition* has been computed to be one hundred and fourteen thousand four hundred and two (114,402). The Editors of that edition were prudent in their use of the obelus, and wisely preferred to prefix too many rather than too few. Indeed, there are not wanting critics who maintain that in many instances lines were thus condemned that admit of satisfactory explanation. The number of obeli errs, therefore, if at all, on the side of fullness. And yet in all these hundred and fourteen thousand and odd lines we find that those marked with an obelus, as hopelessly corrupt, number about one hundred and thirty, which means that there is only one obstinately refractory line, or passage, in every eight hundred and eighty. It is small wonder that the denunciation of Shakespeare's defective text is become gradually of the faintest. We cannot be far astray, if, hereafter, we assume that his text has descended to us in a condition which with truth may be characterised as fairly good.

The most recent criticism of the Folio text has been so pessimistic, that the reasoned optimism of these two statements surely deserves all possible emphasis.

CHAPTER VIII. THE FOLIO OF 1623:—IV. THE PRINTING

SOMETHING must now be said of the First Folio edition of Shakespeare's plays regarded simply as a piece of printing. On its titlepage it is stated to have been "Printed by Isaac Iaggard and Ed. Blount," and, as Blount was not a printer, this leaves Jaggard as its sole producer. Mr Sidney Lee has indeed suggested that while the "main part" of the First Folio was printed at Jaggard's printing-office "probably some presses of Jaggard's friends were requisitioned for parts of the volume." It is almost inconceivable, however, that this should have been the case, as not only the same type and the same ornaments, but even the same brass rules, may be found in use in different parts of the book, whereas had separate printers been employed, each would certainly have used his own rules, and probably his own type and ornaments. It must be remembered also that the Jaggards were the main promoters of the book, their names standing first both on the titlepage and in the colophon. Their interest would be to keep their own presses busy, not to share the work with other men, and there is no evidence that they did otherwise. It may even be doubted whether there is any proof forthcoming for Mr Lee's positive statement that "to economize time the text of the plays was meanwhile printed and made up in three separate and independent sections." The division, though Mr Lee calls it a "clumsy device," was probably editorial rather than typographical, and a plain man might think that there was a good deal to be said in its favour. Granting that the division of the plays into Comedies, Histories and Tragedies was the work of the editors, the printers would naturally give each section separate pagination and signatures, but it by no means follows that they used the opportunity thus offered to print the different sections simultaneously. Mr Lee is doubtless right in saying that "the best printed folios of the time" were not set up in this manner, for over and above the fact that very few of them would have lent themselves so easily to such a division, the conditions of printing in Shakespeare's time were quite different from those which had obtained in the early years of the invention, when simultaneous printing by sections was almost a rule in the case of large books. Few successful printers in the fifteenth century had less than four presses, and six seems to have been the common number, while Anton Koberger had twenty-four. But the Star Chamber Decree of July, 1637, which restricted the number of printers to twenty, and the number of presses in each printing house to two (or in the case of the Master and Wardens to three), only revived the earlier ordinance of 1585. Thus we have no reason for believing that Jaggard owned more than two presses, and if so it is tolerably certain that the three sections of the book were not printed off simultaneously. A reason will be offered a little further on for believing that while a few quires may now and again have been printed at a second press, the work was mainly carried on at a single press without regard to the sections. Jaggard, moreover, printed other books in 1622 and 1623, and, although the Shakespeare Folio, while it was in progress, was doubtless his chief concern, it would be rash to assume that he allowed it to monopolize his whole office.

Two other statements which are sometimes made as to alleged typographical habits which affected the printing of the Folio seem to me very difficult to prove. The first, which has no practical importance, is that compositors used to set up work in their own homes; the second that the copy was read out to them, thus accounting for a fairly numerous class of misprints which alter the wording of a phrase while reproducing, closely or exactly, its sound. Until some positive evidence is produced that these customs were in use in London in Jaggard's day we may well be slow to believe in them. The amount of space which a compositor needs for his work is not so great that there would have been any difficulty in accommodating half a dozen in quite a small room. Type metal is very heavy to carry about, and the accidents of the streets would surely have often resulted in unlocked formes and type scattered in the mire. Each compositor would have had to keep a large quantity of type in his own house, and secret printing (which the Government was bent on repressing) would have been greatly facilitated. Against the theory that the copy was read out to the compositors there are fewer objections, but the one fact that it would double the number of men employed with certainly no commensurate increase of output may surely suffice. It is much simpler to believe that misprints of the class which the theory is introduced to explain were caused by compositors trying to carry too many words at a time in their heads, and reproducing the impression of sound which they had formulated instead of that of the sense. It may be added that in old wood-cuts and engravings of printing, the compositor is nearly always represented as working within a few feet of the press, and that his copy is generally shown as held up before him by a stick.

As regards the printing of the Folio itself there is no evidence of any special preparations having been made for its production. The roman type used for the text, which is slightly smaller in size than modern pica, belonged to a fount, probably of Dutch origin, which by 1623 had been in use for many years in England, and had already been employed by W. Jaggard for the quarto plays printed by him in 1619. In those plays, as in the Folio, it is sometimes found mixed with upper-case letters (majuscules), of a slightly larger face, from the old fount, of practically the same body, inherited by Jaggard from Roberts and by Roberts from Charlwood. The large italics used in the dedication and the running titles can be traced back to the time of John Day. All the other types used in the book are of a quite ordinary character.

As regards the ornaments, I take this opportunity of printing in full a memorandum which I sent to Mr Lee when he was engaged in writing his introduction to the Oxford Facsimile. Mr Lee gave quite as much space to the subject as the ornaments are worth in their own right, but in view of attempts made to discover secret meanings in everything connected with Shakespeare it is as well to show somewhat fully in how many other books they were used.

The ornaments used in the Folio are five different headpieces, three tail-pieces, half an alphabet of small capitals, three capitals of another alphabet, and five others all from different sets. Nearly all these may be found in earlier books printed by Isaac or William Jaggard.

(1) HEADPIECES

(a) Archer headpiece, as on Sig. A₂. In an earlier form in which the work is much more open, this design is found in a variety of books such as Sidney's *Arcadia* (1598), the *Book of Common Prayer* (1603), Gwillim's *Heraldry* (1610), etc. A variation very like that used by Jaggard, but distinct from it, is found in the *Amadis* of 1619 printed by Nicholas Okes. Jaggard's block was used as early as 1613 in Mexia's *Treasurie of Auncient and Moderne Times*, and is found again in 1622 in Augustine Vincent's *Discoverie of Errours in the Fourth Edition of the Catalogue of Nobilitie* published by Raphe Brooke.

(b) Headpiece with the Double Rose, as on Sig A₃. Found also in André Favyn's *Theater of Honour and Knighthood*, printed by William Jaggard in 1623.

(c) Zigzag headpiece, as over Jonson's verses "To the Memory." Found both in Vincent's *Discovery* (1622) and Favyn's *Theater* (1623).

(d) Sheaf headpiece, as over Holland's verses. An old block, the top of the sheaf, which has here disappeared, having been separated from the rest as early in 1611, when it is found in Bunny's *Of the Head Corner Stone*. The piece was finally broken off during the printing of Howard's *Defensative against the Poyson of Supposed Prophecies* in 1620, the block occurring in this book in both states. It was afterwards used in the English version of the *Decamerone* (1620), in Burton's *Description of Leicestershire* (1622), in Vincent's *Discovery* (1622), and Favyn's *Theater of Honour* (1623). It reappears in the Shakespeare Folio of 1632 with a new top on the sheaf.

(e) Headpiece with a single rose, as over Digges's verses. I have not found this in any earlier book.

(2) TAILPIECES

(a) Large tailpiece as on p. 84 and elsewhere. This is found in Brooke's *Catalogue and Succession of the Kings, Princes and Dukes, &c., of England* (1619), and in the *Decamerone* of 1620.

(b) Small block of Royal Arms and Amoretts (see page bearing "The Actor's Names" after *Timon of Athens*, p. [99]). Found also in Milles's *Catalogue of Honour* (1610) and Favyn's *Theater* (1623).

(c) A much worn block, in the centre of which is a horned head, and at the left a trumpeter (see below "The Actor's Names" facing *Henry V*, page 69). This (which I could not find when communicating with Mr Lee) occurs also in the quarto Henry V, with the imprint "Printed for T. P. 1608," really printed by Jaggard in 1619.

(3) CAPITALS

(a) Half alphabet of small initials used at beginning of plays: viz., A, B, C, E, G, H, I, N, O, P, R, S, T. Some of these are found also in Vincent's *Discovery* (1622).

(b) The letters L, H, M, T, let into ornamental borders: T found also in Bunny's *Head Corner Stone* (1611) and in Howard's *Defensative* (1620).

(c) Large letter W on Sig. A₂. Found also in Vincent's *Discovery* (1622).

(d) Large letter F on Sig. A₃. Found also in Milles's *Catalogue of Honour* (1610), p. 763, and in the *Decamerone* (1620).

(e) Medium-sized I within azured ornament (see beginning of *Taming of the Shrew* and *Lear*). Found in Bunny's *Head Corner Stone* (1611), p. 15.

(f) Foliated W (see pages 131, 152). Found also in Brooke's *Catalogue* (1619).

(g) Floral Y (see page 369).

Allusion has already been made to the brass rules which divide the columns of the First Folio, form a rectangle round the type-page and a separate enclosure for the running-title. In trying to understand the typographical habits of Jaggard's office I turned my attention to these, and the evidence which they offer, though it would be difficult to tabulate and is far from easy to explain in words, is of some importance. It will be best to take it in connexion with that offered by the running headlines. As a good example we may take the first sixteen pages of *The Second Part of Henry the Fourth*, which are interesting also for another reason. It will be found that on page 75 a roman n has found its way among the italic of the word *fecond*. On page 78 this word is quite regular, but the serifs at the foot of the *P* in *Part* are broken off. On pages 79, 81, 83, 85, 87, we continue to find the wrong fount n in *fecond*; on pages 80, 82, 84, 86, we continue to find the defective *P* in *Part*. Clearly, then, these headlines were not set up afresh for each page, but were either transferred from forme to forme, or were left in the forme and the new letterpress placed below them. If now we examine the brass rules in these pages we shall find (we must remember that each rule was a separate piece and would naturally sometimes get shifted a little when disturbed) that the same rules used on page 75 are found again on pages 77, 79, 81, 83, 85 and 87, while the rules found on page 76 are repeated on pages 78, 80, 82, 84, and for a long succession of pages with even numbers, though now and again there is a doubtful case, and pages not made up with the ordinary two full columns almost always have different rules surrounding them. Sometimes instead of the same headlines and rules reappearing on a succession of pages there are frequent changes, and both the regularities and the irregularities in skilful hands should render interesting evidence as to the order of printing. From a pusillanimous dislike to breaking up even a facsimile Folio into its component sheets—an indispensable preliminary— I have not myself carried the inquiry very far, but it is surely not without significance that the same lower rule which we find on sigs Z_1, Z_2 of *Twelfth Night* recurs throughout *The Winter's Tale*, disappears during the printing of *King John*, is found again in *Richard II* and continues in use until the middle of *Richard III*, when it disappears again until we come to *Coriolanus*. All three sections of the Folio are thus linked together, while, on the other hand, we are free to account for the temporary disappearance of a rule by the use of a second press for a few successive gatherings. It seems, indeed, quite certain that the whole work was printed in one printing office, and mainly on one press, but with occasional help from another. But Jaggard's journeymen do not appear to have worked with the uniformity which the bibliographer desires, and it is impossible to feel sure even that they always began to print a quire at the same point. Thus a mistake which at first seems purely senseless or wanton offers a rather pretty proof that they printed the comedies two pages at a time, beginning from the inside of the quire. The last two pages of *The Two Gentlemen of Verona* have the running headline of *The Merry Wives of Windsor*. If the printer had been printing straightforward the blunder would have been almost impossible, but if they began by printing the inner pages of quire D, pp. 42-43, then took 40 and 45, and

then 38 and 47, nothing would be simpler than to leave the headline of
The Merry Wives of Windsor in the forme and thus affix it to page 38, where
it has no business. When the sheets were perfected, the same system of
working backwards would apply it quite naturally to page 37. Some of the
numerous mistakes in pagination may also be accounted for in this way. But
I do not feel sure that this method of working back from the inmost sheet
of a quire was always pursued.

ACCIDENTS DURING PRINTING

The typographical course of the First Folio cannot be said to have pro-
gressed smoothly. It is interrupted by many needless misprints in the
signatures and pagination and some in the headlines, which suggest that all
these appurtenances were added by the pressmen immediately before the
page was to be printed, and thus never received any revision from the corrector. But in addition to these trivial disfigurements there is evidence that
the normal course of printing was interrupted by more serious accidents,
which have left their mark on its arrangement.

The fact that the second play in the volume, *The Two Gentlemen of Verona*
begins on a left-hand page, and that *Loves Labors Lost, The Taming of the
Shrew* and *All's Well that Ends Well* do the same, shows that there was no
theory in Jaggard's office that a play must necessarily begin on a recto. When,
therefore, we find the page which follows the end of *Twelfth Night* left blank
and *The Winter's Tale* beginning opposite to it, we are confronted either with
a mere blunder or with the result of an accident. It so happens that the
thirteen comedies which end with *Twelfth Night* exactly fill the quires
signed A-Z, and *The Winter's Tale*, therefore, necessarily begins a fresh set
of signatures. As only this one more comedy had to be printed, there is
nothing surprising in the simpler lower-case signatures a-x being reserved
for the histories, and the more elaborate Aa-Cc being used for the three
quires. The play itself is fully divided into acts and scenes, its stage-
directions have been purged from all trace of the prompt-copy, and, according
to Dr Furness, it is unusually carefully printed. Save for the blank page which
precedes it, there is nothing to excite suspicion, and the blank might easily
have been produced by a miscalculation of half a page in the amount of
space needed for *Twelfth Night*.

It so happens, however, that an entry under the date of August 19, 1623,
in the office book of Sir Henry Herbert, Master of the Revels, first quoted
by Malone (*Life of Shakespeare*, p. 462, and *Var. Shaks.*, III, 229), suggests
that the play may have been omitted from the comedies as originally arranged owing to the disappearance of the copy. The entry reads:

> For the King's players. An olde playe called Winters Tale, formerly allowed of Sir
> George Bucke and likewyse by mee on Mr. Heminges his worde that there was nothing
> prophane added or reformed [*sic*], thogh the allowed booke was missing: and ther-
> fore I returned it without a fee this 19° of August, 1623.

The date of this entry is just three months before that of the licensing of
the First Folio. If only one manuscript of the play was available, and that
was wanted for use in the theatre when the end of the comedies was reached,
there may have been a delay in printing this one play, which was then begun

on a new quire, instead of the last page of quire Z being passed once more through the press. But we cannot be sure that we have here anything more than a coincidence. The careful editing and printing of the play itself seems to exclude the idea of hurry and accident, and the argument from the blank page is capable of being neatly reversed, since, if this obliges us to believe anything, it obliges us to believe that *The Winter's Tale* was set up and printed before *Twelfth Night* was ended, as on any other supposition the blank page was avoidable. In this case we cannot be sure what happened.

We have a more convincing proof of the occurrence of some serious accident when we find a quire of unusual length (eight leaves instead of six) interpolated between Sigs g and h in the Histories with the signature gg. The contents of the quire begin in 2 *Henry IV*, Act III, sc. 2, and contain the rest of the play, while a whole page at the end is devoted to an Epilogue, and another to the Actors' Names, the extravagance of this offering a clear proof that the next play (*Henry V*) was already in print, so that the last leaf of the quire had to be filled with any materials that could be found. The problem is complicated by the fact that the headline on the first page of quire gg has the same wrong fount roman n (*The Second Part of King Henry the Fourth*) as the rectos in the previous quire, and the brass rules are also the same, and yet this page is signed with the irregular signature gg. At what moment this particular page was printed off baffles conjecture. The disturbance generally might be explained, with the aid of the brass rules, by supposing that when the pressmen were half-way through *Henry IV*, Part 2, they were called off to print *The Winter's Tale* (which has the same rules); that the unfinished condition of *Henry IV*, Part 2, was then temporarily forgotten, and that it was only completed when the Histories had reached about the end of *Henry VI*, Part 3, or the beginning of *Richard III*, where again the rules agree. But, as it is hardly certain that *The Winter's Tale* was not printed about its proper time, this theory is proportionately weak.

The last and most serious accident arose in connexion with *Troilus and Cressida*. Originally, this began on the back of the last page of *Romeo and Juliet*, and in one of the copies of the First Folio belonging to the late Baroness Burdett-Coutts the original leaf thus printed has survived instead of the cancel by which it is usually replaced. The cause of the play being uprooted from its position was not merely a desire to change its position; it was clearly intended to be cancelled, since even as late as the time when the Catalogue of Plays was printed in the preliminary quire, its name was omitted. Only a difficulty as to copyright, as far as we can see, could have caused so serious a change, and for this, as has already been noted (see supra, page 116), a possible explanation is suggested by a phrase in the preface to the second quarto. Mr Sidney Lee, who has explained all the circumstances of the uprooting of *Troilus* with more fullness than anyone else, has also shown, with much ingenuity, how *Timon of Athens* was used to fill up the gap caused by its removal, though even after a whole page had been devoted to the Actors' Names another had still to be left blank. When, at the last moment, the obstacle to the inclusion of *Troilus* was removed, the page originally occupied by the end of *Romeo and Juliet* was filled with a

Prologue unearthed for the emergency; the original paging, 79 and 80, was accidentally left to tell its tale on the second leaf; the other leaves were printed without pagination, and the special signatures ¶, ¶¶, and ¶¶¶ were given to the quires, the last of which consisted of only a single leaf.

In addition to these larger accidents which came upon the printers from without, and the misprints which are found in all copies, various smaller mishaps of a kind common at this period have left their mark on individual copies. Letters and figures were pulled out of place by the balls used for spreading the ink on the forme, and wrongly replaced, and in one or two cases the printing of a page was begun and then stopped for it to be corrected. Mr Lee has made this subject so peculiarly his own in connexion with his valuable and interesting Census of Copies that it seems best only to mention the fact here and to refer to his Census and preface to the Oxford Facsimile for details.

The Preliminary Leaves

As in almost all first editions, the preliminary leaves of the First Folio were printed after the text, and their arrangement, which differs in different copies, has given rise to some controversy. The Grenville copy is now bound uniformly with the three later folios in the same collection in full red morocco, with a handsome doublure, by Lewis. A note, however, in Mr Grenville's handwriting, and with his initials, states positively, "This first edition of Shakespeare is an original and perfect copy and was purchased by me in its first binding and in its original state. T. G." That one of the greatest benefactors the library of the British Museum has ever had, from a mere desire for neatness and uniformity, should have stripped a First Folio of its original covers is a sad example of "the mistakes of the good," which no wisdom in their successors can repair. But, despite the crime to which he thus naively confesses, there is no reason to doubt Mr Grenville's statement, and the order of the nine leaves in his copy, when rightly interpreted, can be shown to be correct. They stand as follows:

1. Ben Jonson's Verses, "To the Reader."
2. Titlepage, with Droeshout Portrait.
3. Dedication. Marked A_2.
4. Address To the great variety of Readers. Marked A_3.
5. Ben Jonson's Verses, "To the memory of my beloved, the Author."
6. Verses by Hugh Holland.
7. A Catalogue of the seuerall Comedies, Histories, and Tragedies contained in this volume.
8. Verses by L. Digges and I. M.
9. The Workes of William Shakespeare, containing all his Comedies, Histories and Tragedies: Truely set forth, according to their first originall. The names of the Principall Actors in all these Playes.

As the preliminaries make up the uneven number nine it is certain that one of them must stand outside a quire or gathering. Our data for determining which this is are

(i) the existence of the printed signatures A_2, A_3.

(ii) the possibility of seeing in loosely bound copies that two leaves form part of a single undivided sheet.

137

(iii) the presence or absence of watermarks on the different pages, one of each pair of leaves in a folio necessarily bearing a watermark, while the corresponding leaf has none.

Taking these data in order we note (i) the fact that the third leaf is marked A_3 shows conclusively that either the leaf containing the verses "To the Reader" or the titlepage must be a single leaf, not forming a part of a quire. Also the fact that while there is an A_2 and an A_3 there is no A_4 makes it probable that the quire of which A_2 and A_3 formed part, like those of which most of the body of the book is made up, was intended to consist of only six leaves, and that thus besides the single leaf there was also a sheet of two leaves outside the quire.

(ii) In the Turbutt copy of the First Folio (originally sent by the Stationers to the Bodleian Library, sold by the Library and now restored by public subscription) and in the Capell copy at Trinity College, Cambridge, it can be seen quite clearly that the leaf marked A_2 containing the Dedication forms a single sheet of paper with the leaf containing the verses by Holland; and similarly that the leaf marked A_3 pairs with that containing Ben Jonson's verses to Shakespeare's memory, and the leaf with verses by L. Digges and I. M. with that containing the name of the Actors.

(iii) The question of which of the first two leaves pairs with the leaf containing the catalogue is settled by the watermarks in the Grenville copy, in which the watermark of a Crown is found on the leaf containing the Verses to the Reader, on that signed A_3 and on those containing Holland's verses and the List of Actors. The other five leaves are without watermark. As the leaf containing the catalogue has no watermark, it must pair off, not with the titlepage, which also has none, but with the first leaf.

We thus get the following arrangement:

Verses to the Reader. Watermarked.
　Titlepage. Unwatermarked. An inserted leaf.*
　　Dedication. A_2. Unwatermarked.
　　　Address. A_3. Watermarked.
　　　Jonson's Verses, To the Memory etc. Unwatermarked.
　　Holland's Verses. Watermarked.

Catalogue. Unwatermarked.
Verses by Digges and I. M. Unwatermarked.
Names of the Actors. Watermarked.

* The position of the titlepage as a single leaf inserted between the first and second leaves of a quire at first sight seems a little haphazard, and it has accordingly been contended that the "Verses to the Reader" were an afterthought, and that these, not the titlepage, form the independent leaf. For the reason given above, which was first pointed out by Mr Greg, this is impossible. Haphazard, moreover, as the position of the titlepage may seem, it can easily be shown that the desire to give a leaf containing an engraving specially careful printing led to a similar arrangement in the case of other books. Thus, in the case of the copy of Browne's *Britannia's Pastorals* in 1613, collated for the Grolier Club Contributions towards a Bibliography of English Literature, the engraved titlepage is a single leaf inserted between a blank first leaf and A_2 containing the dedication. In the British Museum copy the blank first leaf has disappeared, but the correctness of the collation can be demonstrated, as the distances between the wire lines proves that the titlepage is printed on quite different paper from quire A, paper which is only used again in the book when another engraving had to be printed. In the same way in Chapman's *Odyssey* of 1614 the engraved title

As regards the two leaves containing the verses by Digges and I[ames] M[abbe] and the Names of the Actors, it is obvious that a binder would consult his own convenience by placing them, as in the Devonshire copy, in the centre of quire A, thus converting it from a quire of six leaves to one of eight, which could still be sewn with a single thread. It is equally obvious, however, that this is one of the worst positions that could be given it. Plainly the verses by Digges and I. M. arrived late, or they would have been put on the back of the leaf containing those of Master Hugh Holland. To bring them in front of Ben Jonson's, but separated from his by the names of the actors, saved the binder some trouble, but was wholly incongruous. Master Wildgoose, the Bodleian binder,* showed little more discernment in choosing the opening between the verses of Jonson [on A$_4$] and those of Holland [on A$_5$]. This was more respectful to Ben Jonson, but left the list of actors separating the verses of Digges and Holland. In many respects the best arrangement is that found in the copy from which was made Booth's "facsimile" of 1862, in which the double leaf is placed immediately before the catalogue. All the verses are thus kept together, and the heading above the names of the actors, which bears some resemblance to a half-title, is only separated from the text by what is practically a list of contents.

While, however, this last arrangement has much to recommend it, there seems no reason to doubt that the order of the leaves in the Grenville copy, in which the added double leaf is placed after the original quire, not inserted in it, is that intended by the publishers. It is found not only in the Grenville but in the Capell, which also, according to Mr Greg, "shows no trace of ever having been tampered with" in modern times, though it is not certainly original, and according to Mr Madan, in a copy in the library of Oriel College, Oxford, in an old, possibly an original, binding, and also in a copy offered for sale by Mr Quaritch in 1905. The treatment of the double leaf

occupies a separate leaf between a first blank and the printed title, after which comes the dedication on A$_3$. Of course, this arrangement was not universal. There are numerous instances in which an engraved titlepage pairs off with another leaf, the two sometimes standing by themselves, less often forming part of an ordinary quire. But the frequency with which an engraved frontispiece in seventeenth-century books forms a single leaf by itself, shows that there was a real preference for printing the sole or most prominent illustration in a book in this way; and in the case of a large folio, like the Shakespeare, there was probably a considerable advantage in so doing.

*While this Turbutt-Bodleian copy, which Wildgoose was employed to bind, is of great interest, if only for its humorous history, I cannot agree with Mr. Madan, when he speaks of it as "the only one which can be regarded as a standard examplar," and as "the copy selected by the publisher for permanent preservation, at a time, when it was seen to be an advantage that some one copy such as this should be accessible in the future for the purposes of reprinting." It is true that when the agreement between Sir Thomas Bodley and the Stationers' Company was made, some twenty years before this, the possibility of a publisher getting back the Bodleian copy, in default of any other to reprint from, was mentioned. But Mr Madan has omitted to quote instances of this remote contingency occurring, and his language hardly accords with human nature. Publishers are still required to deliver certain copies to public libraries for permanent preservation, and it is happily unusual for them to try to evade this obligation or to pick out a specially bad copy, or even to delay delivery till the last possible moment. But they do not hasten to put a copy beyond the risk of destruction at the earliest possible moment, and as for "selecting" it may safely be guessed that the store-keeper hands over the copy that is on the top of a pile, at a moment when a boy can be spared to take it. Exactly how the publishers regarded the obligation in the case of the First Folio is shown by the fact that they economically delivered their copy in sheets instead of ready bound!

avowedly as an afterthought, if not particularly ingenious, is at least straight-forward, and also brings the half-title heading the names of the actors as near as possible to the text.

As regards the engraved portrait of Shakespeare by Martin Droeshout, as about everything else connected with the First Folio, some controversy has arisen. Droeshout must presumably have had some model to work from, and an attempt has been made to find this model in the oil-painting of Shakespeare presented by Mr Archibald Flower to the Stratford Trust, and hence colloquially known as the Flower Portrait. The engraving exists in at least two states. In the earlier of these, or proof, the moustache is small and the eyebrow fair; in the ordinary prints the moustache is large and the eyebrow dark. In both the proof and the prints the ear is a deformity; in the picture it is natural. Mr M. H. Spielmann thinks it clear from this that the hypothetical picture or limning from which the engraving was made must not be identified with the Flower portrait, but that this was itself copied from the engraving and a little improved in the process. Mr Lionel Cust, the Director of the National Portrait Gallery, regards the Droeshout proof as a careless copy of the Flower portrait, and the prints as corrected from this by the aid of the Flower portrait in some particulars (e.g., the moustache and the eyebrow), but not in others (e.g., the ear). Either explanation will account for the facts, and although when the two experts argued the question out, very amusingly, before the Bibliographical Society in January, 1908 (*Transactions*, vol. IX, p. 118 sq.), Mr Spielmann seemed to have rather the better case, it is hardly possible to arrive at any positive proof.

Price, and Number Printed

According to George Steevens, quoting as an authority an entry in the accounts of a contemporary bookseller, the published price of the First Folio was twenty shillings, and, as a single play in quarto was priced at sixpence, the thirty-six which it contains might clearly have been sold in sheets at twenty shillings with some profit. A second edition was printed as early as 1632, and the book must thus have been bought very readily, far more so, for instance, than Ben Jonson's *Works*, of which the first edition was published in 1616 and the second not until 1641. As to how many copies were printed in 1623 we have, unfortunately, no information. On this subject Mr Lee writes: "The number of extant copies of the volume, which amounts to at least 156, shows that the book was in great demand, and that the edition was a very large one. It could hardly have fallen short of 600 copies." Mr Lee has clearly never heard of the well-known maxim that the proportion of the copies of a book likely to escape the hands of time varies, not directly, but inversely, with the number printed. The more difficult a book is to obtain, the more carefully will it be kept; the easier it is to obtain, the more readily will it be destroyed. A large book like the First Folio will stand a deal of wear; and the fact that, even when damaged both at the beginning and the end (the fate which has befallen so many copies), it would still retain thirty-four out of the thirty-six plays in a readable condition, would give it a great advantage over such a book, for instance, as Sidney's *Arcadia*, which has probably again and again been destroyed as

140

useless for a much smaller degree of imperfection. The rapid rise and steady increase, moreover, in Shakespeare's reputation would of themselves give his Plays a great advantage over the *Arcadia*, which enjoyed an amazing popularity for a century and then, save for literary antiquaries, became a dead book. It is thus quite probable that not more than 500 copies of the First Folio were printed in 1623; but if Mr Lee can produce any evidence for his suggested extra hundred, or any one else prove that 750 was the number, or even a thousand, the higher figures may be accepted, not only without incredulity but with pleasure. For, on the whole, Messrs Jaggard and Jaggard, Blount, Smethwick and Aspley, and Messrs Heming and Condell also, seem fairly to have earned any profit which we can imagine as having accrued to them from the Folio. They printed it on suitable paper and with suitable types; they bedecked its titlepage with an engraved portrait; above all—unless this study has been written wholly in vain—it has been proved that they took considerable pains in forming the Shakespeare canon and selecting the best materials from which to print. It is true that their editorial ideals were merely formal and ceremonial, and that even these were only partially carried out. They seem to have left the proofs of the text to take care of themselves, while they tinkered at stage directions and inserted not always accurate divisions into acts and scenes. In the end, either from anxiety to get the book finished, or because they grew tired of an unaccustomed task, they passed some plays for press with the barest minimum of revision, and others with only a little more, and allowed their arrangement of the plays to be influenced by a tradesmanlike desire to put their newest and showiest material in the best positions. In a word, they were very human persons, soon weary of well doing, and with not a conception that they were dealing with the greatest of all English books. But they preserved some twenty of Shakespeare's plays from total destruction and printed greatly improved texts of several others, and for these inestimable benefits, had each of the venturers received the whole proceeds of the edition as his share of the profits, who shall say that they would have been overpaid?

j. ASSIGNMENTS. 1623-1632

4° *August* 1626.

4° August 1626
Edward Brewster
Robert Birde

Assigned ouer vnto them by Mistris Pavier and Consent of a full Court of Assistantes all the Estate right title and interest which Master Thomas Pavier her late husband had in the Copies here after mencioned.

xxviij^s

vizt.

[1] *The pathway to the Knowledg of Arithmaticke*
[2] *The history of Henry the Fift and the play of the same.*

[10] *Master Pavier's rights in Shakespeares plaies or any of them.*

[26] *Sir John Oldcastle a play*

[30] *Tytus and Andronicus*

[37] *Historye of Hamblett*
[38] *Euriolus and Lucretia*

[On or after 19 June 1627]

Thomas Cotes
Richard Cotes

Assigned ouer vnto him by Dorathye Jaggard widowe and Consent of a full Court holden this Day, All the Estate right title and Interest which Isaacke Jaggard her late husband had in the Copies following.
. . .

xj^s vj^d

vizt.

[1] *Wilsons workes*

[22] *Bills for players*
[23] *her parte in Shackspheere playes.*
[24] *Seaven godly sermons vpon the temptacon &c.*

1mo *Marti* 1627 [1628]

Master Richard
Hawkins

Assigned ouer vnto him by Thomas Walkley, and Consent of a Court holden this Day all the estate right title and Interest which he hath in these Copies following.

xviij^d

vizt.

A kinge and no kinge
Philaster or love lies ableeding
Orthello the more of Venice

29 *Januarii* 1629 [i.e. 1630]

Master Meighen.

Assigned ouer vnto him by master Johnson and Consent of Master Purfoote Warden, All the said master Johnsons Estate in the 4 Copies hereafter menconed.

ij^s

142

vizt.

vizt.

Cupids Whirlegeig
Michalmas terme
The merry Wiues of Winsor
The Phenix.

8° Nouembris 1630

Richard Cotes

Assigned ouer vnto him by master Bird and Consent of a full Court holden this day All his estate right and interest in the Copies hereafte menconed. iiij^s
Henrye the Fift.
Sir John Oldcastle
Titus and Andronicus
Eureolus and Lucretia
Yorke and Lancaster
Agincourt
Persiles
Hamblet
Yorkeshire Tragedie.

16 Nouember 1630

Master Allott.

Memorandum master Blount assigned ouer vnto him all his estate and right in the Copies hereafter mencioned as appeareth by a note vnder master Blountes hand, Dated the 26 of June 1630 *in the time of master Warden Purfoote, his hand is subscribed thereunto.* vij^s
The Tempest
Two gentlemen of Verona
Measure for measure
Comedie of Errors
As you like it
All^s well that endes Well
Twelfe night
Winters tale

3 part of Henry. 6^t
Henry: the 8^t

Coriolanus
Timon of Athens
Julius Cæsar
Mackbeth
Antony and Cleopatra
Cymbolyne

ij. THE THREE FOLIOS
Second Edition
M^R· WILLIAM | SHAKESPEARES | COMEDIES, | HISTORIES, and | TRAGEDIES. | Publiſhed according to the true Originall Copies. |

The ſecond Impreſſion. [Portrait signed: Martin Droeshout sculpsit London.] *LONDON,* | Printed by *Tho. Cotes,* for *Robert Allot,* and are to be ſold at his ſhop at the ſigne | of the blacke Beare in Pauls Church-yard. 1632.

*** In what would appear to be either an uncorrected proof of this, or more proba-bly a copy struck off after an accident to the forme carelessly repaired and subsequently corrected to variant B, the comma is omitted after "Histories"; "according" is misprinted "accodring"; "*Jmpreſſion*" has already become "*Impreſſion*"; there is no stop after "*Tho,*" and the second line of the imprint reads, "of the blacke Beare in *Pauls* Church yard, 1632."

(B.) Mᴿ· WILLIAM | SHAKESPEARES | COMEDIES, | HISTORIES, and | TRAGEDIES. | Publiſhed according to the true Originall Copies. | *The ſecond Impreſſion.* [Portrait.] *LONDON,* | Printed by *Tho. Cotes,* for *Robert Allot,* and are to be ſold at the ſigne | of .he Blacke Beare in Pauls Church-yard. 1632.

Variant Imprints: Printed by *Tho. Cotes,* for *William Aspley,* and are to be ſold at the ſigne | of the Parrat in Pauls Church-yard. 1632.
   Printed by *Tho. Cotes,* for *Richard Hawkins,* and are to be ſold at his ſhop | in Chan-cery Lane, neere Serjeants Inne. 1632.
   Printed by *Tho. Cotes,* for *Richard Meighen,* and are to be ſold at his ſhop at the middle | Temple Gate in Fleetſtreet. 1632.
   Printed by *Tho. Cotes,* for *Iohn Smethwick,* and are to be ſold at his ſhop | in Saint *Dunstans* Church-yard. 1632.

Colophon (in all copies): Printed at *London* by *Thomas Cotes,* for *John Smethwicke, Wil-liam Aſpley* | *Richard Hawkins, Richard Meighen,* and *Robert Allot,* 1632.

Head-title: The Workes of William Shake- | ſpeare, containing all his Comedies, Hiſto- | ries, and Tragedies: Truly ſet forth, according to their first Originall.

Collation: A⁶⁺⁴, 10 leaves, unpaged; A-Z Aa Bb⁶ Cc², 152 leaves, paged 1-275, 277-303; pages [276] and [304] blank; a-y⁶, 132 leaves, paged 1-45, 48-100, one leaf unpaged, 69-232; aa-zz, aaa-ccc⁶ ddd⁴, 160 leaves, paged 1-168, 269-419, page [420] blank. Total, 454 leaves.

Misprints in Signatures: A₃ (preliminary) misprinted as A₂; i as I, i₃ as I₃, l₃ as h₃; m as M; m₂ as m₃; u₃ as v₃; gg₂ as gg₃.

Misprints in pagination: (First pagination:) 46 misprinted as 64; 58 as 80; 153 as 151; 194 as 494; 249, 250 as 251, 252; 265 as 273; (second pagination:) the numbers 47, 48 omitted, 89, 90 misprinted as 91, 92; the number 69-100 repeated, 88 (in the repeats) being misprinted as 87, 94 as 49 and 95 as 59; 164 misprinted as 194; 209 as 120; (third pagination:) 96 misprinted as 67, 154 as 134; the number 169-268 omitted; 286, 287 misprinted as 186-187; 341, 342 as 143, 144; 351, 352 as 151, 152; 355 as 335; 389 as 399.

Contents. Preliminaries: Ben Jonson's verses, leaf 1ᵇ (recto blank); titlepage with por-trait, 2ᵃ (verso blank); Dedication, 3 (sig. A₂); address To the great variety of Readers, 4ᵃ (sig. A₄, verso blank); verses "Vpon the Effigies of my worthy Friend, the Author, Master William Shakeſpeare, and his Workes [Anon.], and "An Epitaph on the admirable Dramaticke Poet, W. Shakespeare" [by John Milton, unsigned], 5ᵃ (verso blank); verses by Digges and I[ames] M[abbe], 6ᵃ (verso blank); head-title and names of the actors, 7ᵃ (sig. *, verso blank); Ben Jonson's verses to Shakespeare's memory, 8 (sig. *₂); verses On Worthy Master Shake-ſpeare and his Poems, signed I. M. S., 9; verses by Hugh Holland, 10ᵃ; A Catalogue of all the Comedies, &c., 10ᵇ.

—*Comedies:* The Tempest, pages 1-19; *The Two Gentlemen of Verona,* 23-38; *The Merry Wives of Windsor,* 39-60; *Measure for Measure,* 61-84; *The Comedie of Errors,* 85-100; *Much Adoe about Nothing,* 101-121; *Loves Labour's lost,* 122-144; *A Mid-sommer Nights Dreame,* 145-162; *The Merchant of Venice,* 163-184; *As You Like It,*

185-207; *The Taming of the Shrew*, 208-229; *All's Well, that Ends Well*, 230-254; *Twelfe Night, Or what you will*, 255-275, followed by a blank page; *The Winters Tale*, 277-303, followed by a blank page.

—*Histories: The Life and Death of King John*, pages 1-22; *The Life and Death of King Richard the Second*, 23-45; *The First Part of Henry the Fourth*, with the Life and Death of Henry Sirnamed Hot-Spurre, 46-73; *The Second Part of Henry the Fourth*, Containing his Death: and the Coronation of King Henry the Fift, 74-100, followed by an unpaged leaf containing the Epilogue and Actors' Names; *The Life of King Henry the Fift*, 60-59[95]; *The first Part of King Henry the Sixt*, 96-119; *The second Part of King Henry the Sixt*, with the death of the Good Duke Humfrey, 120-146; *The third part of King Henry the Sixt*, with the death of the Duke of Yorke, 147-172; *The Tragedy of Richard the Third:* with the Landing of Earle Richmonde and the Battell at Bosworth Field, 173-204; *The Famous History of the Life of King Henry the Eight*, 205-232.

—*Tragedies: The Tragedie of Troylus and Cressida*, preceded by its Prologue, pages 1-29; *The Tragedy of Coriolanus*, 30-59; *The Lamentable Tragedy of Titus Andronicus*, 60-81; *The Tragedie of Romeo and Iuliet*, 82-106; *The Life of Tymon of Athens*, 107-127, followed by the Actors' Names, 128; *The Tragedy of Iulius Cæsar*, 129-150; *The Tragedie of Macbeth*, 151-168, 269-271; *The Tragedy of Hamlet, Prince of Denmarke*, 272-302; *The Tragedy of King Lear*, 303-329; *The Tragedy of Othello, the Moore of Venice*, 333-359; *The Tragedy of Anthony and Cleopatra*, 360-388; *The Tragedy of Cymbeline*, 389-419.

Size: Good copies measure $13\frac{1}{2} \times 8\frac{3}{4}$ inches.

THIRD EDITION

First Issue.

MR. WILLIAM | SHAKESPEARES | Comedies, Histories, and Tragedies. | Published according to the true Original Copies. | *The Third Impression.* | [Droeshout's portrait.] *LONDON,* | Printed for *Philip Chetwinde,* 1663.

₊ In a variant of this issue, instead of the portrait there is a blank space. In all copies the verses on the portrait face the title as in the previous editions, and the text ends with *Cymbeline*, page 877, the succeeding page being blank. Otherwise, this issue agrees with that of the succeeding year described below.

Second Issue.

MR. WILLIAM | SHAKESPEAR'S | Comedies, Histories, and Tragedies. | Published according to the true Original Copies. | *The third Impression.* | And unto this Impression is added seven Playes, never | before Printed in Folio. | *viz.* | *Pericles* Prince *of Tyre.* | The *London Prodigall.* | The History of *Thomas* Ld *Cromwell.* | Sir *John Oldcastle* Lord *Cobham.* | The *Puritan Widow.* | A *York-shire* Tragedy. | The Tragedy of *Locrine.* | [Device with motto: Ad ardua per aspera tendo.] | *LONDON,* Printed for P.C. 1664.

Head-title: The VVorks of William Shakespeare, containing | all his Comedies, Histories, and Tragedies : | Truely set forth according to their | first Original.

Collation: A⁶ b⁴, 10 leaves unpaged; A–Z⁶Aa⁶Bb⁸, Cc–Zz Aaa⁶, Bbb–Zzz Aaaa–Dddd⁶ Eeee⁴, 444 leaves paged 1–877, pages 276, 304 and 878 blank; a⁶b⁴, 10 leaves paged 1–20; ₊, ₊₊, *₊*, *₊₊*⁴, ¶A ¶B⁶ ¶C–¶F⁴ ¶G⁶, 50 leaves paged 1–100. Total 514 leaves.

Misprints in Signatures: A₃ misprinted as A₂; Ddd₃ unsigned; ¶B₃ misprinted as ¶B₂.

Misprints in pagination (copies vary): 39 misprinted as 36, 108 as 56, 196 as 194, 201 as 103, 203 as 103, 373 as 374; 428 as 433, 433 as 428, 560–568 repeated, 576 misprinted as 556, the number 608 omitted, 619 misprinted as 617, 659–666 as 657–664, the numbers 714, 715 repeated; 779 misprinted as 787, 798 as 799, 858 as 859, 861 as 961, 868 as 669, 873 as 973, 875 as 879, 876 as 990; also in the last pagination 18 misprinted as 16, 41 as 36, 49–52 as 50–53.

Contents: Preliminaries: Engraved Portrait and Ben Jonson's verses on it, 1ᵇ (recto blank), titlepage, 2ᵃ (verso blank); dedication, leaf 3 (sig. A₂, for A₃); address, leaf 4; commendatory verses, 5–9 (sig. b₁–[b₅]); head-title and Names of the Actors, 10ᵃ; Catalogue of all the Comedies, &c., 10ᵇ; *Comedies*, pp. 1–303; *Histories*, pp. 305–568; *Tragedies*, pp. 560–877.

—*Additional plays:* The much admired Play, called *Pericles, Prince of Tyre.* With the true Relation of the whole History, Adventures, and Fortunes of the faid Prince. Written by W. Shakespeare, and publifhed in his life time, pp. 1–20.

The London Prodigal. Written by W. Shakefpeare, pp. 1–16.
The Hiftory of the Life and Death of Thomas Lord Cromwell, pp. 17–32.
The Hiftory of Sir John Oldcaftle, the good Lord Cobham, pp. 33–54.
The Puritan: or The Widow of Watling-ftreet. pp. 55–74.
A York-fhire Tragedy. Not fo New, as Lamentable and True, pp. 75–81.
The Tragedy of Locrine, the eldeft Son of King Brutus, pp. 82–100.

Size: Good copies measure 13½ × 8¾ inches.

FOURTH EDITION

Mᴿ· William Shakefpear's | COMEDIES, | HISTORIES, | AND | TRA-GEDIES. | Publifhed according to the true Original Copies. | Unto which is added, SEVEN | PLAYS, | Never before Printed in Folio: | *VIZ.* |

Pericles Prince of *Tyre* 〉 〈 Sir *John Oldcaftle* Lord *Cobham*.
The *London Prodigal.* 〉 〈 The *Puritan Widow.*
The Hiftory of *Thomas* Lord 〉 〈 A *Yorkfhire* Tragedy.
  Cromwel. 〉 〈 The Tragedy of *Locrine.*

| *The Fourth Edition* | [Device or Ornament.] | *LONDON,* | Printed for *H. Herringman, E. Brewfter*, and *R. Bentley*, at the *Anchor* in the | *New Exchange*, the *Crane* in St *Pauls* Church-Yard, and in | *Ruffel*-Street *Covent-Garden.* 1685.

Variant Imprints: Printed for *H. Herringman, E. Brewfter, R. Chifwell* and *R. Bentley*, at the *Anchor* | in the *New Exchange;* and at the *Crane*, and *Rofe and Crown* in St. *Pauls* | Church-Yard, and in *Russel*-Street *Covent-Garden.* 1685

Printed for *H. Herringman*, and are to be fold by *Jofeph* Knight | and *Francis Saunders* at the *Anchor* in the Lower Walk | of the *New Exchange.*

Head-title: The Works of WILLIAM SHAKESPEAR; containing *all his Comedies* | *Hiftories and Tragedies; Truly fet forth according to their firft Original.*

Collation: [∗²] A⁴, six leaves unpaged; A–Y⁶Z⁴, paged 1–272 with errors and omissions; Bb–Zz⁶, *Aaa–*Ddd⁶*Eee⁸, paged 1–328; Aaa–Zzz Aaaa–Bbbb⁶, Cccc², paged 1–303, the last page blank. Total: 458 leaves.

Misprints in Signatures: Quires Bb and Cc are signed B and C, Dd₃ is misprinted as D₃, Oo as Pp, *Aaa₃ as *Aa₃, *Eee and *Eee₂ as Eee and Eee₂.

Misprints in pagination (copies vary): (First Pagination), 33 misprinted as 23; the numbers 97, 98 omitted; 107 misprinted as 109; 109 as 111; the numbers 161, 162 omitted; 120, 191 misprinted as 186, 187; 219 as 221; 246 as 234; 255 as 243; the numbers 254 and 255 repeated, the two pages (only the second blank) after p. 272 unnumbered; (third pagination) 67 misprinted as 76.

Contents : Preliminaries: Engraved Portrait and Ben Jonson's verses on it, 1ᵇ (recto blank); titlepage 2ᵃ, verso blank; Dedication, leaf 3 (sig. A₁); address, leaf 4ᵃ; commendatory verses, in double columns, the last two with headlines across the page, 4ᵇ–5ᵇ; head-title; names of actors, and catalogue of all the comedies, etc. (not includ-

ing the seven additional plays), 6ᵃ (verso blank). *Comedies*, pp. 1–272; *Histories*, 1–232;
Tragedies: Troilus, Coriolanus, Titus Andronicus, Romeo and Juliet, 233-328; *Timon-Cymbeline*, 1–192; *Pericles* and the six spurious plays, 193-303.
Size: Good copies measure 14¼ × 9⅛ inches.

iij. QUARTOS AFTER 1623

THE | MERRY | VVIVES | OF WINDSOR. | With the humours of Sir *Iohn Falſtaffe*, | As alſo the ſwaggering vaine of Ancient | *Piſtoll*, and Corporall *Nym*. | Written by *William Shake-Speare*. | [Rule] | *Newly cor-rected*. | [Rule] | [Ornament] | [Rule] | *LONDON:* | Printed by *T. H.* for *R. Meighen*, and are to be ſold | at his Shop, next to the Middle-Temple Gate, and in | *S. Dunſtans* Church-yard in *Fleet-ſtreet*, | 1630.

Collation : A–K⁴, unpaged.
Head-title: THE | MERRY VVIVES | OF VVINSOR.
Running-title: The merry Wiues of Windſor.

Loues Labours lost. | A WITTIE AND | PLEASANT | COMEDIE, | As it was Acted By his Maieſties Seruants at | *the* Blacke-Friers *and the* Globe. | *Written* | By WILIAM SHAKESPEARE. | [Smethwick's device.] | *LONDON,* Printed by *W.S.* for *Iohn Smethwicke*, and are to be | ſold at his Shop in Saint *Dunſtones* Church- | yard vnder the Diall. | 1631.

Collation: A–I⁴K², unpaged.
Head-title: Loues Labour's loſt.
Running-title: Loues Labour's loſt.

The moſt excellent | Hiſtorie of the Merchant | of *VENICE.* | With the extreame crueltie of *Shylocke* | the Iewe towards the ſaid Merchant, in | cutting a juſt pound of his fleſh: and the ob- | taining of PORTIA by the choice | *of three Cheſts.* | As it hath beene divers times acted by the | *Lord Chamberlaine his Servants.* ‖ [rule] Written by WILLIAM SHAKESPEARE. [rule] ‖ [ornament.] ‖ LONDON, | Printed by *M.P.* for *Laurence Hayes*, and are to be ſold | at his Shop on Fleetbridge. 1637.

Collation: A–I⁴, unpaged.
Head-title: The Comicall Hiſtory of the Mer- | chant of *Venice.*
Running-title: The Comicall Hiſtorie of | the Merchant of Venice.
    The Actors' Names occupy the back of the title.

The moſt excellent | HISTORIE | OF THE | Merchant of Venice: | With the extreame cruelty of *Shylocke* | the *Jew* towards the ſaid Merchant, in cutting a | juſt pound of his fleſh: and the obtaining | of *Portia* by the choyce of three Cheſts. | As it hath been diverſe times acted by the | *Lord Chamberlaine his Servants.* ‖ [rule] Written by WILLIAM SHAKESPEARE. [rule] ‖ [A crown.] ‖ *LONDON:* | Printed for *William Leake*, and are to be ſolde at his ſhop at the | ſigne of the Crown in *Fleetſtreet*, between the two | Temple Gates. 1652.

    This is a reiſſue of the edition of 1637, with a new titlepage, on the back of which are "The Actors Names" and a liſt of ſeventeen books "Printed and ſolde by William Leake."

A WITTIE | AND PLEASANT | COMEDIE | Called | *The Taming of the Shrew.* | As it was acted by his Maieſties | *Seruants at the* Blacke Friers |

147

and the Globe. | *Written by* Will. Shakeſpeare. | [Smethwicke's device.] | *LONDON,* | Printed by | *W. S.* for *Iohn Smethwicke,* and are to be | ſold at his Shop in Saint *Dunſtones* Church- | yard vnder the Diall | 1631.

Collation: A-I₄, unpaged.
Head-title: THE | Taming of the Shrew.
Running-title: The Taming of the Shrew.

THE | HISTORIE | *OF* | Henry the Fourth: | VVith the battell at *Shrewesbury,* be- | tweene the King, and Lord *Henry Percy,* | ſurnamed *Henry Hotſpur of* | *the North.* | [rule] | With the humorous conceits of *Sir* | *Iohn Falstaffe.* | [rule.] | Newly corrected, | By *William Shake-ſpeare.* [rule] | *LONDON,* | Printed by *Iohn Norton,* and are to bee ſold by | *William Sheares,* at his ſhop at the great South doore | of Saint *Pauls-*Church; and in Chancery-Lane, | neere *Serieants-Inne.* 1632.

Collation: A-K⁴, unpaged.
Head-title: The Hiſtory of | *Henry the Fourth.*
Running-title: The Hiſtory of | Henry the Fourth.

THE | HISTORIE | *OF* | Henry the Fourth: | VVITH THE BAT-TELL AT | *Shrewsbury,* betweene the King, | and Lord *Henry Percy,* ſurnamed | *Henry Hotſpur* of the | *North.* | [rule] With the humorous conceits of Sir | Iohn Falstaffe. | [rule] *Newly corrected,* | By | William Shakespeare. | [rule] *LONDON,* | Printed by John Norton, and are to be ſold by | Hvgh Perry, at his ſhop next to Ivie-Bridge | in the Strand, 1639.

Collation: A-K⁴, unpaged.
Head-title: THE | HISTORY OF HENRY | the Fourth.
Running-title: The Hiſtory of | Henry the Fourth.

THE | LIFE AND | DEATH OF KING | *RICHARD* THE | SECOND. | With new Additions of the | *Parliament Scene,* and the | Depoſing of King *Richard.* | [rule] As it hath beene acted by the Kings Majeſties | Servants at the *Globe.* | [rule] By *William Shakeſpeare.* | [rule] [ornament] [rule.] *LONDON,* | Printed by Iohn Norton. | 1634.

Collation: A-K⁴, unpaged.
Head-title: The Life and Death of | King *Richard* the ſecond.
Running-title: The Life and Death | of Richard the ſecond.

THE | TRAGEDIE | *OF* | KING RICHARD | *THE THIRD* | Con-tayning his trecherous Plots, againſt | *his brother* Clarence: *The pittifull murther of his ino-* | cent Nepthewes, his tiranous vſurpation: with the whole | courſe of his detefted life, and moſt | *deſerued death.* | As it hath beene lately Acted by the Kings Maiesties | *Seruants.* | Newly agmented. | By *William Shake-ſpeare.* | [Ornament.] | *LONDON.* | Printed by *IohnNorton,* and are to be ſold by *Mathew Law* | dwelling in *Pauls* Church-yeard, at the Signe of the | *Foxe,* neere Sᵗ. *Auſtines* gate, | 1629.

Collation: A-L⁴ M², unpaged.
Head-title: None.
Running-title: The Tragedie | of Richard the Third.

THE | TRAGEDIE | *OF* | KING *RICHARD* | THE THIRD | Con-tayning his treacherous Plots, a- | gainſt his brother *Clarence:* The pitifull

| murder of his innocent Nephewes: his | tyranous vſurpation: with the | whole courſe of his deteſted life, | and moſt deſerued death. | [rule] *As it hath beene Acted by the Kings | Maieſties Seruants*. | [rule] Written by *William* Shakeſpeare. | [rule] [Ornament, Fleur-de-lys.] | *LONDON,* | Printed by IOHN NORTON, 1634.

Collation: A-L⁴ M², unpaged.
Head-title: None.
Running-title: The Tragedy | of Richard *the Third.*

THE MOST | EXCELLENT | And Lamentable Tragedie | of ROMEO and | IVLIET. || As it hath beene ſundrie times publikely Acted, | by the KINGS Maieſties Seruants | at the GLOBE. | *Newly Corrected, augmented, and amended*. | [Smethwick's device.] | *LONDON,* | Printed for *Iohn Smethwicke,* and to bee ſold at his Shop in | Saint *Dunſtanes* Church-yard, in Fleete ſtreete | vnder the Dyall.

Variant title: In this the words " Written by W. Shake-ſpeare " (in italics) precede " Newly corrected," etc.
Collation: A-L⁴, unpaged.
Head-title: THE MOST EXCEL- | LENT AND LAMENTABLE | Tragedie of ROMEO and IVLIET.
Running-title: The moſt Lamentable Tragedie | of Romeo *and* Iuliet.
Printer: Not ascertained. The date may be any year after 1611.

THE MOST | EXCELLENT | And Lamentable Tragedie | of ROMEO and | JULIET. | As it hath been ſundry times publikely Acted | by the KINGS Majeſties Servants | at the GLOBE. | Written by *W. Shake-ſpeare*. | *Newly corrected, augmented, and amended.* [Smethwick's device.] *LONDON,* | Printed by *R. Young* for *John Smethwicke,* and are to be ſold at | his Shop in St. *Dunſtans* Church-yard in Fleetſtreet, | under the Dyall. 1637.

Collation: A-L⁴, unpaged.
Head-title: THE MOST EXCEL- | LENT AND LAMENTABLE | Hiſtorie *of* ROMEO and | Juliet.
Running-title: The moſt lamentable Tragedy | of Romeo *and* Juliet.

THE | TRAGEDY | OF | HAMLET | *Prince of Denmarke.* | Newly Imprinted and inlarged, according to the true | and perfect Copy laſtly Printed. | BY | WILLIAM SHAKESPEARE. | [Smethwick's device.] | LON-DON, | Printed by *W. S.* for *Iohn Smethwicke,* and are to be ſold at his | Shop in Saint *Dunſtans* Church-yard in Fleetſtreet: | Vnder the Diall.

Collation: A-N⁴, unpaged, last blank.
Head-title: THE | TRAGEDIE | OF | HAMLET | PRINCE | OF DENMARKE.
Running-title: The Tragedie of Hamlet | *Prince of* Denmarke.
Printer: William Stansby. This undated edition may have been printed any time after 1611.

THE | TRAGEDY | OF HAMLET | PRINCE OF | DENMARK. | Newly imprinted and inlarged, according to the true | and perfect Copy laſt Printed. | [Rule] *By* WILLIAM SHAKESPEARE. [Rule] [Smethwick's device] [Rule] *LONDON,* | Printed by *R. Young,* for *John Smethwicke,* and are to be ſold at his | Shop in Saint *Dunſtans* Church-yard in Fleet-ſtteet, | under the Diall. 1637.

Collation: A–N⁴, unpaged.
Head-title: THE TRAGEDY OF | HAMLET | PRINCE OF | DENMARK.
Running-title: The Tragedy of Hamlet | Prince of Denmarke.

M. William Shake-fpeare, | *HIs* | True Chronicle Hiftory of the life | and death of *King Lear*, and his | *three Daughters.* | *With the Vnfortunat Life of* EDGAR, | fonne and heire to the Earle of *Glocefter*, and | *his fullen affumed humour of* TOM | of Bedlam. | *As it was plaid before the Kings Maiefty at Whit-Hall, vp* | *on S. Stephens night, in Christmas Hollldaies.* | By his Maiefties Servants, playing vfually at the | *Globe*, on the *Bank-fide.* | [Ornament] | *LONDON.* | Printed by *Jane Bell*, and are to be fold at the Eaft-end | of *Chrift-Church.* 1655.

Collation: A–L⁴, unpaged.
Head-title: M. William Shake-fpeare | *HIS* | Hiftory of King Lear.
Running-title: The Hiftory of King Lear.
  On the back of the titlepage is a list of 22 "Books Printed; | And are to be Sold by *Jane Bell* at the East end | Of Christ-Church."

THE | Tragœdy of Othello, | The Moore of Venice. | *As it hath beene diuerfe times acted at the* | Globe, and at the Black-Friers, by | *his Maiesties Seruants.* || *Written by* VVilliam Shakefpeare. | [Device of Phaethon.] *LONDON,* | Printed by *A. M.* for *Richard Hawkins*, and are to be fold at | his fhoppe in Chancery-Lane, neere Sergeants-Inne. | 1630.

Collation: A–M⁴; leaves 2–48 recto mispaged 1–92, the last page blank.
Head-title: The Tragedy of Othello the Moore | of Venice.
Running-title: The Tragedy of Othello | the Moore of Venice.

THE | Tragœdy of Othello, | The MOORE of VENICE | *As it hath beene divers times Acted at the* | Globe, and at the Black-Friers, by | his Majefties SERVANTS. | *Written by* William Shakefpeare. | *The fourth Edition.* [Rule] [Device of Crown.] [Rule] *LONDON,* | Printed for *William Leak* at the *Crown* in *Fleet-* | *ftreet,* between the two Temple Gates, 1655.

Collation: A–M⁴, leaves 2–48 recto, paged 1–93.
Head-title: The Tragedy of OTHELLO the Moore | of Venice.
Running-title: The Tragedy of Othello | the Moore of Venice.
  On the last page is a list of 44 books, 'Printed or fold by *William Leake*.'

THE LATE, | And much admired Play, | CALLED | Pericles, Prince of | Tyre. | *With the true Relation of the whole Hi-* | ftory, aduentures, and fortunes | of the fayd Prince: | Written by WILL. SHAKESPEARE: | [Fleur-de-lys device.] | *LONDON,* | Printed by *I. N.* for *R. B.* and are to be fould | at his fhop in *Cheapfide*, at the figne of the | *Bible.* 1630.

Collation: A–H⁴ I², unpaged.
Head-title: The Hiftory Of | Pericles, Prince of Tyre.
Running-title: Pericles Prince of Tyre.

THE LATE, | And much admired Play, | CALLED | Pericles, Prince of | Tyre. | *With the true Relation of the whole Hi-* | ftory, aduentures, and fortunes | of the fayd Prince: | Written by WILL. SHAKESPEARE. | [Fleur-de-lys device] | *LONDON,* | Printed by *I.N.* for *R.B.* 1630.

Collation: A–H⁴ I², unpaged.
Head-title: The Hiſtory Of | Pericles, Prince of Tyre.
Running-title: Pericles Prince of Tyre.

THE LATE, | And much admired Play, | CALLED | Pericles, Prince of | Tyre. | *With the true Relation of the whole Hi-* | ſtory, adventures, and for- | tunes of | the ſaid Prince. | Written by W. SHAKESPEARE. [Printer's de- | vice.] | Printed at *London* by *Thomas Cotes*, 1635.

Collation: A–H⁴ I².
Head-title: THE | HISTORY OF | Pericles, Prince of Tyre.
Running-title: Pericles Prince of Tyre.

iv. QUARTOS OF SPURIOUS PLAYS ADDED IN 1664
LOCRINE
Entry in the Stationers' Register:
xx° die Iulij [1594]. *Thomas Creede. Entred for his Copie vnder thandes of the Wardens, The Lamentable Tragedie of Locrine, the eldest sonne of Kinge Brutus. discoursinge the warres of the Brittans, &c.* vjᵈ.

FIRST EDITION
THE | Lamentable Tragedie of | *Locrine*, the eldest ſonne of King *Brutus*, discour- | ſing the warres of the *Britaines*, and *Hunnes*, | with their diſcomfiture: ‖ *The Britaines victorie with their Accidents, and the* | *death of* Albanact. *No leſſe pleasant then* | *profitable.* ‖ Newly ſet foorth, ouerſeene and corrected, | By *W. S.* | [Creed's device.] LONDON | Printed by Thomas Creede. | 1595.

SIR JOHN OLDCASTLE
Entry in Henslowe's Diary:
This 16 *of October* [15]99. *Received by me, Thomas Downton, of phillip Henslow, to pay Mr. Monday, Mr. Drayton, and Mr. Wilson and Hathway, for the first pte of the lyfe of Sʳ Jhon Ouldcasſtell and in earnest of the second pte: for the use of the company, ten pound, I say receved . . .* 10ˡⁱ.

Entry in the Stationers' Register:
11 *Augusti* [1600]. *Thomas pauier. Entred for his copies vnder the handes of master Vicars and the wardens. These iiij copies viz.*

    The first parte of the history of the life of Sir John Oldcastell lord Cobham.
    Item the second and laste parte of the history of Sir John Oldcastell lord
       Cobham with his martyrdom.

FIRST EDITION; SECOND EDITION.
Reduced facsimiles of the titlepages have been given on pages 90 and 91.

THOMAS LORD CROMWELL
Entry in the Stationers' Register:
11° *Augusti* [1602]. *William Cotton. Entred for his Copie vnder thandes of master Iackson and master waterson warden A booke called the lyfe and Deathe of the Lord Cromwell as vt was lately Acted by the Lord Chamberleyn his seruantes.* vjᵈ.

151

FIRST EDITION

THE | True Chronicle Hi- | ftorie of the whole life and death | of *Thomas* Lord *Cromwell.* | As it hath beene fundrie times pub- | *likely Acted by the Right Hono-* | rable the Lord Chamberlaine | *his Seruants.* | Written by W.S. | [Eld's device.] | Imprinted at London for *William Iones*, and are | to be folde at his houfe neere Holburne con- | duict, at the figne of the Gunne. | 1602.

SECOND EDITION

THE | True Chronicle Hi- | ftorie of the whole life and death | of *Thomas* Lord *Cromwell.* | As it hath beene fundry times pub- | likely Acted by the Kings Maiefties | Seruants. | [rule.] | *Written by* W.S. | [rule.] | [Printer's device.] | *LONDON*: | Printed by THOMAS SNODHAM. | 1613.

Collation: A-G⁴, unpaged.
Head-title: The life and death of the Lord | *Cromwell.*
Running-title: *The Life and Death* | *of the Lord* Cromwell.

THE LONDON PRODIGAL
Entry in the Stationers' Register: *None.*
FIRST EDITION
THE | LONDON | Prodigall. | As it was plaide by the Kings Maie- ‖ fties feruants. | By *William Shakefpeare.* | [Creed's device.] | LONDON. ‖ Printed by T. C. for *Nathaniel Butter*, and | are to be fold neere S. *Auftins* gate, | at the figne of the pyde Bull. | 1605.

A YORKSHIRE TRAGEDY
Entry in the Stationers' Register:
2ᵈᵒ *die Maij* [1608]. *Master Pauvyer Entered for his Copie vnder the handes of master Wilson and master Warden Seton A booke Called A Yorkshire Tragedy written by Wylliam Shakespere* vjᵈ.

FIRST EDITION
A | YORKSHIRE | Tragedy. | *Not fo New as Lamentable* | and true. | *Acted by his Maiefties Players at* | the *Globe.* | *Written* by VV. Shakfpeare. [Device, with motto " Sic crede."] | AT LONDON | Printed by *R. B.* for *Thomas Pauier* and are to bee fold at his | fhop on Cornhill, neere to the exchange. | 1608.

SECOND EDITION
A reduced facsimile of the titlepage has been given on page 89.

THE PURITAN WIDOW
Entry in the Stationers' Register:
6 *Augusti* [1607]. *George Elde Entred for his copie vnder thandes of Sir George Bucke knigt and the wardens a book called the comedie of the Puritan Widowe.* vjᵈ.

FIRST EDITION
THE | PVRITAINE | Or | THE VVIDDOVV | of Watling-ftreete. | *Acted by the Children of Paules.* | Written by W. S. | [Device.] Imprinted at London by G. ELD. | 1607.

CHAPTER X. THE LATER FOLIOS AND QUARTOS, 1623–1685

IN the Folio of 1623 and the quartos by which it was preceded we have the only documents which can pretend to any original authority for the formation of Shakespeare's text. The subsequent quartos are of little or no interest save as showing the hold upon the reading public exercised by certain plays. The three Folios are in a different position. To the student of the history of Shakespeare's text they are indispensable. No scholar was called in to edit any one of them; and when we remember the result of letting loose Richard Bentley, the greatest scholar of the next century, upon the text of Milton, we may well rejoice that this was so. The suggestions that Milton himself or Ben Jonson may have been responsible for some of the changes in the Second Folio are based upon nothing but the facts that both men were alive and wrote verses in Shakespeare's honour, and that the imagination is tickled by the idea of their playing the part which the hypothesis assigns to them. Had either of them taken up such a task, it is possible that Bentley's audacities would have seemed but an anticlimax. The actual editors of the successive Folios, probably in each case the printer's ordinary corrector of the press, took a humble, but not altogether timorous, view of their functions. They subjected the spelling of the First Folio to a continuous modernization, and various slight grammatical or syntactical irregularities are smoothed away. All this was, of course, of the nature of what we are pleased to call emendation. There is not the slightest reason to believe that any new original sources were brought into use for improving the text. Had such sources been discovered, we can hardly doubt that they would have been vaunted on the titlepages and that prefaces would have been written to assure the reader that now at last they might be confident that the author's true text was placed before them. The nature of the changes, moreover, even when a percentage of a somewhat more ambitious nature is taken into account, does not encourage such a theory. On the other hand, changes made anonymously in the ordinary course of their work by men of Shakespeare's own century, accustomed to the business of proof-correcting, start with many advantages over the conscious emendations of their more pretentious successors. In any case there is no room for doubt that the labours of the earlier "correctors" were considered beneficial in their own day and for some generations after it. It is not until we come down as late as Dr Johnson that we find any clear recognition of the superiority of the First Folio over the later ones. We now know that the Second Folio was a reprint from the First, the Third from the Second, the Fourth from the Third. According to Dr Furness, Nicholas Rowe printed his edition from the Fourth Folio; Pope used Rowe's text and Hanmer Pope's; Theobald's shows signs of having been set up from Pope's second edition, and his own second edition was used in the same way by Warburton, while Warburton's work was used by Johnson, whose admiration for the First Folio did not persuade him to forgo the convenience of sending a modern text to the printer. Thus, while each editor, in order to justify his existence, made certain changes to which he drew attention, and tinkered, or let his printer tinker, at spelling and punctuation in silence, he took over from his predecessors a text to which, from 1632 onward, similar contributions had been continuously made, so that unless every edition is available for comparison the responsibilities of the different printers and editors cannot be ascertained.

For some five or six years after its publication the First Folio completely satisfied the demand for Shakespeare's plays. At last, in 1629, John Norton printed a quarto of *Richard III*, which was sold by Matthew Law. In 1630 R. Meighen, who had obtained the copyright from Arthur Johnson on January 29 of that year, reprinted *The Merry Wives of Windsor*, and Richard Hawkins produced a new quarto of *Othello*, which had been transferred to him by Thomas Walkley on March 1, 1628. In 1631 John Smethwicke, who had contributed to the First Folio, of which he was one of the publishers, the copyright of the old play, *The Taming of A Shrew*, which he had acquired from Nicholas Ling, now took back his own with interest by printing a quarto of *The Taming of the Shrew* which follows the Folio text.* He also, in the same year, reprinted *Loves Labors Lost*, the copyright of which he had acquired from Ling, who had obtained it from Cuthbert Burby, the publisher of the quarto of 1598, since when it had never been printed separately. Lastly, in 1632 (whether before or after the Second Folio we have no means of proving, but probably before) John Norton printed a quarto (the seventh) of *Henry IV*, which was sold by Willam Sheares. Thus, whereas the six years 1623-1628 had produced no quartos, in these four, 1629-1632, as many as six were put on the market. The proprietors of the Folio doubtless found in this revived activity of the quarto-owners an encouragement to bring out a new edition, and the fact, though only a small one, may be added for what it is worth to the other evidence of the constant and continuous character of Shakespeare's popularity.

Between 1623 and 1632 several changes took place among the owners of copyrights in the Shakespeare Folio. Of the three chief promoters of the First Folio the two Jaggards had both died before 1632, and Blount in that year was giving up business and soon followed them to the grave. Whatever interest William Jaggard had possessed in the copyright of the plays first entered in 1623, must have passed to his son Isaac, who in his own right had none, since he was only the printer of the book. An undated entry in the Stationers' Register for 1627, following one dated June 19, is placed against the names " Thomas Cotes, Richard Cotes," and reads, "Assigned ouer vnto him by Dorathye Jaggard and Consent of a full Court holden this Day. All the estate right title and interest which Isaacke Jaggard her late husband had in the copies following," " the copies following " being twenty-four in number (two of which must have been taken as one, since only twenty-three sixpences were charged), and the twenty-third item being " her parte in Shackspheres playes."

In 1630 Richard Cotes made another purchase. On August 4 Edward Brewster and Robert Birde had acquired from Mrs Pavier upwards of sixty copies (the number of sixpences charged was fifty-six) belonging to her late husband, the enterprising Thomas. Among these are mentioned: (2) *The History of Henry the Fift* and the play of the same, (10) Master Pavier's

---

* Mr Tucker Brooke, in his excellent *Shakespeare Apocrypha* (1908) has overlooked this change of text when in his list on page ix he writes: " 8. *The Taming of a Shrew*. Ascribed to Shakespeare in Smetwick's [*sic*] reprint of 1631. The first edition is anonymous."

rights in Shakespeare's plaies or any of them, (26) *Sir John Oldcastle* a play, (30) *Tytus and Andronicus* and the *Historye of Hamblett*. On November 8, 1630, Richard Cotes purchased from Bird "*Henrye the Fift, Sir John Oldcastle, Titus and Andronicus, Yorke and Lancaster, Persiles* [*sic*], *Hamblet, Yorkshire Tragedie*." Eight days later a memorandum was registered of a transfer privately made from Blount to Robert Allott on the preceding June 26 of all the plays first registered in 1623, while at earlier dates Richard Hawkins had acquired from Walkley his interest in "*Orthello, the More of Venice*" (March 1, 1627/8) and Richard Meighen had bought from Arthur Johnson "*The Merry Wives of Winsor*" (January 29, 1629/30).

The text of all these transfers will be found quoted in full from Dr Arber's transcript of the Stationers' Register in the Bibliography which precedes this chapter. They are here mentioned to enable us to account for the five names which we find connected with the Second Folio. We find that Thomas Cotes had acquired (by his own action or through Richard Cotes) all the rights of the Jaggards and had added to them others derived from Pavier. He was thus naturally the printer of the new edition. Robert Allott had stepped into the shoes of Blount, and was thus, equally naturally, its chief publisher. Two of the old venturers, Smethwick and Aspley, were still alive, and two new men, Hawkins and Meighen, owners respectively of *Othello* and *The Merry Wives*, were allowed to take shares, which were probably insignificant compared with those of Allott. We can thus fully account for the new colophon: " Printed at London by Thomas Cotes for John Smethwick, William Aspley, Richard Hawkins, Richard Meighen and Robert Allot, 1632."

According to a fashion which had been common in France, and of which there are instances in England, in the sixteenth century, each of the five publishers of the Second Folio had a titlepage printed for the copies which he took as his share, giving his own name and address and omitting those of his partners. Titlepages with the imprint, " Printed by Tho. Cotes for Robert Allot," are in an overwhelming preponderance (indicating, doubtless, the importance of his share in the venture) and are found in what would appear to be three successive states. The first of these, of which there is a copy in the Lenox collection at New York, is obviously only an uncorrected proof of the second, while the third differs only in adopting different forms of "I" and "J," and the form, "at the signe of the Blacke Beare," instead of the longer, "At his shop at the signe of the Blacke Beare " (see the entry of the Second Folio in the Bibliography). In this final form the title reads:

MR WILLIAM | SHAKESPEARES | COMEDIES, | HISTORIES, and | TRAGEDIES. | Published according to the true Originall Copies. | *The second Impreſsion.* | [Portrait.] | *LONDON,* | Printed by *Tho. Cotes,* for *Robert Allot,* and are to be ſold at the ſigne | of the Blacke Beare in Pauls Church-yard. 1632.

Four other variants are distinguished by the imprints of the Stationers taking part in the venture, to whom they were allotted for sale. The rarest of these are apparently those bearing the names of William Aspley and Richard Meighen, of each of which Mr Livingston only records the sale of a single copy as against over forty (doubtless including several reappearances) of copies with the Allot titlepages. Of copies bearing the " Hawkins " imprint Mr Livingston records three sales, and of those with the "Smethwick" five.

155

As regards the changes made in the text of the Second Folio record has already been made of the generally accepted view that in no case have they any authority behind them and that in themselves they are unimportant. The precise degree of this unimportance remains indeterminate, as (so far as I know) no conspectus of its new readings has ever been published, and the only person who seems to have collated the texts of 1623 and 1632 with a view to ascertaining their general relations is Mr C. Alphonso Smith, of the Louisiana State University, whose remarks on the subject (published in *Englische Studien*, Band 30, pp. 1-20, 1902) are sufficiently useful, and also entertaining, to invite quotation. He writes:

The Second Folio differs widely from the First, critics to the contrary notwithstanding; but the differences are not in the domain of exegesis proper, but of syntax. Those who expect to find in the Second Folio critical attempts to clear up the obscure passages of the First Folio will surely be disappointed. The editors entered upon their task with no such purpose in view; indeed, it was not until the time of Nicholas Rowe, in the beginning of the eighteenth century, that a serious attempt was made to "edit" Shakespeare in the modern sense of the word. Passages in the First Folio that one would think even a child might have interpreted and rectified are left by the editors of the Second Folio just as they found them. For example, in the First Folio of 2 *Henry IV* (III, i, 9-12) the famous apostrophe to sleep is written thus:

Why rather, sleep, liest thou in smoky cribs,
Upon uneasy pallets stretching thee
And hushed with buzzing *night*, *flies* to thy slumber,
Than in the perfumed chambers of the great?

A mere reading of this passage aloud would seem to be sufficient to displace the comma between *night* and *flies* and to make a compound of the two; but the editors of the Second Folio repeat the senseless reading and are in turn slavishly followed by the editors of 1664 and 1685. Again, in the First Folio of *King John* (v, vii, 15-18), Prince Henry is made to say of the king's dying condition:

Death, having prey'd upon the outward parts,
Leaves them invisible, and his siege is now
Against the *wind*, the which he pricks and wounds
With many legions of strange fantasies.

This error of *wind* for *mind* is repeated by all the other folios, though the prince had already suggested the right reading by saying that the king's *brain* was seriously affected.

These citations are taken at random and could be multiplied *ad libitum;* but even a superficial acquaintance with the contents of the Second Folio will suffice to show the reader that the editors made little attempt at exegesis, and that the controlling purpose of their new edition is not to be sought in the realm of conjectural readings or of brilliant emendations. This purpose must be sought in the realm of syntax. It is true, as White says, that "neither of the last three folios is of the slightest authority in determining the text of Shakespeare"; but the Second Folio is of unique service and significance in its attempts to render more "correct" and bookish the unfettered syntax of the First. The First Folio is to the Second as spoken language is to written language. It must not be thought that the language had materially changed from 1623 to 1632. The supreme syntactic value of Shakespeare's work as represented in the First Folio is that it shows us the English language unfettered by bookish impositions. Shakespeare's syntax was that of the speaker, not that of the essayist; for the drama represents the unstudied utterance of people under all kinds and degrees of emotion, ennui, pain and passion. Its syntax, to be truly representative, must be familiar, conversational, spontaneous; not studied and formal. Men do not speak as they write.

Shakespeare shows in the few formal letters and studied orations that he introduced
into his plays that he felt instinctively the stylistic grades that should be preserved.
But in the one-volume edition of 1623 Shakespeare's dramas entered upon a new
sphere of service: they became popular not only as stage material but as reading material. Hence a new edition was called for, in which the chief burden of the endeavor
should be to make the language conform to the needs of written style rather than to
the demands of oral delivery.

There is a rich humour in the suggestion that Messrs Allott, Cotes,
Smithwick, Aspley, Hawkins and Meighen were responding in 1632 to a
call for a new edition "in which the chief burden of the endeavor should
be to make the language conform to the needs of written style rather than
of oral delivery," instead of merely reprinting in the ordinary course of business
a successful book. But, apart from this pleasantry, Mr Smith's general remarks
are much to the point, and his special investigation into the changes made
in the concord of subject and predicate in the Second Folio are interesting.
Thus he tells us that of 235 passages in the First Folio in which an ordinary
plural subject is followed by a singular predicate fifty-nine are corrected in the
1632 edition, while of sixteen instances of the opposite concord eight are
changed. In more complex cases there is far less innovation; thus with 188 compound subjects with singular predicates only two are changed, and of fifty-six
plural relative clauses only eight. In another class, that of the use of a verb
in the third person instead of the first or second, out of forty-six cases about
eighteen are said to be changed. If these instances, as Mr Smith asserts,
comprise "the vast majority of the changes" made in the text of the 1632
Folio, they are even slighter than have been supposed.

If we listen to Dr Howard Furness when he is comparing the two Folios
in a play, such as *As You Like It*, where the text of the First Folio is itself
satisfactory, we shall have this impression confirmed. Here he writes:

Practically the text of the four Folios is one and the same. The discrepancies
between the First and the Fourth are mainly such as we might expect in the changes
of languages within the dates of publication. In the last century Steevens professed
to give to the Second Folio a preference over the First. But I doubt if this preference
sprang from any very deep conviction; I am not sure that Steevens did not profess it
mainly for the sake of annoying Malone, whose "learning and perspicuity" Steevens
extolled chiefly for the sake, I am afraid, of calling him in the same sentence his
"Hibernian coadjutor," a cruel little stab at one who had tried to obliterate his
nationality, it is said, by dropping, with the letter y, the accent on the final vowel of
his name. In the present play there are two or three instances where unquestionably
the Second Folio corrects the First. For instance, Oliver says (IV, iii, 150), "I briefe,
he led me to the gentle Duke"; this trifling typographical error is corrected in the
Second Folio to "*In* brief he," etc. Again, in line 163 of the same speech, Oliver
says, "this napkin died in this blood," where the Second Folio reads, "died in *his*
blood." But these are insignificant, and not beyond the chance corrections of a good
compositor, who, however, overshot the mark when he changed Rosalind's words
(IV, iii, 71) from "false strains" to "false *strings*," and did even worse for Orlando,
when one of the finest sentences in the whole play was converted into limitless bom-
bast. "I will chide no breather in the world," says Orlando in the Second Folio,
"but myself, against whom I know *no* faults." It is a little singular that what is
always in the First Folio "Monsieur" is in the Second and following Folios "*Moun-
sieur*." Whether this indicates a change in general pronunciation from Elizabeth's
time to Charles the First's, or is merely peculiar to one compositor, I do not know.

Thus, in *As You Like It*, we find the compositors or press-correctors of the Second Folio making a handful of emendations, some obviously right, others as obviously wrong. On the other hand, in the case of a play, such as *Macbeth*, which started with an exceptionally faulty text, we find references to "the numerous corrections (decidedly and unquestionably so) made by the editors of F²,"* and we have to recognize that the Second Folio did not merely alter the First in order now and again to make the colloquial syntax more regular, as Mr Alphonso Smith has proved with so much industry, or to improve lines in which the loss of a word had spoilt the metre, as has been pointed out by Tieck and others, but in a real sense began the work of lawful and necessary emendation. It is obvious that the emendation was done at haphazard and that numerous glaring misprints and blunders in punctuation passed unnoticed. Nevertheless, it was in 1632 that a start was made in re-editing the First Folio, and thus no survey of the history of Shakespeare's text can be complete which does not take into account the work of these anonymous compositors and correctors.

The publication of the Second Folio only checked the issue of quartos for a couple of years. In 1634 we find Norton reprinting *Richard II* and *Richard III*. In 1637 Smethwicke brought out new editions of *Romeo and Juliet* and *Hamlet*, and Laurence Heyes, after an eighteen years' interval, exercised the right he had claimed in 1619 to reprint *The Merchant of Venice*. In 1639 Norton reprinted *The History of Henry the Fourth*. That there were not more quartos during these years was probably due to Cotes having acquired the copyrights of Pavier and his unwillingness to do anything which would delay the profitable job of printing a new edition of the entire Folio. That he was not indifferent to such profits as might be made from a quarto is shown by his issuing in 1635 a new edition of *Pericles*, not yet, it will be remembered, included in the volume.

After 1639 political troubles spoilt the market for plays, and there are no more editions to record till 1652, when William Leake, a publisher much interested in dramatic literature, reissued the 1637 edition of *The Merchant of Venice* with a new titlepage. Laurence Heyes had evidently waited too long before bringing out his edition, and in the bad times that followed 1637 some of it had remained unsold, so that Leake was able to acquire the stock. In 1655 Leake published a new edition of *Othello*, calling it the fourth, and in the same year Jane Bell reprinted *King Lear*. Leake had obtained his copyright in *Othello* as early as 1638 by assignment from Robert Mead and Christopher Meredith, with other books that had belonged to Richard Hawkins. How Mrs Bell became proprietress of *King Lear* we shall not know until Mr H. R. Plomer has completed his transcript of the Stationers' Register for this period. She was successor and, therefore, almost certainly the widow of Moses Bell, who died about 1649, after having been in business on his own account for about ten years."†

* Hunter, quoted by Dr Howard Furness.
† From 1628 to 1638 Moses worked with Henry Bell, probably a brother; but as all their copyrights were transferred to Haviland and Wright in September, 1638, the interest in *King Lear* must have been acquired later than this. See Plomer's *Dictionary of Booksellers and Printers*, 1641-1667.

When the king had obtained his own again and the Cavaliers had had a year or two to recruit their fortunes, a new Folio Shakespeare became once more a possibility. This time only a single name was associated with it, that of Philip Chetwind, who, after the death of Robert Allott in 1636, had possessed himself of his copyrights by the usual expedient of marrying his widow. Thomas Cotes, who printed the Second Folio, had died in 1641, and his brother Richard thus became sole proprietor of the business in 1753. His will makes specific mention of his rights in Parkinson's *Herbal*, but not, apparently, of those in the Shakespeare. His business was now in the hands of his widow, Ellen Cotes; but it was apparently not by her, as we should expect, that the Third Folio was printed. On its titlepage this bears a device of twisted serpents with the motto "Ad ardua per aspera," and this is found on numerous works printed about this time by Roger Daniel, at one time printer to the University of Cambridge, but now at work in London. Pending further evidence, it is thus to the press of Daniel that the Third Folio must be tentatively* assigned. After the Restoration it became less common for books to bear the name of their printer, and there is no colophon in the Folio to eke out the meagre imprints, "Printed for Philip Chetwinde," "Printed for P. C.," found on the titlepages of 1663 and 1664. But the fact that not only the portrait (which would belong to the publisher) but some of the ornaments of the previous editions reappear points to the probability of a legitimate succession.

As to the minor partners in the Folio of 1632 the biographies in Mr H. R. Plomer's useful *Dictionary of Booksellers and Printers* 1641-1667 suggest that the rights of John Smethwick would have passed to Miles Fletcher or Flesher, a very important printer who was Master of the Stationers' Company for the fourth time in 1663. Aspley cannot be traced. Hawkins, as we have seen, was now represented by Leake. Richard Meighen had died in 1641, and his business, after being carried on for several years by his widow Mercy, was now in the hands of Gabriel Bedell. Whether Chetwinde had to make arrangements with any of these firms we have no information. Apparently he alone took the risk of the publication.

The most notable feature of the Third Folio, the inclusion of seven plays which the original editors left out of the Shakespeare canon, was clearly an afterthought. No mention is made of them in either of the variant titlepages of 1663, and the pagination is not continued on from the end of *Cymbeline*. The bibliographical evidence, indeed, points to two stages in Chetwinde's plans, in the first of which he intended to include only *Pericles*, which has a separate pagination (1-20) and separate signatures ($a^6\ b^4$). As a second afterthought the other six plays were added, with pagination 1-100, and the very inconvenient† signatures $*$, $**$, $^*_**$, $****^4$ ¶A ¶B^6, ¶C-¶E^4, ¶G^6. Modern criticism has confirmed and extended the distinction thus made by admitting *Pericles* into the canon, where indeed it has a better right than *Titus Androni-*

---

* In 1661, apparently, the same device was used on the titlepage of Abraham Wright's *Commentary on the Psalms*, "Printed by I. R. for William Grantham." This raises a new claimant, but I can find no printer with these initials.

† One sheet of the fifth quire is signed with five asterisks, but it was easily realized that this system had to be abandoned as the last quire would have needed eleven.

cus, though both plays might with advantage be relegated to an Appendix.

Chetwinde would have been well advised if he had stayed his hand, as he seems at first to have intended, after the insertion of *Pericles*. But we may be sure that the evidence which appealed to him was not the style or craftsmanship of the plays, but the fact that they had been allowed to pass under Shakespeare's name or initials either during his life or within a few years of his death, and had recently been attributed to him in booksellers' catalogues. Having once thrown over the authority of the First Folio, he had indeed every temptation to add other plays besides *Pericles*. Even for the error for which he is most easily convicted, the inclusion of *Sir John Oldcastle*, which we know from Henslowe's Diary (see the entry quoted in the Bibliography, p. 151) was written by Anthony Munday, Michael Drayton, Robert Wilson and Thomas Hathway, Chetwinde had great excuse. He set up his text from the quarto of 1619 with the spurious date 1600, and very probably had never seen the genuine quarto of 1600 printed by Valentine Sims, which makes no attribution of the play to Shakespeare. In the absence of the first quarto, even if he had suspected the date of the second to be spurious, he might easily have imagined that the assertion that the play was "Written by William Shakespeare" was reprinted, along with the rest of the title, from the original. We now know that this was not the case, and that the insertion of these words in 1619 was one of the most impudent of the Jaggard-Pavier frauds. But with all the original venturers in the First Folio dead, so that there was no one to give the reasons on which they had acted in accepting or rejecting plays claiming Shakespeare as their author, the evidence of a titlepage apparently printed in the full heyday of Shakespeare's activity was naturally accepted as sufficient.

In the case of the *Yorkshire Tragedy* we are ourselves confronted with the same dilemma which, owing to a spurious date, sufficed to procure the inclusion of *Oldcastle*. The *Yorkshire Tragedy* was not only published in 1608 with "Written by W. Shakspeare" on its titlepage, but the same statement ("Wrytten by Wylliam Shakespere") appears in the quite regular entry (May 2, 1608) in the Stationers' Register which preceded the first edition. Shakespeare's authorship of this play between August, 1605 (the date of the murderer's execution), and 1608 being quite inconceivable, there are only two alternatives to choose from. We may treat Pavier as merely a lying pirate, or we may believe that he had some inch of authority for the statement and that his conscience easily permitted him to convert this into an ell. The King's Players themselves probably were not ill pleased when a new and anonymous play was attributed to their best author. If they did not spread such a rumour themselves, they probably took no pains to correct it when started by others. There is the likelihood that any play written for the king's company at this date would have been submitted to Shakespeare for him to read it, to make suggestions, to supervise it, and out of this managerial connexion with a play whispers of his authorship, if no other name were attached to it, would easily arise. It is even possible, supposing Pavier to have paid for his "copy," that the inch of authority was supplied to him not merely by an uncontradicted rumour, but by vague statements of any agents with

160

whom he may have negotiated for its purchase. And we need not doubt that
the smallest hint that Shakespeare had touched the play would have sufficed
to stir Pavier to attribute it to him in the most formal manner.

None of the other plays lightheartedly attributed to Shakespeare in the
Third Folio has the double authentication of a precise statement on an early
titlepage and also in a perfectly regular entry in the Stationers' Register.
The only other spurious play of which an early edition bore Shakespeare's
name in full is *The London Prodigall* "printed by T. C. [i. e. Thomas Creede]
for Nathaniel Butter" in 1605. This was preceded by no entry in the Stationers' Register, and is thus more likely than Pavier's venture to have been
a merely lying piracy.

The three remaining plays are all alike in having been entered at Stationers'
Hall without any suggestion of their authorship, and printed, not as by William Shakespeare, but as "Written by W. S.", or in one case "Newly set
foorth, ouerseene and corrected, By W.S." It is "The Lamentable Tragedy
of Locrine . . . Printed by Thomas Creede. 1595" in which the ascription
is thus limited to one of editorship. The play had been duly registered in
July of the preceding year, the year 1594, when, on account of the closing
of the theatres, so many plays appear to have been sold by the companies,
and this raises a strong presumption that it was honestly bought. As it was
thought worth while in that year to attribute *Titus Andronicus* unreservedly
to Shakespeare, his name must be considered as already reckoned an attrac-
tion, and in dishing up this old play (critics are fairly agreed that it was probably written some ten years before its publication) Creed probably thought
himself a model of moderation in merely asserting that it was "ouerseene
and corrected, By W. S." It is notable, however, that in none of the three
lists of plays published by booksellers before 1664 is it attributed to Shakespeare. In that of Rogers and Ley (1656) it is entered as *Locrinus Tragedy*,
by Archer (1656) as *Locrinus*, by Kirkman in 1661 as by "W. S." It was
only in Kirkman's revised list of 1671, after the appearance of the Third
Folio, that it figures as "*Will Shakespear*. Lockrine, Eldest Son of K. Brutus,
T [i.e. Tragedy]." Nevertheless it was very probably the entry in 1661 which
caused its inclusion in the Third Folio, from whence this attribution to Shakespeare was subsequently borrowed.*

* The practice of using a blank page or leaf in a new book to advertise other publications began about 1649 and speedily became common. As has been noted in the Bibliography, lists of this
kind are to be found in William Leake's reissue of *The Merchant of Venice* in 1652 and Jane
Bell's edition of *King Lear* in 1655. In the years 1650 to 1661 over a dozen lists of this kind
containing plays are appended to books published by Humphrey Moseley, William Leake, Bedell
and Collins, and Andrew Cooke. All these were confined to plays published by the advertisers.
But as, after the subsidence of the Civil War, interest in the drama revived, booksellers began to
collect stocks of the old plays and published much more extensive catalogues of them. Two of
these were printed in 1656, appended respectively to *The Careless Shepherdess* published by Rogers
and Ley, and to the *The Old Law* published by Edward Archer. A third, by Francis Kirkman,
which is of great importance in its probable effect on Chetwinde, appeared in 1661 appended to
the "second impression" of *Tom Tyler and his Wife*. This (which was reprinted, with additions
in 1671), is headed: "A True, perfect and exact Catalogue of all the Comedies, Tragi-Comedies,
Pastorals, Masques and Interludes, that were ever yet printed and published, till this present year
1661, all which you may either buy or sell at the several shops of *Nath. Brook* at the Angel in
Cornhil, *Francis Kirkman* at the *John Fletchers Head*, on the Backside of *St. Clements*, *Tho. Johnson* at the Golden Key in St. *Pauls* Churchyard, and *Henry Marsh* at the Princes Arms in *Chan-*

Thomas Lord Cromwell, after entry in the Stationers' Register in August, 1602, was published the same year by William Jones, its titlepage bearing the words, " As it hath beene sundrie times publikely Acted by the Right Honorable the Lord Chamberlaine his Seruants. Written by W. S." With the change of the company's name to the " King's Maiesties Seruants" the same phrases occur in the reprint of 1613, " Printed by Thomas Snodham." By Rogers and Ley in 1656 it was catalogued without any author's name, but in Archer's list of the same year it appears as " Cromwells historie. H[istory]. *William Shakespeare.*"

Lastly *The Puritaine or the Widdow of Watling Streete* was entered in August, 1607, and published the same year as " Acted by the Children of Paules. Written by W. S. Imprinted at London by G. Eld." It is not catalogued by Rogers and Ley, but appears in the lists of Archer and Kirkman with the name of " Will. Shakespeare" printed against it.

After this brief review of the facts as regards these seven plays it should be clear that we have no need, or right, to suppose that Philip Chetwinde, or his advisers, considered their claims to be admitted into the Shakespeare canon in any critical spirit. No one had as yet begun to play at the fascinating but rather unprofitable game of assigning authors to anonymous plays, or parts of plays, solely on principles of what may be called literary connoisseurship, as early pictures are nowadays transferred from one painter to another according to the pronouncements of our cocksure critics of art. Attention had recently been drawn to these seven plays by the attribution, in dealers' catalogues, of six of them to Shakespeare and one to W. S. On examination four of them were found to bear the name of Shakespeare on the titlepages of early editions (or in the case of *Sir John Oldcastle*, what seemed to be an early edition) and the other three his initials. Chetwinde might have taken his stand on the fact of the rejection of these plays by the editors of 1623, but his position in doing so would have been weakened firstly by the absence of any explicit allusion to these plays as spurious in the First Folio and secondly by the incompleteness of the original editions of the rival folios of Ben Jonson and Beaumont and Fletcher. He seems at first to have intended only to include *Pericles*, the most popular of the seven, but afterwards added the other five which had been claimed as Shakespeare's, and even *Locrine*, for which no such claim had yet been made. From a bookselling point of view he was probably wise, but if the circumstances were as we have supposed the inclusion of the seven plays in the volume of 1664 cannot be taken as in any substantial degree strengthening their claims to admission into the Shakespeare canon.

Some two years after the publication of the Third Folio a great part of central London was destroyed by fire, and, as the stationers nearly all had their premises in this district, their printed stock suffered heavily. On the basis of the number of copies which have come under the hammer in

cery-lane near *Fleet street*. 1661." For a full account of these lists see W. W. Greg's *Lists of Masques, Pageants, &c.*, supplementary to a *List of English Plays*, Bibliographical Society, 1902. The attribution of spurious plays to Shakespeare in booksellers' lists almost compelled Chetwinde to include them in the Third Folio, unless he was prepared to defend himself against a charge of incompleteness.

London during the ten years 1897 to 1906, taken from Mr. William Jaggard's very useful *Index to Book-Prices Current*, we may estimate the loss from this cause in the case of the Third Folio as fully half the edition, a guess which for a book which had been on the market for a couple of years seems fairly in accordance with the probabilities from a publisher's standpoint. By this time, however, the trade in the old books was pretty well organized in London, and with copies of the First and Second Folios, as well as the Third, coming from time to time on the market, it is not surprising that it was over twenty years before a new edition appeared a profitable venture. If any enterprising publisher who chose had been free to print the works of Shakespeare, no doubt not merely one but several editions would have appeared before 1685, but although the details of the succession from Chetwinde to Herringman have not, as far as I know, yet been unearthed from the Stationers' Registers, where they probably lie hid, it must be remembered that the works of Shakespeare were still copyright, and might have remained so for ever had it not been for the copyright law under Queen Anne and the view taken of it by the courts. That a publisher while he feels himself secure in his rights will often be slow in exercising them, we have had recent proofs in the languid treatment of the works of such writers as Miss Austen, Peacock and George Borrow, while they remained in the hands of the original owners of the copyrights, as compared with the number of editions published as soon as competition became possible. Throughout the seventeenth century it rested, at any given moment, with a single tradesman to determine what opportunities of buying the works of Shakespeare should be offered to the English public, and it is perhaps not very surprising that the tradesmen, with the conservative instincts of our race, thought that their interests would best be served by bringing out a succession of large folios at safely distant intervals. For the total cessation of the quartos of single plays we may find explanations firstly in Shakespeare being now on his way to the position of a classic, so that the demand would be for complete editions, not for haphazard quartos, and secondly in the gradual dying out of the few firms which had the right to issue them. As we have seen, Cotes had bought up Pavier's "copies," and in no case had any one of the succession of chief proprietors used his rights to bring out separate editions of single plays.

The Fourth Folio was announced in the "Catalogue of Books printed and published at London in Easter Term, 1685" by the following entry (Arber's *Term Catalogues*, II, 122):

Mr. William Shakespeare's Comedies, Histories and Tragedies. Published according to the true original Copies. The Fourth Edition. Folio. Printed for *H. Herringham;* and sold by *J. Knight* and *F. Saunders* at the Blew Anchor in the Lower Walk of the New Exchange.

This announcement, curiously enough, corresponds to the least common of the three variant imprints found in different copies of the titlepage, only three sales being recorded by Mr Livingston and only two in Mr Jaggard's *Index to Book-Prices Current*, 1897-1906. In the great majority of copies (forty-three sales are recorded by Mr Livingston) the imprint runs, "Printed for *H. Herringman, E. Brewster* and *R. Bentley*, at the *Anchor* in the *New Exchange*, the *Crane* in St *Pauls* Church-Yard, and in *Russel*-Street *Covent-*

The Later Folios and Quartos

163

Garden," while in a sub-variety of this (seven sales being recorded by Mr Livingston) the name of another bookseller, Chiswell, comes between those of Brewster and Bentley. Thus altogether, in addition to Herringman, who had obviously taken the place filled by Blount, Allot and Chetwinde in previous editions, five other firms were engaged in the venture, to which probably they were admitted by Herringman rather to lessen his own risk than as having any claims such as had apparently procured the inclusion of Aspley, Smethwick, Meighen, etc., in the first and second editions. The titlepage bears a small device of a fleur-de-lys upon a dotted background in an oval frame, which may indicate the printer but at this date can hardly be relied on as doing so. The portrait, which is retouched, is placed, as in the 1664 issue of the Third Folio, facing the title, with its verses beneath it. The commendatory verses are printed in double columns.

As regards its text, the Fourth Folio is very little removed from being a mere reprint of the Third, which it copies, rather unluckily, even in the mention on the titlepage of the "Seven Plays Never before printed in Folio." It has its own interest, however, as the last of the series of the great folios, in whose columns can be noted exactly what was left for the eighteenth-century critic-editors to accomplish, and itself marks the completion of the task of the printer-editors of Shakespeare's own century. We must not claim too much for these printer-editors. It cannot be said that they rose to the height of their opportunities, either in purging Shakespeare's text of obvious errors or in providing the British public with attractive editions likely to win for him fresh readers. But with all their lack of enterprise they did enough to show that they were confronted by a greater demand than existed for the works of any other Elizabethan playwright, and these four large folios, in addition to upwards of seventy quarto editions of single plays, should surely suffice to dispel the myth that either in his lifetime or at any subsequent period Shakespeare was other than the most popular of English dramatists.

ADDITIONAL APPENDIX TO CHAPTER IV.
MR G. W. COLE'S CENSUS OF THE QUARTOS OF 1619.

ON page 85, after showing with the aid of Mr Lee's figures how much commoner the 1619 *Pericles* is than any of the other early quarto editions I wrote, "when a complete census of all the known Shakespeare quartos is produced, similar, if not quite so striking results will probably emerge in the case of all the quartos of the volume." Based on his investigations for the notes to his fine catalogue of the Church Collection Mr George Watson Cole, of Riverside, Conn., has now produced such a census for all the quartos of 1619, and has most kindly placed his figures at my disposal. The following table represents the facts arrived at in the Church Catalogue, the index figures giving the number of duplicates in each collection.

LIBRARIES AND COLLECTIONS.	Merchant of Venice (1600). Roberts.	Midsummer Night's Dream (1600). Roberts.	Sir John Oldcastle (1600). T.P.	King Lear (1608). Butter.	Henry V (1608).	Merry Wives of Windsor (1619).	Yorkshire Tragedy (1619).	Whole Contention. Part I. (1619).	Whole Contention. Part II. (1619). No titlepage.	Pericles (1619).	TOTALS (Pavier Editions).
Bodleian Library	1	1	1	2	1	1	1	1	1	1	10[1]
British Museum	2	2	2	3	1	2	3	2	2	2	10[11]
Trinity College, Cambridge . . .	1	1	1	1	1	1	1	1	1	1	10
Devonshire, Duke of	1	1	1	1	1	1	1	1	1	1	10
Church, E. Dwight.	1	1	1	1	1	1	1	1	1	2	10[1]
Huth, Alfred H.	1	1	1	1	1	1	1	1	1	1	10
White, William A.	–	1	1	1	–	1	1	1	1	1	8
Boston Public Library (Barton) . . .	1	1	1	1	1	1	1	1	1	1	10
Ellesmere, Earl of	–	–	–	–	–	1	–	–	–	1
Lenox Library	1	1	1	1	1	1	1	3	3	2	10[5]
Dyce Collection	–	–	1	–	1	1	1	1	1	1	7
Hoe, Robert	1	1	1	1	1	1	1	1	1	1	10
Edinburgh University (Halliwell) . .	1	1	–	1	1	–	1	–	–	–	5
Eton College	1	1	1	1	1	–	–	1	1	1	8
Stratford Shakespeare Memorial . .	2	1	1	1	–	1	–	–	–	–	5[1]
Perry, Marsden J. (Gwynn copy) . .	1	1	1	1	1	1	1	1	1	1	10
Halsey, Fred. R.	1	1	–	1	–	–	–	–	–	–	3
Trowbridge, F. K.	1	–	–	–	–	1	–	–	–	1	3
Furness, H. H..	1	–	–	1	2	–	–	–	–	1	4[1]
Howe, Lord (copies)	1	1	1	1	1	1	1	1	1	1	10
Morgan, J. Pierpont	–	1	1	1	1	1	1	1	1	–	8
Library of Congress	–	1	–	–	–	–	–	–	–	–	1
Bute, Marquis of	–	1	–	–	–	–	–	–	–	–	1
Wrenn	–	–	1	–	–	–	–	–	–	–	1
Birmingham Free Library	–	–	–	–	1	–	–	2	1	–	3[1]
Brown, John Carter, Library . . .	–	–	–	–	1	–	–	–	–	–	1
Van Antwerp	–	–	1	1	1	–	–	1	1	1	6
TOTALS . .	19	20	19	22	20	17	18	21	20	20*	196

* Mr Sidney Lee locates **17** copies, and mentions six unlocated.

Since drawing up this table Mr Cole has traced two more quartos in private collections, and six in booksellers' hands, while 18 others have been sold at auction. He can thus now account for 222 copies as follows:

PAVIER QUARTOS.	Located in Church Catalogue.	Located since.	In Booksellers' hands.	Sales during seasons of 1906-8 other than above, so far as known.	TOTAL.
Whole Contention, Part I.	21	—	1	4	26
Whole Contention, Part II.	20	—	1	4	25
Midsummer Night's Dream	20	—	2	1	23
Sir John Oldcastle	19	1	—	3	23
Merchant of Venice	19	—	—	—	19
Henry V.	20	—	1	—	21
King Lear	22	—	—	1	23
Pericles	20	—	—	3	23
Merry Wives of Windsor	17	1	1	—	19
Yorkshire Tragedy	18	—	—	2	20
	196	2	6	18	222

The first point brought out by these tables is the close approximation in the number of copies of each of these quartos, there being, in the entire series, not less than 19 nor more than 26 of any one play. In the second place the fact, already pointed out on pages 85 and 98, that copies of these editions are much more frequently met with than those of other Shakespeare quartos is brought into still greater prominence. Mr Cole's researches have been extended to the twin quartos which pair with those of 1619, and of the "Heyes" *Merchant of Venice* he has located as many as 14 as against 19 of the "Roberts," but of the Fisher *Midsummer Night's Dream* only 7 as against 23; of *Sir John Oldcastle*, 2 against 23; of *King Lear*, 8 against 23, or a total of 31 extant copies as against 88. No explanation of this striking difference in rarity has yet been put forward, save that here propounded that the "Quartos of 1619" were preserved in greater numbers by being bound together in volumes.

INDEX

Fisher's, see *M.N.D.*, 1600; Ling's, see *Hamlet*, 1603, 1604; Smethwick's, see *Hamlet*, 1611; Okes', see *King Lear*, 1608 (Pied Bull), *Othello*, 1622

Devil's Charter, by Barnabe Barnes, its titlepage quoted, 71

DEVONSHIRE COPY of First Folio, order of preliminary leaves in, 139

DOOR, use of the word in stage directions, 126

DRAMATIS PERSONÆ, lists of in First Folio, 128

DROESHOUT, Martin, his portrait of Shakespeare in the First Folio, 140

ECCLESTONE, William, probably owner of initial E in stage directions to *All's Well*, 127

ELD, George, printed *Troilus and Cressida*, q.v.; also 1602 *Cromwell* and 1607 *Puritan*, 152

ELIZABETH, Queen, *Loves Labors Lost* and *Merry Wives of Windsor*, acted before, 32, 45

ENGRAVED TITLEPAGES, sometimes part of a quire, sometimes not, 138 note

Every Man in his Humour, publication of "stayed," 67; subsequent entry and edition of, 68

FISHER, Thomas, published *Midsummer Night's Dream*, q.v.

FOLIO OF 1623, bibliographical description of, 108-110; the collection of the copy, 111-122; the editing, 123-130; the printing, 131 seqq.; accidents during printing, 135 seq.; the preliminary leaves, 137 seqq.; price and number printed, 140 seq.

FOLIO OF 1632, bibliographical description of, 143 seq.; circumstances of its publication, 153 seqq.; its text compared with that of the First, 156 seqq.

FOLIO OF 1663-1664, bibliographical description of, 145 seq.; circumstances of its publication, 159 seq.; inclusion of spurious plays in, *ibid.*; part of the Edition destroyed by fire, 162

FOLIO OF 1685, bibliographical description of, 146 seq.; circumstances of its publication, 163 seq.

FULKE, Rev. William, payments to for his commentary on the Rheims New Testament, 6

FURNESS, Dr Howard, quoted as to stage directions in *Midsummer Night's Dream*, 126; as to relation of Quarto and Folio texts, 129; as to excellence of Folio text, 129 seq.; his statement as to the genealogy of Editions of Shakespeare, 153; on the textual changes in the later Folios, 157

GARRICK, David, his set of the Quartos of 1619, 83

GLOBE SHAKESPEARE, its evidence as to excellence of Shakespeare's text, 130

GLOBE THEATRE, fire at in 1613, 117, 119; plays by Shakespeare in repertory of in 1623, 119 seq.; mentioned on titlepages of *Romeo and Juliet* (1609), *King Lear*, *Pericles* and *Othello*, q.v.

GOSSON, Henry, publisher of 1609 *Pericles*, q.v.

GOUGH, Robert, probably owner of initial G in stage directions to *All's Well*, 127

GREENE, R., his literary earnings, 5

GREG, Mr W. W., the author's obligations to, vi, 82, 111; his proof by watermarks that the Quartos of 1619 were all printed at one time, 93; ditto by numerals in imprints and by devices, 94

GRENVILLE, Thomas, rebinds his First Folio, 137; its evidence as to the order of the Preliminary Leaves, 137

GWYNN, Edward, his volume of Shakespearian plays, 81 seqq.

174

128. *Titus Andronicus*, quarto editions of described, 14 seqq.; entered in Stationers' Register, 64; assignment of, *salvo jure cuiuscunque*, 66; exceptional fullness of its stage directions, 72, 75; rival claims to copyright of, 114; 1611 reprint used for First Folio, 121. *Troilus and Cressida*, quarto editions of described, 56 seqq.; entered in Stationers' Registers, 65; provisional entry to Roberts, 66; meaning of this entry discussed, 76 seqq.; its preface quoted, 77; the two issues of its first edition, 77 seq.; probable difficulties as to its inclusion in the First Folio, 116; temporarily omitted from Folio, 136. *Twelfth Night*, excellent text of, 128. *Two Gentlemen of Verona*, goodness of its text, 128; headline of *Merry Wives* used for in First Folio, 134 seq. *Winter's Tale*, excellent text of, 128; loss of "booke" of may have caused its temporary omission from First Folio, 135

SEGAR, Master, Deputy to Sir G. Buck, licensed *Troilus and Cressida*, 56

SHORT, Peter, printed 1598 *Henry IV*, q.v.

SIDNEY, Sir Philip, his refusal to allow his writings to be printed, 7, 65; his *Arcadia* more easily made useless to readers than the Folio Shakespeare, 140

SIMS, Valentine, evidence for his having printed the first edition of *Hamlet*, 73 seq.; printer of 1597 *Richard II*, 1604 *Henry IV*, 1600 *Henry IV*, Part 2, 1597 *Richard III*, 1600 *Much Ado*, q.v.

SINCKLO, actor, use of his name in stage direction to 2 *Henry IV*, 68; so also in 3 *Henry VI*, 127

Sir John Oldcastle, entry and title quoted, 151; its inclusion in the Third Folio, 160

SMETHWICK (SMITHWEEKE), John, owner after 1607 of copyright of

Loves Labors Lost, Romeo and Juliet, Hamlet and *Taming of A Shrew*, q.v.; one of the publishers of the First Folio, 112; also of the Second, 144, 155

SMITH, C. Alphonso, on the editing of the Second Folio, 156 seq.

SNODHAM, Thomas, printer of 1613 *Cromwell*, 152

Spanish Tragedie, titlepage of first extant edition quoted, 70

SPELLING, evidence from as to the dates of the two "1600" editions of the *Merchant of Venice*, 98

SPIELMANN, Mr M. H., on portraits of Shakespeare, 140

SPURIOUS PLAYS, attributed to Shakespeare, printed in 1664 Folio, 145 seq.; previous editions and entries in Stationers' Registers, 151 seq.; their inclusion in the Third Folio discussed, 159 seq.

STAFFORD, Simon, printed 1599 *Henry IV*, and 1611 *Pericles*, q.v.

STAGE DIRECTIONS, included in the bibliography of the early quartos, Chapter II; occurrence of names of actors in, 68, 126; when very descriptive suggest piracy, as in first *Romeo and Juliet*, 69, 72; when imperative, as in second *Romeo and Juliet*, suggest playhouse copy, 70, 72; treatment of in First Folio, 125 seq.

STATIONERS' COMPANY, the alleged unscrupulousness of its members, 3; its functions, 4 seq., 65 seqq.; entries of Shakespeare's Plays in quoted, Chapter II *passim;* plays so entered have good texts, 65 seqq., 78, 79; conditional entries in its Registers and cases of plays being stayed, 66 seqq.; no entry in its Registers needed after a piracy, 69; nor for adaptations of plays already entered, 112; obligation on Stationers to present books to the Bodleian, 139 note; entries of transfers of Shakespeare's plays 1626, etc., quoted, 142 seq.